MW00907725

THE STORY OF
GANNON UNIVERSITY
EDUCATION ON THE SQUARE

Rev. Dr. Robert Barcio
Mrs. Grace Davies
Dr. Carl Lechner
Dr. Thomas Szendrey
Mr. Gerard P. Walsh
Rev. Dr. Robert Levis, Chairman

TABLE OF CONTENTS

Library of Congress Catalog Card Number: 85-81770
Printed in the United States of America
ISBN 0-936063-00-9

© Copyright 1985
Gannon University Press
Perry Square
Erie, PA 16541

CHAPTER I

ERIE, WHERE IT ALL BEGAN

Erie, the Gem City of the Great Lakes, a quiet little lake town equidistant from Cleveland and Buffalo, is the site of this story and the home of Gannon University. Our history of Gannon begins with a brief background of the religious, commercial, political, and educational aspects of the city, especially during the 20's and 30's, the time when Gannon's founders wrestled with the idea of a men's college.

At the turn of the twentieth century, a large percentage of immigrants arriving in the United States were Polish, Slavic, and Italian, and, generally, Catholic. While the Immigration Act of 1924 slowed it, this immigration was never fully interrupted, and succeeding generations increased the numbers of Catholic immigrants. In the Erie Diocese, the Catholic population increased from 118,829 in 1925 to 128,093 in 1935. In 1910, 29% of the population of Erie was Catholic; in 1925 36%; and by 1940, 45%. *The Catholic Directory* reported gradual increases in the number of Erie priests during this decade: 203 priests in 1925 increasing to 215 in 1935.

The politics of the first third of the twentieth century also reflect these nationalities. At the turn of the century, the population of Erie primarily consisted of Anglo-Saxons and Germans, while the three new ethnic groups had increased to about 40% of the city's population. At the beginning of the century, politics were controlled by the upper-class Germans, who were predominantly Protestant and Republican. In the late 1930's Irish Catholics dominated Erie politics, with the year 1940 as their peak influence. Thus, during the 1920-1940 period, the increase in appointments of Irish, Italian, and Polish constituents was a harbinger of the coming era of their influence.

1

Citizens and their elected politicians had their share of problems in the early 1930's. Paramount was the Depression, triggered by the stock market crash in October 1929. Even though Erie had diversified industries, the city was hard hit during the depression years. Every group and every individual did all that was possible to overcome the desperate problems affecting Erie and the nation.

Employment levels plummeted.

The Community Chest assumed much of the responsibility in easing the burdens of poverty, unemployment, and discouragement. Schools, often through heroic efforts of teachers and staff, provided hot lunches and clothing and performed diverse service for the local community.

One of the noblest united efforts was the project of the Uplift Society of Erie, a temporary relief agency composed of community-minded businessmen. With contributions of money and produce from the community, they provided, for a very small fee, a dish of meat stew, bread, and coffee for the unemployed.

By 1933, economic conditions had worsened and resulted in the declaration of a bank holiday by President Roosevelt on March 6. Four Erie banks did not reopen: The Second National Bank, Erie Trust, American State Bank, and The Bank of Wesleyville. Six others did return to normal business: First National, Marine Bank, Security Peoples, Union Trust, Bank of Erie Trust, and the Lawrence Park National Bank. These events shocked the financial foundations of the community to such an extent that in 1934 *Fortune* reported that forges and foundries were idling, and Erie was feeding 18,000 of its citizens.

Despite these hard times, standing tall on the northwest corner of 10th and Sassafras Streets as a stone beacon, the spire of St. Peter's Cathedral pierced these dark clouds and became a symbol of hope to the people of Erie. Bishop John Mark Gannon, an Erie native himself, had been installed as Bishop of Erie on December 16, 1920. He was a builder. As one of the youngest Bishops in America, he began his successful career by supplying schools, churches, rectories, and convents for his growing flock. The crash of 1929, while slowing his pace, never dulled his architechtonic overview of his diocese. Holy Rosary Parish was established in 1923; ground was broken for St. Hedwig's in 1927; and St. Paul's

Church was founded in 1928. On February 27, 1925, the diocesan newspaper, the *Lake Shore Visitor,* read, "Drive for mission in Girard reaches $10,195"; "New high school in St. Marys, PA blessed by Bishop"; "Contract to be let for North East Church"; "Trinity Cemetery to be beautified". Thus, by 1933, the year Cathedral College had opened, there were 15 parochial schools with 6,655 students, a decided increase over the 1913 count of 4,100 students in 11 parochial schools: All of this growth had been stimulated by the energetic, young, Bishop John Mark Gannon from whom Gannon University would eventually take its name.

In the realm of higher education for women, Villa Maria College opened in 1925, the fruit of the successful Villa Maria Academy, founded in 1892 by the Sisters of St. Joseph. Mercyhurst College for women, founded by the Sisters of Mercy, welcomed its first students in 1926, and like Villa Maria, offered a four-year program. The St. Vincent Hospital School of Nursing, started in 1901, boasted a new nurse's residence in May 1924.

However, men of the Erie area who desired higher education in Catholic institutions were less fortunate than women. There was Kanty College, a high school and small junior college for men of Polish descent, opened in 1911, under the direction of the Missionary Fathers of Saint Vincent de Paul. The Sacred Heart Mission at Girard provided high school and junior colleges, but was restricted to preparing boys for the missionary priesthood in the Society of the Divine Word. Likewise, St. Mary's College, founded in 1881, a preparatory seminary at North East, educated only boys who aspired to the priesthood in the Redemptorist Order.

The growth of the city in the late 1920's was reflected not only in the construction of parochial schools under Bishop Gannon, but also by new public schools. John C. Diehl served as Superintendent of Erie Schools from May 1922 until June 1935, and his teaching and administrative career with the School District spanned 48 years. He built three new elementary schools: Jefferson at 37th and Holland Streets; Edison at East Lake Road and Bacon Street; and Cleveland at Mill Road and Marion Street. Four other elementary schools were enlarged: Irving, Wayne, Roosevelt, and Burton. Wilson Junior High was opened in 1927. Strong Vincent High School started classes in 1930. Originally designated as West

High School, the name was changed to honor General Strong Vincent of Civil War fame. East High School, the other high school in the city, had been built in 1921. Students who had attended Central High School, on the southeast corner of 10th and Sassafras Streets, could now go to Strong Vincent or Academy High School, which had opened in 1920.

The Central High building would either be rented to the University of Pittsburgh, which had established a junior college in Erie in 1928 on State Street, or be remodeled for a technical school. However, the market price of the building decreased when the Depression hit in 1929. The Erie Diocese made an offer to purchase the Central High building with plans to transfer Cathedral Prep facilities from across the street to this building. Eventually the decision was made to remodel the Central High facility into the Technical High School, which opened February 2, 1931.

A Department of Special Education was created by the Erie School Board on August 11, 1929. The supervisor's responsibilities included 26 full-time special classes besides part-time classes to teach lip reading and to correct speech defects. The School District directed the Public Library, too, for Erie had been the first city in Pennsylvania to take advantage of an 1895 law which permitted Boards of Education to organize and operate public libraries. Located in a classic, turn-of-the-century building at South Park Row and French Street, the library included an art gallery on the second floor and a museum in the basement.

In the 20's and early 30's, the increase in the number of facilities for children and young people in the diocese was not limited to educational institutions. The million-dollar St. Joseph's Home for Children, on West Sixth at Kahkwa Boulevard, whose design was personally donated to Bishop Gannon by Detroit's Henry Ford, ministered to 360 children when it was dedicated in 1924. The Home had outgrown St. Joseph's Orphan Asylum at 218-234 East Third Street, built in 1871-1872. This building would later be known as St. Mark's Hall and, in 1945, would become St. Mark's Seminary from which seminarians traveled to Gannon College for daily classes. In 1925, the Eichenlaub Home at 209 East Ninth Street was acquired to become the Erie Day Nursery, providing day-care for the children of working mothers.

Furthermore, the diocese provided services for older children. Harborcreek Training School for Boys was an outgrowth of the Protectory started by Msgr. H. C. Wienker in 1911. Gannondale, a residential training school for girls, opened with one cottage in 1934 and developed into an estate-like compound on East Lake Road. The dedication of Camp Glinodo, on Lake Erie and East Lake Road, initiated a new camping concept in July 1930. Continuing this awareness of the needs of young people, the Department of Youth Activities was founded by Bishop Gannon in 1933, having as its purpose the protection and salvation of the youth of the diocese. The celebration of Vocations Day, especially to encourage more young men to enter the priesthood, began in 1934.

In addition to St. Peter's Cathedral, several other church buildings were part of the downtown Erie religious community in the second decade of the twentieth century. Across from St. Peter's Cathedral, at 225 West 10th Street, was the new Luther Memorial Church, a modern stone edifice dedicated in 1926. It was erected by the congregation to replace their former church at the southwest corner of 11th and Peach Streets. Also near the Cathedral, at 135 West 10th Street, was the First Baptist Church, dedicated in 1922. This new church combined the congregations of the First Baptist Church and the 1896 offshoot of that church, the Calvary Baptist Church. The inspiration for the original First Baptist Church in 1831 had come from revival meetings at the First Presbyterian Church, and the First Baptist Church building on the northwest corner of Fifth and Peach Streets was dedicated in 1835. That building was sold eventually to St. Patrick's Church, and the Calvary Baptist building at the West 10th Street site was razed when the new church was built in 1922 for united congregations.

The First Presbyterian Church had been a mother church to several other churches in Erie and the Erie area. Organized in 1815, one early meeting place was the "Yellow Meeting House" given to the congregation by Judah Colt in 1819. Located on Sassafras Street between Sixth and Seventh Streets, this site was later, in 1922, the location of what John Elmer Reed called a "fine temple," the First Church of Christ Scientist. A more permanent building of the First Presbyterian Church was erected on Peach

Street between Fifth and Sixth Streets in 1824; and that building was demolished in 1859 to construct a new church. This finer building, whose spire and entrance faced the northwest corner of the West Park, burned in 1944 and the church was rebuilt in 1950. The adjoining Selden Chapel, on the southwest corner of Fifth and Peach Streets, was dedicated in 1892. The building complex now houses the Pontifical Center for Catechetical Studies, and the Campus Ministry in the Selden Chapel. The church proper has become the Gannon University Chapel, while the Education Building is occupied by the offices of Student Personnel Services.

The congregation of the original First Presbyterian Church branched out into two additional churches. One, the Park Presbyterian Church, was organized in 1855. Its church-home on South Park Row, adjacent to the old City Hall, was erected in 1857, and a chapel and Sunday School rooms were added in 1877. The second, the Central Presbyterian Church, was founded in 1871, and the church was built in 1873 at the northeast corner of 10th and Sassafras Streets. Although this church burned in 1888, a new church was ready for worship in 1889. The Park and Central churches were merged February 8, 1929 forming the Church of the Covenant (Presbyterian). This imposing Gothic structure extends from 247 West Sixth Street to 250 West Seventh Street. This building was dedicated December 14, 1930.

The merger of downtown Presbyterian churches was completed when, on January 1, 1981, the First Church and the Church of the Covenant merged to become the present First Presbyterian Church of the Covenant. The vacated Peach Street First Church became part of the Gannon University campus in March 1981. Two years later, the First Church of Christ Scientist building, at 618 Sassafras Street, was also purchased by Gannon University.

Other close neighbors of Gannon University are the First United Methodist Church and the St. Paul's Episcopal Cathedral and diocesan headquarters. The First Methodist Church began in 1826 with the establishment of a Methodist class. Their first church building, dedicated January 1, 1839, was on the north side of Seventh Street between Peach and Sassafras Streets. When the congregation outgrew that church, called "Wesley Chapel," a new sanctuary was built at the site of the present church, the southeast corner of Seventh and Sassafras Street and dedicated in 1860.

The first Episcopal parish in Erie was formed in 1827. Their first building, a wooden structure, was consecrated in 1834. The present gray stone church at the same site, 133-143 West Sixth Street, was consecrated in 1860. It has been extensively renovated twice in the past fifty years, and a new pipe organ was installed in 1983. St. Paul's is the Cathedral church for the Episcopal Diocese which was established in 1910, having been a part of the Diocese of Pittsburgh. In 1967, a new headquarters for the Episcopal Diocese of Northwestern Pennsylvania was built at 145 West Sixth Street. The parish Chapter House, at 134 West Seventh Street, was erected in 1928.

What was the City of Erie like in the 20's and 30's? The religious and educational structure has been described. To provide further background for the birth of Cathedral College, its eventual growth into Gannon University, and the contributions of the University to the community, a look at the city's building profile, commercial life, and recreational facilities will be provided.

A new community Play House opened in 1929, the year of the stock market crash, at 128 West Seventh Street. Gannon College purchased that building in March of 1963 and continues to use it as a theatre. The Erie County Courthouse added its east wing in 1929 also and its west wing, originally built in 1855, was remodeled to match the classic Greek structure of the addition. In 1931, the Warner Theatre at Eighth and State Streets was built as a kind of fantasy escape for the hungry, the depressed, the unemployed of the city. That same year, the Boston Store, which opened at 1604 Peach Street, was forty-six years old. That same year it expanded its property holdings in the 700 block on the west side of State Street and completed the present six-story building. In 1950, its Peach Street building would be added; and in 1955 its Eighth Street building. On July 7, 1979, the year Gannon became a University, its doors would close.

Another downtown Erie department store, Trask, Prescott, and Richardson was erected as an investment by Jerome F. Downing in 1892 on the northeast corner of Ninth and State Streets, in a very modern six-story building. The Downing office building on the northwest corner of Ninth and Peach Streets had been built in 1883 as headquarters for his extensive business and later as the office of his estate. This six-story structure was one of the many investments of Jerome Francis Downing (1827-1913), outstanding lawyer, businessman, church leader, and citizen, who had come to Erie from Massachusetts in 1855. Downing has been described as "the grand old man of Erie." His home, in its heyday, was one of the most attractive in the city. Located at 225 West Ninth Street, it was purchased by Bishop Gannon in 1925 for the expansion of Cathedral Prep administrative offices and the library. After September 1933 some of its shabby but spacious rooms would be used for classes for the new Cathedral College. All these buildings are gone: the office building has been replaced by a thirteen-story apartment edifice; the Downing home site is part of Cathedral Center; the Insurance Block was razed during downtown urban renewal.

Another elegant downtown building, the Scott Block, bore the name of an earlier businessman whose wealth would provide a mansion for his daughter, Annie Scott Strong, until 1928. Fifty years after his death, this mansion became the home of Gannon School of Arts and Science. William L. Scott (1828-1891) came to Erie in 1848; as a page in Congress he had been encouraged to come by General Charles M. Reed, Congressional representative from the Erie district. Scott's career brought him the titles of Railroad King and Coal King of the United States. Also a successful politician, he was chosen mayor of Erie in 1866 and 1871, and elected to Congress in 1884. Fame came also from the development of his two-thousand-acre bayfront estate, for his Algeria Farm was regarded as one of the best horse breeding farms in the world. He purchased the world's finest stallion, Rayon D'Or, one of whose descendants was Man O'War. John Carney wrote that the Scott colors were as well known then as are the later ones of Belmont, Whitney, and Bradley.

Much of the business for these enterprises was transacted at the northwest corner of 10th and State Streets, where, since 1875, had stood the proud Scott Block, the grey limestone building with its

Doric, Ionic, and Corinthian pillars, its mansard roof crowned with an iron fence, its elegantly corniced windows, its Scott's Music Hall with the 25-foot-high ceiling, crystal chandeliers, parquet floor, silken walls. Various merchants occupied its street level and lower floors. In 1924, the W. T. Grant Company opened in the Scott Block and remained there until 1954. A parade of offices on the upper floors handled varied businesses that were part of the Erie scene for more than fifty years. However, the unique structure was never the same after it was gutted by fire on December 20, 1944. In remodeling, the mansard roof and the embellishments were removed, along with the sheen of the dream that had been William L. Scott's in excavating the original building in July 1873. The building was totally demolished in March 1969, along with the Lawrence Hotel, a landmark since 1911, and Shea's Theatre, whose organ Gannon University now owns. The Hilton Hotel would use the north side of 10th Street, from State to Peach Streets, when it opened October 15, 1976. Diagonally across the intersection from the Scott Block, at 1001-7 State Street, the fourteen-story Erie Trust Company building became Erie's only skyscraper in 1926.

During this same period, in two small rooms on the third floor of the Scott Block, a giant was being humbly born. The Erie Insurance Exchange lists its birthday as April 20, 1925, at noon. Its co-founder, H. Orth Hirt, became president of the thriving insurance business in 1931. Expansion took the business to 101 East Sixth Street from 1938 until 1956. The next move to 144 East Sixth Street would presage the award-winning headquarters of the Erie Insurance Group. In 1984 this building would become a most impressive partner of Gannon University in downtown Erie's urban renewal.

John Nolen in *Greater Erie* called Erie "the meeting place of iron ores from the upper lake regions and coal from the Pennsylvania fields." Thus, by the late 20's, overall diversified companies were firmly established in Erie industry. These included such firms as Jarecki Manufacturing Company (1852), Erie Malleable Iron Company (1880), American Sterilizer Company (1894), Hammermill Paper Company (1898), Continental Rubber Works (1903), Lord Corporation (1919), Griswold Manufacturing Company (1897), Zurn Manufacturing Company (1900), Erie City Iron Works (1894), Reed Manufacturing Company (1896), General Electric (1911). The Erie Resistor Corporation began in 1928; and in the same year, Bucyrus-Erie Company was formed by the consolidation of the Bucyrus Company and the Erie Steam Shovel Company. In a 1930 report of industry, the *Erie City Directory* 1932 reads: "Over 326 manufacturing establishments, employing 22,694 men and women, paying wages of $36,963,000 annually, and having products valued at $113,772,800 annually."

The fishing business prospered in Erie, with an average catch of 30,000 tons a year during the 1895-1920 period. However, the still unexplained disappearance of ciscoes in 1925 helped to diminish this successful fishing trade.

The lake front, Presque Isle, the bay, and streams have helped shape Erie's character and destiny. Presque Isle became a state park in 1921; and in 1926, the Perry Monument was built at Crystal Point beside Misery Bay. Through the good offices of Jerome F. Downing, land had been acquired and improved for Glenwood Park. Mill Creek, running through the park, had been controlled in 1921 with debris-catchers and the Mill Creek tube. In 1929, a large animal house was built at the Glenwood Zoo.

Erie boasts many recreational facilities as well. The Memorial Stadium at Academy High School, dedicated to the veterans of World War I on Armistice Day, 1924, provided facilities for outdoor events, mostly sports. Another large meeting place was the Carney Auditorium at 1024 French Street. Opening in 1927, it accommodated more than two thousand people for lectures, concerts, sports, marathon dances, cooking schools. Many famous personalities appeared at the auditorium, including: Billy Sunday, Marion Talley, Gladys Swarthout, Lawrence Tibbett, Rosa Ponselle, Governor Gifford Pinchot, Secretary of Commerce Herbert Hoover, Clarence Darrow, Miss America 1930, Jack Dempsey, Admiral Richard E. Byrd and Paul Siple, the Erie Boy Scout who was selected to accompany the Byrd expedition to the South Pole. Siple would receive an honorary degree at the Gannon College commencement ceremony in 1958.

Transportation was also flourishing in Erie during the 1920's and 1930's. Back in 1909 the first round trip air flight was made over Erie, from Four-Mile-Creek to City Hall. On March 16, 1926, Dr. Robert Hutchings Goddard launched the first liquid-propellant rocket at Auburn, Mass., taking 2.5 seconds to travel 184 feet. The next year, May 21, 1927, a young hero named Charles Augustus Lindbergh piloted a very small airplane, "The Spirit of St. Louis", across the Atlantic Ocean alone and non-stop, and later over Erie. As a result of this activity, ten years later the Works Progress Administration constructed the Port Erie Airport.

In the meantime, such seasoned world travelers as Bishop John Mark Gannon would travel by rail and luxury liner; the Bishop's first air flight was to the Eucharistic Congress in Sao Paulo, Brazil in September 1942. The lighter-than-air dirigibles came and went with the Shenandoah being torn to pieces by a thunderstorm in 1925; the Akron being lost in a storm over the Atlantic in 1933; her sister ship, the Macon, crashing into the Pacific in 1935. Only the proud Hindenburg remained, but later burned at Lakehurst, New Jersey in 1937.

The Erie Railways Company was formed in September 1924 to take over the street car system, and the following year this parent firm organized the Erie Coach Company to operate a bus line. On December 7, 1925, the first motor bus left Perry Square driven by the father of Fr. Robert Levis of the University, and the last trolley completed its run on May 12, 1935. Downstate in the diocese, the trolley line between Reynoldsville and Punxsutawney was abandoned on September 30, 1927 after twenty-eight years of service.

As railroads continued to be important to the city, the new Union Station at 14th and Peach was built in 1926. The new post office and Griswold Plaza to the north completed the beautification of this area. One could take the Pennsylvania Railroad to Kanty College from 1912 until 1926 when that stop was discontinued. However, Shannon Road was cemented in 1928, making access somewhat easier. Small communities were somewhat accessible by rail. One traveler's story tells of a woman who asked the Pennsylvania Railroad conductor, "Is this the accommodation that stops at Belle Valley?" He replied, "It would have to be an accommodation to stop there!"

During this time, when Cathedral College began (1933), the first Erie talkies were shown in 1927, and, by 1934 one could enjoy not only Shirley Temple, Tom Mix, and Hoot Gibson, but news-reels, big news in 1933, which included Hitler's election to Chancellorship of Germany, Congress' legalizaton of 3.2% beer, and the repeal of Prohibition, in effect since 1920.

Those having phones during this decade probably would be doing business with the Mutual Telephone Company at 19-21 East Ninth Street, then would watch the company expand its operating territory to communities of the county, and erect its new exchange office building at 20-26 East 10th Street in 1926. In 1930 the corporate name was changed to Pennsylvania Telephone Corporation, and as additional subscribers were acquired, the dial operation gradually expanded. Telegrams were still a convenient way to communicate and uniformed young men were on service.

The people of Erie have always been sports-minded and have faithfully supported all of the University's sporting events since their beginnings. What was the Erie sports picture in the 20's and 30's? John C. Carney's *Saga of Erie Sports* depicts this scene.

Gus Anderson, one of Erie's earliest famous athletes, started his career at Colgate University, and returned to Erie to coach at East High School and, in 1930, coached at Millcreek High School. His track team at East was one of the best balanced teams in Erie track history; and in 1926, East's basketball team went to state finals. Anderson Field at McDowell High School represents the affection and esteem of Anderson's Millcreek Township fans.

Lowell Drake was head athletic coach at Academy High School from 1923 until 1945, then became the coordinator of physical education and athletics in the Erie School District. His contributions to Erie sports include development of the track programs; and in 1931, arrangement of the first football game under lights at the stadium. Football at Cathedral Prep School was started in 1925, four years after the school opened. Under the coaching of Father Walter Conway, in 1932 the team was neither tied nor beaten. Another benchmark in high school football was accomplished by William (Demmy) Demorier in 1926 when he arranged for one of the first intersectional games in the country, scheduling Academy to play Atlanta, Georgia. Carney credits this versatile promoter with putting Erie sports on the map.

The YMCA was also actively promoting sports. In the lobby of

Msgr. Joseph J. Wehrle, S.T.D.

Cathedral College, 1933-1941.

Msgr. Wilfrid Nash, Archbishop Gannon, and Dr. Joseph Wehrle.

Most Rev. Alfred M. Watson.

Old Main, winter view.

Founder's Day, February 19, 1960. Pa. Superior Court Judge William Hirt, Archbishop J.M. Gannon, Rev. Dr. Wilfrid J. Nash.

Erie Club (across from Old Main) and First Presbyterian Church around 1890. The church later burned and was replaced. Student Services and the Pontifical Center are presently housed there.

Archbishop J.M. Gannon and President Nash with Dr. Paul Siple, with his mother and wife.

the downtown "Y" is a picture and plaque honoring J. D. (Doc) Ainsworth as Athletic Director 1914-1937. "Doc" advocated the American Crawl and his champion swimmers included Olympic team members. Gus Pulakos was on Doc's first swimming teams, and Achilles, one of Gus' sons, was the last great swimming star coached by Ainsworth during two generations of service.

The first city golf tournament had been held in 1921, the year the Lawrence Park Golf Club was organized. Golf was introduced to Erie by Joseph Metcalf who returned home in 1897 with a set of golf clubs after he had seen the game played in Scotland.

There was exciting action in the world of tennis, for the 20's saw a new group of champions. Byron Baur, now an attorney and still winning championships, played winning doubles with Joe Schmid, now retired, and for whom Schmid Towers is named. Baur, Schmid, and several other young players were members of the Erie Tennis Club which played at Hunter's Lodge after about 1922 when they built six tennis courts on the property they subleased from a riding club. Hunter Willis had purchased the Major Parker property on Parker Road (now Schultz Road) and remodeled and enlarged the homestead to make the Lodge. Charles LeSueur, then president of the Tennis Club and associated with the Erie Conservatory of Music located at 156 West Seventh Street, is recognized as an important force in promoting the popularity of tennis during this period.

This was Erie in the 20's and 30's, when Gannon College first took roots through the vision of the Bishop of Erie, John Mark Gannon, who had been himself a poor local boy, but one who never forgot the lack of education and cultural advantages which beset him. John Mark Gannon (1877-1969) was the seventh of nine children, the fourth son, born to Thomas Patrick Gannon (1832-1894) and Julia Dunlavey Gannon (1841-1930) of Erie. His education in Erie included parochial school at St. Patrick's, his home parish, and graduation from Clark's Business College in 1892. After working at the Erie City Iron Works for two years as a bookkeeper, he left for St. Bonaventure College in Allegany, New York, in 1894 and received his Bachelor of Arts degree from that institution in June 1899. Studies at the Catholic University of America earned him a bachelor degree in Sacred Theology in 1902 and a licentiate in Sacred Theology in 1904. With studies in Europe he earned doctoral degrees in Canon Law and Sacred Theology from Appolinare University in Rome, Italy. The first of several honorary degrees was conferred by Notre Dame University in 1927.

Father John Mark Gannon was ordained December 21, 1901. His experience with parish life began with duties at St. Joseph's Church in Oil City, St. Francis Xavier in McKean, and St. Stephen's in Oil City during the summers of 1903 through 1905. In 1907 he was assigned to St. Anthony's, a new parish at Cambridge Springs, and remained there until 1916, when he was assigned to St. Brigid's in Meadville. His final local parish service was at St. Andrew's in Erie, from 1917 through 1919 while he was Auxiliary Bishop. He was consecrated Bishop on February 6, 1918. Bishop John E. FitzMaurice died on June 11, 1920 and Auxiliary Bishop John Mark Gannon was installed as Bishop of the Diocese of Erie on December 16, 1920.

As parish priest and bishop he was known as a builder and an innovator; St. Anthony's Church, the parochial school at St. Brigid's, the rectory at St. Anthony's, the starting of Cathedral Prep in 1921 were early portents of a most productive episcopate.

There was yet another facet to Father John Mark Gannon's abilities, for he had been appointed Superintendent of Schools of the Diocese on February 13, 1912. An active administrator, he worked on standardization of elementary schools in the diocese and on a system of certification for teachers.

In spite of the precipitous condition of the American economy in the wake of the stock market crash of 1929 and the ensuing Great Depression, some of the efforts of the Catholic Church in the realm of education proved to be quite successful. Naturally, this was not achieved without struggle and sacrifice. Among these successes was the extension of the Catholic school system not only in Erie but in much of the nation. The extent of this venture, strongly supported by many bishops to fulfill the mandates of the Council of Baltimore to establish a school in every parish, contributed mightily to creating a demand for secondary and higher education under the auspices of the Catholic Church. Numerous Catholic institutions of higher learning were established in the

1920-1950 era to meet this educational need; it might be added that this was also the age of the expansion of higher educational opportunities in the country as a whole. Beginning with the establishment of Georgetown in 1789, as the first Catholic university in the new nation, this number had grown by 1932 to 162 institutions with 2,768 professors providing an education for 105,926 students. The pace of development increased in the 1930's and after and by 1982 there were 237 colleges and universities serving 533,080 students.

CHAPTER II

THE NEWSBOYS' COLLEGE

"Now, Dr. Wehrle, don't start a college when I'm away!" Bishop Gannon insisted just before leaving for his *ad limina* visit to Rome.

"By no means, Your Excellency," "Doc" Wehrle assured him.

The very next day "Doc" Wehrle consolidated final plans to open a men's college. The retired Ordinary of the Diocese of Erie, Bishop Alfred M. Watson, with a smile, so described the mandate under which Cathedral College opened its doors, a few yards west of the bishop's residence, September 18, 1933.

It would be pleasing to think that Gannon University was founded upon the great wealth of noteworthy, successful Erie entrepreneurs, or developed from the congealing of lofty educational objectives of Erie's respective constituencies, or from the collective conviction of ecclesiastical advisors to the local church. It didn't. It resulted from the profound and invincible convictions of two local churchmen, with long experience in education, who were convinced that something had to be done for the education of poor boys in Erie. These churchmen were Archbishop Gannon and "Doc" Wehrle.

If Archbishop Gannon had any interest at all in the improvement of his diocese, it would have been in the area of education. Whether this interest came from his experience as Superintendent of Schools of the Diocese starting in 1912, or whether it came from a deeper personal conviction is difficult to evaluate. His statements made in the latter years of his life tend to reflect his conviction that education was the most important tool anyone could use to rise from humble happenings; to actualize for himself the great American dream of self-fulfillment; to have a voice in the economic, social, and political life of America. When plans for Gannon

17

School of Arts and Science were announced in 1941, the Bishop
wrote:

> The sons of a working man, no matter how virtuous or talented, are
> forced to give up hope of a college education. I do not think the right
> to a college education should be based on wealth or social standing.
> I think the right to a college education should be based on virtue and
> talent . . . . the college should be open to young men of any creed or
> color. They shall receive an education and at a minimal cost — a
> cost which they can well defray by a paper route.

Archbishop Gannon, as he looked west to the dilapidated, gray,
weathered site of Cathedral College, must have mused often about
its humble start as well as its problematic future, but he encouraged,
supported, and underwrote the efforts of the man who laid the
foundation stones of a great university.

Dr. Joseph J. Wehrle is the hero in the story of Gannon University's origins. His driving energy, his invincible tenacity, and his
unbelievable courage undergirded the first efforts to establish an
Erie college for men.

"Doc" Wehrle was a dignified, modest, erect, statuesque
schoolman, about six feet tall, with a mop of very blonde hair. In
his younger years he might be described as modestly handsome.
He always wore clerical black. His only concession to fashion was
a rather long suit coat which had to be custom-made and fashioned
by a tailor. He wore a white, very high clerical collar which
distinguished him from other clerics. This is the way he predictably
appeared in public, generally neat, but with long, wavy blonde
hair almost always windblown.

However, his students usually observed him in his office without
coat and collar, in a white shirt, clean but wrinkled, collar turned
down and sleeves to the wrist. He was wont to sit back in a relaxed
way in his battered swivel chair with his feet up on a desk covered
with papers, correspondence, books, periodicals, and ashtrays
filled with cigarette butts. One or the other shoe often sported a
hole. In his younger years, he swam in Lake Erie. His infrequent
recreation was a walk with his large dog, which was the center of
loving attention on the part of his students. He was almost always
a solitary figure with few intimate friends, and these were generally
clerics. His living quarters, never of importance or concern to

him, were spare and monastic. Until the end of his life, he enjoyed robust health. This might have resulted from his spartan diet of buttermilk and soda crackers which he almost habitually substituted for meals most of his adult years.

In 1921 he became Founder and Headmaster of Cathedral Preparatory School. Most students related to him in a deep and devoted way, with loyalty that perdured a lifetime because he related best to his students. He continued his educational relationships with secular and ecclesiastical officers with precision and dignity; he knew the great men and women of Erie's society and beyond, but his warmth and sympathy and love and real self were reserved for students. This is more true of his high school tenure than of his college presidency. A Prep High School student, apprehended for gambling, truancy, or scholastic indifference, caught the fire of his disapproval; the punishment he meted out rarely reflected rancor or bitterness, but instead a loving, intimate and personal concern by "Doc."

Dr. Wehrle was born in Punxsutawney, Pennsylvania on September 15, 1891, the son of a jeweler, and one of five children, two daughters and three sons. After graduation from St. Vincent's Seminary in Latrobe, Pennsylvania, he was sent to Rome for his theological studies and was awarded the Doctorate of Sacred Theology. Ordained on October 28, 1915, his first assignment was to St. John's Parish, 26th at Wallace Street, Erie. After three years, he was appointed Pastor of St. Francis' Church, McKean, Pennsylvania. In December 1919, he was appointed Superintendent of Schools of the Diocese of Erie. This onerous and responsible position he held while he was both Headmaster of Cathedral Preparatory School and President of Villa Maria College.

"Doc" was notorious for his absent-mindedness. The Rev. William Martin, one of his closest colleagues for many, many years and aide to "Doc" during the waning years of Cathedral College and infancy of its successor institution, the Gannon School of Arts and Science, enjoyed reporting "Doc's" dismay at having his car, (generally a large and heavy one), stolen while on a trip to Buffalo, New York. Dr. Wehrle had driven to Buffalo for an overnight meeting and forgot that he had driven his car and so returned in a friend's car. After returning to Erie, he noticed his car had been "stolen" and so reported it to the Erie police who dutifully recovered it in Buffalo in the same parking lot where "Doc" had left ît. Father Martin had the humorous task of getting to Buffalo and driving the "stolen merchandise" home to Erie.

As previously noted, "Doc" was a heavy smoker. Not infrequently he would light his cigarette from the car lighter and discard the lighter out the open window.

The students of Cathedral Preparatory knew "Doc" much more intimately than the students of Cathedral College or the Gannon School of Arts and Science. With the older men he was generally more formal and correct, but with the secondary schoolboys, he was forever threatening sanctions of the direst nature if they were to be apprehended in the midst of their boyish pranks. For example, a typical warning from him was: "If any of you students of the Cathedral Preparatory School of Boys is caught smoking on the premises, you will be subject to immediate suspension!"

Such culprits would be suspended for a few hours until their embarrassed parents would be interviewed in "Doc's" office and reinstated. Another of his famous warnings would be: "If any of you seniors is caught gambling on these premises, you will be subject to immediate dismissal without possibility of reinstatement!"

"Doc" often would "raid" the lads "shooting craps" in out-of-the-way corners of the basement school. Like a black condor, he would swoop down upon the unfortunate gamblers to take off with the prize — eighteen cents, a quarter, occasionally even thirty-seven cents. Generally that same day "Doc" would be chuckling as he munched a hotdog and Coke in the miniscule "cafeteria" in the basement of Cathedral College, then run by Bob Riddle (who later owned and operated Sunset Inn on the banks of the south shore of Lake Erie for thirty years).

Time meant little to him. Occasionally he was so preoccupied with a book, often times an old medieval tome, that he would spend all evening and all night reading it. He wouldn't sleep at all. When the Prepsters were remiss in their studies, he thought nothing of keeping them after school for an hour or more. The worst of these scholastic criminals were sentenced for a week to "serve time" sometimes in "Doc's" office since he had office work to do. These occasions generally created a loving relationship between "Doc" and the culprit, which lasted a lifetime. Volumes could be written of the stories Prepsters tell of their first Headmaster and their run-ins with him.

Personal money meant less than nothing to him. For years he would meet institutional expenses out of his own meager salary. This was especially true in the 30's when the dark days of the Great Depression grew even blacker. He was always a soft touch for every "down-and-outer" who approached him. One winter day, a poor man approached "Doc" for some money for clothes. He immediately took off his brand-new woolen overcoat and gave it to the man.

Sister Julia Marie Carey, the former Miss Ruth Carey, who served for years as secretary to Dr. Wehrle at Cathedral College, has contributed some interesting anecdotes about "Doc." She described his bi-monthly rampage when he would rage about a point of scholarship or discipline that he felt was being eliminated or overlooked by students. During this time, he thought nothing of throwing an eraser, a piece of chalk, or a book at some distracted student.

She recalls "Doc's" detective work in rounding up two Prep boys one afternoon, whose pockets "Doc" demanded be emptied. Out squirmed a couple of garter snakes on his desk, to the concealed amusement of the priest.

His relationship with women was definitely shy and generally nervous. When some angry mother would phone him to discuss the failures of her son, he quickly told his secretary, "Tell her I have another appointment, can't talk to her now."

Housekeeping in old Cathedral College was a luxury few of the faculty or the students considered necessary. Generally one or two students would be designated "superintendent" and haphazardly slide a worn out broom across the floor in an unscheduled fashion, and wash the blackboards occasionally. Falling leaves often blew into the building and would collect in the corners of the halls and other errant places. One day, "Doc" got very excited when the leaves started to burn in the open floor registers where they had collected. "Call the fire department! Call the fire department!" "Doc" roared. Of course the students welcomed the intermezzo from class as the firemen extinguished the little blaze.

Sister Julia Marie recalls "Doc's" dogs better than most of his acquaintances, probably because she often took care of them. For example, Prince, a pure-bred English Setter, loved to chase cars, bicycles, motorcycles, and anything else that moved fast. He was actually a very pious dog inasmuch as he loved to look for his master in St. Peter's Cathedral where he would often find him celebrating the liturgy. At communion time, Prince would bound over the marble communion railing to assist his master by picking up the lower part of either alb or chasuble as "Doc" walked back and forth distributing communion (to the absolute consternation of all the pious parishioners of St. Peter's). "Doc" would usually convince somebody to take the dogs when they were old and sickly and so, eventually, Prince was given to his secretary. Several years after receiving Prince, "Doc" insisted in giving his secretary another pointer, "Go on, take it home with you, she is a nice dog! You will like her!" In no time at all, the secretary became midwife to a litter of pointers, in which, of course, "Doc" was not interested in the least.

"Doc" owned Sinbad I, a mammoth German Shepherd, while at Gannon School of Arts and Science. Everybody knew and loved Sinbad, whose ferocious appearance masked his extreme laziness and excessive weight. No student would refuse to share his lunch with Sinbad. Generally wherever "Doc" went, his dog followed, and the scene of both master and beast presented an interesting picture in the classroom with "Doc" seated high on his wooden desk and the dog perched beneath it.

In the Spring of 1925, the first graduates of Cathedral Preparatory School, financially unprepared to continue their education, were frequent petitioners of "Doc's" help concerning their future. Bishop Alfred M. Watson was one of those students. There were forty-two boys in that graduation class, only a handful of whom were capable financially of enrolling in college. Dr. Wehrle never doubted that somehow he would help them all. He conceived the idea of establishing a junior college for men to complete what had been begun on the secondary level.

However, if Dr. Wehrle conceived the college in his mind, it would be many years in gestation before delivery. The religious women of the diocese simultaneously were moving to create two separate facilities for the higher education of women in the area. In 1926, Mother Mary Borgia, R.S.M., instituted Mercyhurst College; and Mother M. Helena, S.S.J., and Sister Stella, S.S.J., established Villa Maria College in 1925. Each institution has been in continuous operation since that time. Since Dr. Wehrle was also Superintendent of Schools, he was directed by Bishop Gannon to aid in the establishment of Villa Maria College and named its President. Dr. Wehrle was pragmatic enough to recognize the impossibility of the diocese establishing two colleges simultaneously, one for women and another for men, and so he shelved his plans for a men's college, but only momentarily and temporarily. Disappointed, he bided his time.

What would he do with the thirty or so Cathedral Prep graduates for whom he was already committed to provide higher education? He decided they would attend Villa Maria College, but only to the despair, embarrassment, and shock of the Sisters. And so they did enroll.

The Sisters strongly resented the enrollment of these male students presumably because this represented a serious departure from tradition. Most Catholic colleges at that time were single-sexed. Certainly no college conducted by religious women was coeducational. However, the Sisters acceded to Dr. Wehrle's arrangements probably out of a general sense of gratitude to him as well as to Bishop Gannon. The men students continued at Villa Maria College for two years, until the early days of June 1927, when they were requested not to return in the Fall. Dr. Wehrle personally interceded on their behalf and their grades and credits were accepted by both St. Bonaventure University, Olean, New York and St. Vincent College, Latrobe, Pennsylvania, even though Villa Maria College was not regionally accredited at the time. In fact, the State of Pennsylvania was not to grant the charter to conduct a college until 1929, the beginning of the Great Depression.

By the Summer of 1933, the possibility of higher education for men in Erie had lessened. If the first graduates of Cathedral Prep School were financially bad off in 1925, by 1933 their condition was tragic. 1933 represented the worst deepening of that economic collapse of the entire country. The smokestacks of Erie factories were clean. Many banks collapsed. Hammermill Paper Company

was distributing food baskets to its idle employees. All the shops
on West 12th Street resembled dirty tombs. Erie fathers cultivated
small plots of land in order to grow vegetables which their spouses
canned to avoid starvation through the winter months. Soup
kitchens were operated not only by conscientious religious groups,
but even by the city administration at Mulligan Hall, the City
Hall Annex. Those bread and soup lines extended around Perry
Square West twice a day for years. Despairing and penniless men
hurled themselves to death out of the windows of the Erie Trust
Company (the present G. Daniel Baldwin Building at Tenth and
State) and from the Commerce Building at Twelfth and State
Streets.

There were thirty-six graduates in Dr. Wehrle's Prep School in
1933, only two of them in any way financially able to plan for
college. Most of the rest of that graduating class literally sat in the
Downing Building where Dr. Wehrle lived and where his office
was located and begged him to help them. Could nothing at all be
done to enable them to go to college?

Dr. Wehrle knew that now was the time to act in spite of the
total lack of any reasonable promise of success. He had conceived
of the idea for his college around 1925 (and possibly before) and he
would witness its birth in 1933. He conferred frequently with
Bishop Gannon throughout the summer about the possibility of
founding a college for men. Naturally, Bishop Gannon was sym-
pathetic, but counseled patience and prudence since funds were
totally lacking.

This was the occasion of the dialogue recounted at the start of
this chapter. Bishop Gannon journeyed to Europe and remained
belatedly in Spain until the end of September. Whether Dr. Wehrle
was moved by private revelation, compassion for his destitute
students, or from impatience no one can ever know. He went
ahead anyhow, presumed permission to start the college he was
forbidden to start in the Bishop's absence, and dared to open the
doors of what he called Cathedral College at his home, the Downing Building, 225 West Ninth Street, thirty-five yards west of the
Bishop's residence. Cathedral College was born!

There are no records of what the returning Bishop Gannon
either thought or remarked about the infant junior college operat-

ing almost in his yard. He must have been disturbed. He probably was angry for a time. One can be sure, interesting conversations took place between the Bishop and the educational pioneer. However, the motives that drove Dr. Wehrle also stimulated the Bishop. If he did not bless the institution, he did not discontinue it. He let it continue but pointedly placed the full burden of administration and management on the tall shoulders of this solitary educational entrepreneur.

The next few years saw Dr. Wehrle at his best. He literally existed for Cathedral College exclusively. There is nothing he would not have done, save sin, to keep it functioning. Friends reported that most of his personal salary, as miniscule as it was, went toward paying off bills. These were the "buttermilk and cracker" years, an era of stark survival.

The first year, 1933-34, Cathedral College operated under the charter of Villa Maria College as a downtown extension for men. Coincidentally, Villa Maria College was facing its first major educational hurdle, accreditation by its regional accrediting body, the Middle States and Maryland Association of Colleges and Secondary Schools (now Middle States Association of Colleges and Universities). The accrediting committee granted that Villa Maria's accreditation hinged on its severing its connection with Cathedral College. Obviously, these educators saw the crowded and inadequate facilities of the dilapidated building in which Cathedral College was housed, not to speak of its other faults. Villa's ties with the downtown men's division had to be severed.

Without delay, Dr. Wehrle immediately journeyed to Harrisburg where he studied laws relating to institutions of higher learning in hopes of finding some Pennsylvania institution whose charter would permit sponsorship of the infant Cathedral College. He discovered that any college in Pennsylvania that held a charter granted before the adoption of Pennsylvania's Constitution of 1873 had almost unlimited educational powers and was not subject to legislative restrictions adopted subsequent to 1873. The Erie Sisters of St. Joseph at one time had possessed such a charter but failed to register a request for its renewal and their privileged charter thus had lapsed. Dr. Wehrle discovered that Duquesne University in Pittsburgh had one of these "grandfather charters" but was not interested in sponsoring Cathedral College. Dr. Wehrle resourcefully returned to where he attended the seminary, to St. Vincent College in Latrobe, and there the Most Reverend Archabbott Alfred Koch, O.S.B., graciously consented to permit Cathedral College to operate under the charter of St. Vincent College. This was the arrangement from September 1934, the second year of operation, to September 1941, when Cathedral College became the Gannon School of Arts and Science and returned once more to function under the charter of the fully accredited Villa Maria College.

Dr. Wehrle was not alone in this project of beginning Cathedral College. A very small handful of laymen, some of whom taught at Cathedral Preparatory School, constituted a nucleus of faculty upon which the whole project depended.

James J. Freeman (1913-1980) started teaching mathematics at the Cathedral Preparatory School under Dr. Wehrle in September 1934 and ended his long and useful teaching career at Gannon University with death on January 12, 1980. He began teaching algebra, trigonometry and eventually differential equations, analytical geometry, and integral calculus at Gannon College in 1945, and his service as teacher of mathematics at Gannon College continued until his death. Tens of thousands of both men and women students attest to his competency in the field of mathematics as well as to his basic pedagogical ability. It was often said, "If Mr. Freeman can't teach you, you can never learn mathematics!" He invested his entire professional life in these institutions originally because of his love and devotion to the person of "Doc" Wehrle and eventually from an invincible love for teaching. His inadequate compensation; the almost complete want of professional perquisites; occasional skirmishes with "Doc"; and the financial needs of his family, never moved him to seek a more favorable professional position in another, more established, educational institution which he could have most easily obtained. Gannon College awarded him an honorary degree, Doctor of Laws, on May 21, 1978.

Francis J. Hermann (1910-1981) also started his teaching career in chemistry at the Cathedral Preparatory School (the exact year is unknown). He started at Cathedral College as instructor of chemistry in September 1935. No Cathedral College student was unfamiliar with the tall figure wearing a black rubber apron who presided over the laboratory in the west rear of the old Downing Building for so long. The very mention of Mr. Hermann recalls the universal smell of sulphur compounds pervading the building. Mr. Hermann made the move with "Doc" from Ninth to Sixth Street in 1941, and left Gannon College in 1951 in order to start an industrial shop in Wattsburg, Pennsylvania, in 1955.

Gerald Raymond Kraus never taught on a regular basis at Cathedral Preparatory School. He started teaching mathematics and physics at Cathedral College in September 1937, after beginning teaching at Mount Mercy College in Pittsburgh where he served as mathematics instructor. He made the move to Gannon School of Arts and Science in 1941, when he added engineering subjects to his customary list of mathematics courses, and where he remained until the early 50's at which time he created the Kraus Manufacturing Company in Erie. He returned to an academic career as Dean of Engineering at Gannon College in 1954. From 1956 to 1972, he served as Dean of Pure and Applied Sciences and Dean Emeritus since that time. No individual contributed more significantly than Dean Kraus toward the establishment of science education at Gannon College or its predecessor institutions. In 1963, Pope John XXIII awarded him the *Pro Ecclesia et Pontifice* award, one of of the highest honors which a Catholic layman can receive. In 1980, Gannon University awarded him an Honorary Doctor of Laws.

John E. Waldron (1911-1979) began his teaching career in the humanities at Cathedral Preparatory School around 1934. His service was very brief at the Prep School since "Doc" asked him to teach Latin, history, and political science at Cathedral College starting September 1936. He moved to Gannon School of Arts and Science in 1941, but entered the military service during the war years (1942-1944), after which he returned to Gannon College as a professor in education. He continued at Gannon until granted a two-year leave of absence (1948-1949) during which he earned his Ph.D. in economics at the University of Pittsburgh. Dr. Waldron was the first of a long list of teachers who interrupted their teaching to pursue a doctorate. He was named by Dr. Wehrle as

Dean of Instruction in 1950, and served with eminent distinction as administrator and professor until his retirement. He also was awarded the *Pro Ecclesia et Pontifice* award by Pope John XXIII in 1963.

Francis C. Weithman left Rensselaer Polytechnic Institute to teach mathematics at Cathedral College when it opened in 1933. At this time he served as administrative aide to Dr. Wehrle in several capacities. He transferred to Gannon School of Arts and Science in 1941, but interrupted teaching to serve as major in the United States Army until the war's end. At this time, he contributed greatly to instruction in business administration and accounting and remained with the college until 1972, when he opened his office as a Certified Public Accountant. His uncountable and indispensible contributions to Cathedral College and its successor institutions can only be estimated, never adequately weighed.

Dr. Wehrle hired Paul B. Hesch to teach economics and accounting. This Titusville native continued to teach at Cathedral College until his entry into the United States Navy; he was killed in the line of duty in the Philippine Islands.

Elmer T. Weibel (Ph.D., Notre Dame University), taught chemistry for a number of years at Cathedral College beginning in 1933.

Francis Darwin Greiner, who attended Cathedral College from 1934-1936, and received his degree from Georgetown University School of Foreign Service in 1938, taught economics at Cathedral College beginning in February 1940. He was the first Cathedral College alumnus to be added to the college teaching staff. Dr. Wehrle rarely missed an opportunity of assessing very intelligent students whom he would invite later to assume teaching positions in his institution.

Gerald J. Weber, currently U.S. District Judge for the Western District of Pennsylvania, a recent graduate of Harvard and the University of Pennsylvania, taught English literature at Cathedral College from 1939 to June 1941. He then served five years in the armed services, some of which was spent in Austria where he met his future wife, Berta, who was to have a distinguished career herself at Gannon College. After the military, he resumed teaching English at Gannon College for only one year, 1947-1948.

Other notable instructors at the college included Harry S. Wilder who taught English for several years beginning in 1933; and George G. Stout who taught accounting for a short time in 1936.

This nucleus of laymen represented most of the faculty of Cathedral College from September 1933 until its termination in June 1941. It has proved impossible to gather a complete record of the total faculty, especially those who served for a while as part-time and adjunct faculty. But these teachers are listed because they represent a body of pioneers who were as dedicated, competent, and committed to this project as its first president. While a priest and clergyman was its inspiration, and while a bishop was considered its founder, the institution was always from the beginning a lay and Christian effort. It flowed from their love of learning and their desire to communicate knowledge to the less gifted and the less privileged. The personal sacrifice and abnegation of these men following behind their leader, "Doc" Wehrle, can only be surmised.

In addition to these lay faculty, three priests especially contributed to Cathedral College in its early days. Father Edward Peter McManaman, Father Alfred Michael Watson, and Father William L. Sullivan.

Rev. Edward Peter McManaman (1900-1964), who later became Auxiliary Bishop of the Diocese of Erie with residence at St. Joseph's Church in Oil City, Pennsylvania, taught religion at Cathedral College from its beginning in 1933. However, his endless duties as Rector of St. Peter Cathedral (1936) prevented intensive activity at the college. His major and permanent contributions to higher education resulted from his being one of "Doc" Wehrle's most important educational advisors. With a Doctorate in Sacred Theology (1931) and many years of experience as Director of the Confraternity of Christian Doctrine, he was well qualified to serve as a competent advisor in various boards of control and other executive councils set up to administer both to Gannon School of Arts and Science and Gannon College. No one was more aware than Rev. McManaman of "Doc's" educational competencies as well as of his administrative weaknesses. He served actively on the Executive Committee of Gannon School of Arts and Science and Gannon College from 1941 until his death in 1964. Bishop

McManaman, for years as Secretary to the Executive Committee of the Board of Control of Gannon College, often advocated changes which seemed revolutionary at the time to Dr. Wehrle. This was painful both to "Doc" as well as to him. He was probably the first serious articulate critic of some of Dr. Wehrle's policies, and first in a series of professional critics who later on would be instrumental in the closing out of "Doc's" educational career.

Rev. William L. Sullivan (1894-1961) was appointed the first resident Chaplain at Mercyhurst College in 1926. Dr Wehrle gave him the title of Assistant Dean of Religion in 1934, and he taught at Gannon for several years. Later, he served on the Executive Council of Gannon School of Arts and Science and on the Board of Incorporators and the Executive Committee of the Board of Control of Gannon College.

Rev. Alfred Michael Watson (1907), while appointed Chaplain and Professor at Mercyhurst College in September 1936, assumed duties as religion teacher at Cathedral College beginning in 1938 and continuing until appointed to the faculty of the Cathedral Preparatory School on October 1, 1941. He was ordained Auxiliary Bishop of Erie on June 29, 1965, and Bishop of Erie on March 19, 1969. He served as secretary, member, and Chairman of the Board of Trustees of Gannon College 1965-1982, and now as Trustee Emeritus. A lifelong friend and admirer of Dr. Wehrle, Bishop Watson must be viewed as being always in support of Dr. Wehrle's first educational efforts as well as a sophisticated, experienced advisor to the maturing institution of Gannon College. A close, personal friend of "Doc," Bishop Watson delivered a poignant tribute to Dr. Wehrle at the homily of his funeral Mass on December 28, 1967, at St. Peter's Cathedral.

Mr. Francis G. Weithman recollects the faculty of Cathedral College at the end of its first year of operation as follows: Dr. Wehrle, Latin; Fr. McManaman, S.T.D., religion; Dr. Duering, Ph.D., German; Paul B. Hesch, B.S., economics and accounting; Harry S. Wilder, M.A., English; J. C. Rischell, A.B., French; T. E. Weible, Ph.D., chemistry; Francis G. Weithman, A.B., mathematics; G. P. O'Connor, A.B., LL.B., business law.

The Cathedral College newspaper, *The Tower*, October 30, 1936, lists the Cathedral College faculty in 1936 as follows:

Rev. Joseph J. Wehrle, S.T.D., religion; Rev. Gottleib Steinwachs, Ph.D., German; The Messrs. Elmer T. Weible, Ph.D., chemistry and physics; Francis G. Weithman, B.S., mathematics; Harry S. Wilder, English; John E. Waldron, M.A., history, political science, and Latin; Gerald P. O'Connor, Ll.B., commercial law; George G. Stout, LL.B., mathematics; Leroy Burgnon, B.S., accounting; John C. Rischell, A.B., French; and Francis A. Hermann, B.S., chemistry.

In 1939, Mr. Waldron listed the faculty as follows:

The Revs. Joseph J. Wehrle, Latin and psychology; Alfred M. Watson, religion; Albert Chapdelaine, Latin and Greek; the Messrs. Gerald R. Kraus, mathematics; Francis G. Hermann, chemistry; Gerald P. O'Connor, business law; Donald Stout, accounting, economics, and political science; and John E. Waldron, history and political science. Other members of the college faculty included the Messrs. Gerald J. Weber, English and American literature; and Francis Greiner, economics.

Looking through the papers of "Doc" Wehrle, one finds the following budget for the third year of the fledgling college, as incredible as it appears.

CATHEDRAL COLLEGE

BUDGET FOR SCHOOL YEAR 1935-36

EXPENSES

Salaries		$5,500.00	
Books　Paid	$457.31		
Due 368.32			
Miscellaneous (Estimated)		150.00	
St. Vincent Contract		200.00	
			$6,725.63

INCOME

Tuition, Books and Lab Fees:			
First Semester	$2,994.11		
Second Semester	2,329.65		
		$5,323.76	
N.Y.A.		755.75	
Chem. Dept. Special		92.93	
Janitor Service on Tuition		50.00	
			$6,222.44
Delayed:			
Tuition, Books and Lab Fees:		$　200.00	
N.Y.A.		280.00	
Janitor Service on Tuition		25.00	
			505.00
			$6,727.00

What was "Doc's" philosophy of education? It is peculiar that, in spite of being President of both Villa Maria College and Cathedral College, and in spite of service as Superintendent of Schools for the diocese for many years, Dr. Wehrle never formally expressed his philosophy of education. However, he entertained one quite clearly as is ascertained through study of the course offerings at Cathedral College and later at Gannon School of Arts and Science and Gannon College. One would think that he would have formulated such a policy in the frequent educational speeches he made in the Erie area and elsewhere, and in the educational meetings he regularly attended and to which he contributed, but no such policy is extant.

Yet his educational principles and philosophy are best surmised by observing his currcula. Liberal arts, the humanities, *belleslettres*, classical education, liberal education — however it be named, was the solid rock of education for Dr. Wehrle. "Doc" would share with his students his open disdain for those educational theories and experiments he heard expounded at national meetings. With relish and full self-assurance, he would rededicate himself to teach the basic principles of logic or mathematics or Latin. These were the indispensible cogs in the gears of his pedagogical machine both at Cathedral Prep School and Cathedral College — the trivium and quadrivium. Dr. Wehrle himself was educated in this classic Western mold, and was completely convinced of its indispensibility in his students' education. He wanted them simply to be able to read, write, speak, listen, think and understand. If they could do these things, they were educated. He would teach them first to be human, the additional benefits of a Gannon education would follow.

And so, every Prepster took four years of English; two years of Latin, Greek, or a modern foreign language; three to four years of mathematics; four years of history; and two to three years of science — biology, chemistry, or physics. Dr. Wehrle never introduced business or even applied science subjects to this classic curriculum. *"Mens sana in corpore sano,"* (A healthy mind in a healthy body) was the motto of Cathedral Prep School, which its founder, Dr. Wehrle, chose in 1921. It is an apt symbol of the goals of liberal education. But woe to the unfortunate guard or quarterback on the Rambler team who failed Latin. He did not play. Dr. Wehrle considered the long walk back and forth to school from home would provide for a sound body, but he had to make stern provisions for the disciplining of a sound mind. This he did.

When confronted with the more complex problems of college curricula, he moved in a predictable and characteristically straight way. Philosophy would be central and would serve as cornerstone to all curricula because it was the most profound, most integrative of all subjects. Theology would also be important, but Dr. Wehrle always expressed a kind of sensitive caution about it since Cathedral College must also serve as the community college for men, many of whom would be Protestants, Jews, and non-believers. He would rather use philosophy to integrate the whole learning process.

Dr. Wehrle realized in 1933 that his Cathedral College was a junior college, a two-year institution. Immediate to his plans was the easy passage of his students on to four-year institutions. Cathedral College would never grant degrees, even of associate kind. In a certain sense, it would be merely a place in Erie where poor boys could least expensively prepare themselves for transfer to other colleges. And so, the courses set at Cathedral College were designed from catalogs of target colleges in which Erie men would enroll.

But still, Dr. Wehrle's total dedication to the humanities was always obvious. The liberal arts would be central to all other studies. This became even more apparent when Dr. Wehrle designed his full college curricula for Gannon School of Arts and Science in 1941. The core curriculum would contain almost eighty semester hours of credit required of all students for the baccalaureate degree — English, grammar and rhetoric, literature, mathematics, science, philosophy, theology, social studies, and a foreign language. Every student would boast of a philosphy minor, consisting of eighteen semester hours of credit.

Simply, Dr. Wehrle defined education chiefly in terms of liberal arts. If not distracted by other more practicable motives, like providing for vocational needs of the Erie community, every degree from his college would be a liberal arts degree. In his practical wisdom, he would make concessions in the direction of careerism, but the overall profile of courses would be prominently and predominantly characterized by the liberal arts.

CHAPTER III

THE VETERANS' COLLEGE

By the second year of its operation, Cathedral College had attracted ninety students who were taught by a faculty of nine teachers. During its brief and gestational existence, the college was never to go beyond 100 men and to accumulate more than nine instructors at any one time. Cathedral College always remained a junior college, with humble two-year programs. Yet in its three basic programs — science, liberal arts, and business —with evening school and summer sessions, the foundation of the future Gannon University was deeply cemented. When Cathedral College moved from West Ninth Street, out of its Victorian, rambling building, to Sixth Street at Perry Square, into its magnificent mansion, the change represented only a more pronounced commitment to the education for men started in 1933.

In 1941, the news that Bishop Gannon had bought what most Erieites considered to be the most elegant building in downtown Erie made the front page of the *Erie Daily Times*. This spacious and magnificent mansion was the pride and joy of the Scott-Strong families, two families which amassed considerable wealth from corporate finances and railroading. The mansion, designed by the famous American architects, Green and Wick, had been the site of Erie's most famous gatherings of national and international celebrities, of the "beautiful people" of the time. A frequently repeated, but undocumented story notes that President Howard Taft, a man of some considerable girth, dined and stayed in the mansion overnight with considerable embarrassment over his inability to get himself unstuck from one of the marble bathtubs!

The Executive Council changed not only the location of Cathedral College but its name. It now became the Gannon School of Arts and Science, still a junior college and, once more, under the charter of Villa Maria College. The new property included not only the mansion, but also two brick buildings which had served as living quarters for domestics and a two-storied carriage house located to the rear. This carriage house and stables buildings eventually would be named Downey Hall and would house science laboratories for many years. Msgr. Thomas B. Downey, Pastor of St. Patrick's Church, Franklin, Pennsylvania, and a life-long friend of "Doc" Wehrle, was most generous to the college in these earliest years when finances were critical. He is also remembered for his generosity toward Notre Dame University as well as to the Holy Cross Fathers who conducted it, inasmuch as several of his parish sons became members of that congregation, one of them Lawrence Graner, C.S.C., Archbishop of India.

In September 1941 the Gannon School of Arts and Science enrolled its first class at its new location on the corner of Sixth and Peach Streets, a class four times larger than any previous one. But this increased enrollment was not to last. In 1941, President Franklin D. Roosevelt, re-elected for an unprecedented third term, by defeating the Indiana lawyer, Wendell Wilkie, declared war on Japan after the Japanese had attacked the American naval base at Pearl Harbor, December 7, 1941. This national calamity affected and almost obliterated the struggling men's college on Sixth Street. The relatively large enrollment of men dropped from 400 students to less than fifty and was to remain at this level until veterans returned in 1947-48.

It was the quiet and enduring sacrifice of the clergy faculty that kept the college alive. Father Wilfrid J. Nash, later to become its second president, carried a superhuman academic load with courses in philosophy, theology, psychology, German, logic, and science. Father Joseph Barry, full-time chaplain for the Sisters of St. Joseph at the Villa Maria Motherhouse, taught economics at the Gannon School. Father Thomas J. Crowell, assistant pastor at St. Andrew's Church, also taught at the school in several areas of business administration. The assistant chancellor of the Diocese, Father Robert D. Goodill, taught several courses in religion. A young attorney, Gerald Weber (now Federal Judge), took time out from a budding law practice to teach courses in English literature, political science, and business law. Msgr. Edward Latimer, assistant pastor at Holy Rosary Parish, taught Greek. And of course, "Doc" Wehrle universally carried a heavy load of classes along with almost all of the administrative duties of the college.

No account of the early days of Gannon College could be complete without a brief mention of the contributions made by Sr. Mary Cornelia McGuire, S.S.J. (1875-1949). Sr. Cornelia was hired by "Doc" Wehrle to teach English at Cathedral Prep School in 1926 and uninterruptedly performed her task until 1941, when she assumed teaching responsibilities at Villa Maria College and at the Gannon School of Arts and Science. In 1944, she returned to serve "Doc" Wehrle at the Gannon School of Arts and Science full time. She authored a book, *The Minimum Essentials of Technical English*, which her students studied probably more intensely than any other text in any other field. Exacting and strict, she was the terror of Prep boys for years. Somebody said of her, "Most dreaded while you have her, most appreciated in after years." She was a tireless educator. Thousands of men and women in all the professions and vocations of life give credit to her for teaching them how to express themselves succinctly, unambiguously, and with flourish. She thought nothing of devoting her life to unappreciative students, because she took joy in their academic and professional successes. She spent her declining years in simple tasks like cleaning the little gold chapel in Old Main, in helping to serve meals to the staff, and in tutoring students in the intricacies of grammar and syntax.

Among the papers of "Doc" Wehrle is the following list of professors at the Gannon School of Arts and Science for the second semester of the scholastic year 1943-1944:

Full-Time Professors

Francis J. Hermann, M.S. — Chemistry
Theresa C. Kaminsky, A.B. — Registrar
Gerald R. Kraus, M.S. — Mathematics & Physics
William D. Martin (Rev.) — Religion
M. Cornelia McGuire, M.A. — English
Rudolph E. Morris, LL.D. — German & French
Wilfrid J. Nash, M.A. — Psychology
*John P. O'Brien, Ph.D. — Biology
Leo T. Phillips, Ph.D. — Latin & Greek
Joseph H. Schauinger, Ph.D. — History

Margaret J. Schauinger, A.B.L.S. — Librarian
Joseph J. Wehrle, S.T.D. — Logic
*John E. Williams, Ph.D. — Politial Science & Sociology

Part-Time Professors

John A. Janowski, M.A., B.L.S. — Assistant Librarian
Mary Suzy Lucas, M.D. — Biology
Gerald P. O'Connor, LL.B. — Business Law
William L. Sullivan, Ph.D. — Philosophy
**Donald F. Stout, M.B.A. — Accounting & Economics
**John E. Waldron, M.A. — Education

*No classes in their fields this semester, due to war, but will have classes in September 1944.

**Will be full-time professors at close of war.

In the darkest days of its beginnings, when the institution was nearly studentless, the junior college was to be converted to a four-year institution under its own charter. This action perfectly symbolizes the conviction, nerve, courage, and drive of "Doc" Wehrle. Application was made to the Pennsylvania Department of Instruction for a separate charter which would authorize the school to confer the degree of Bachelor of Arts and Bachelor of Science. This charter was granted on November 2, 1944, and on December 1, 1944, the Gannon School of Arts and Science became Gannon College, with all due rights and prerogatives to grant the baccalaureate degree. With the success of the American war effort in Europe and Asia, and the signing of the peace treaties in 1945, the hostilities of World War II mercifully ended. Then began a phenomenal period of growth for the young Gannon College with the return of thousands of veterans who enjoyed the privilege of veterans' educational benefits guaranteed by PL 346 and PL 16 of the 78th Congress. In 1947, Gannon College again boasted of 400 students, thirty-four faculty members, and a physical plant of two buildings. The mansion served as nucleus and housed the offices of the administration, library, chapel, cafeteria, and nine classrooms. The Carriage House, now named Downey Hall of Science, was fitted with several laboratories, a few offices, and an assembly hall large enough to accommodate 200 persons.

After World War II, enrollment in the nation's colleges reached 2,028,000 as compared to 1,365,000 in 1939. The growth of Gannon

was, of course, intimately related both to the need for a Catholic
higher education for a larger number of young people as well as to
the burgeoning veteran population on the campuses in 1946 and
subsequent years. The further national growth of the percentage
of young men and women continuing higher education (21% of
the 18-21 age group attended college in 1930 compared to 32% by
the late 1950's) contributed to the solidification of Gannon and
many other institutions of higher learning.

Before a review of the growth of Gannon College, both in
buildings and student population, a mention of Ferdinand Waldo
(Fred) Demara is necessary. No history of Gannon's early days
would be complete without this interesting personality. In response
to Dr. Wehrle's frequently repeated advertisement in educational
journals of the day which solicited the invaluable services of
college professors most scarce by reason of the War, Fred Demara
appeared.

Demara was a tall, brush-cutted, heavy-set, imposing, and dom-
ineering personality who swept Dr. Wehrle and the infant Gannon
College like a tidal wave. When he presented his credentials
which were actually those of Robert Linton French, Ph.D. in
psychology from Stanford University, and a M.A. from the University of Michigan, with Post-Doctoral studies at Yale University,
"Doc" Wehrle understandably drooled. "Doc" had the embarrassing capacity of giving an applicant for a teaching position practically anything he wished at the time of a first interview. The
longer one served at the college, the more his titles and perquisites
were diminished. Demara insisted that he be hired as Dean of the
School of Philosophy. "Doc" Wehrle hesitated only momentarily,
not even considering the problem that Gannon College did not
have a School of Philosophy. He granted Demara the title, who in
turn, printed up his personal professional card not only describing
himself as Dean of a nonexistent School of Philosophy, but also
listing Gannon University as his employer (anticipating the
expansion of the college by some 35 years).

He was to teach psychology along with Father Wilfrid Nash,
who soon was to doubt Demara's competence when he would ask
Nash, generally right before class, some rudimentary question
about psychology. Dr. Joseph Zipper, Chairman of the Biology

Department at the time, also was shocked when he was informed by Demara that since a shipment of amoebae was arriving, Demara had prepared some rat cages he discovered in the top floor of Downey Hall so that there would be a minimal loss of amoebae life.

Demara didn't stay long at Gannon College, from October 1945 to March 1946. A most engaging speaker, he was very much in demand at Rotarian meetings, American Legion conclaves, and other community gatherings when he spoke on the topic, "Growing Gannon and its Role in Erie."

Professional incompetence was not the reason for his academic demise at the college. Rather, it was his prodigal misuse of purchase orders. Having been moved from the second floor of Old Main to the third floor, a sign and symbol of demotion, he compensated by outfitting his new quarters in lavish fashion which he judged his positon as Dean deserved. In those days, little piqued "Doc" Wehrle more than carelessness in the use of the college's money.

All in all, Demara, before his death on June 8, 1982, served as a science instructor in an Arkansas Boy's School; a Trappist monk in several monasteries; a Navy surgeon in the Royal Canadian Navy during the War in Korea (he actually performed surgery on sailors); a Latin master at North Haven High School in Maine; a deputy warden at Huntsville State Penitentiary in Texas; a college founder who helped get Notre Dame Normal School in Maine accredited as a four-year institution; an auditor at the Lemar Hotel in Houston; and as a teacher of Eskimos at a school at Point Barrow, Alaska.

Robert Crichton wrote two books about Demara, *The Great Imposter* (New York: Random House, 1959) and *The Rascal and the Road* (New York: Random House, 1959). The actor, Tony Curtis, starred as Demara in a movie entitled *The Great Imposter* in 1961.

The completion of the library building and Commons, the first new buildings on campus, occurred in 1948. A fundraising campaign had been inaugurated under the direction of the Auxiliary Bishop of the Diocese, Most Rev. Edward P. McManaman, at that time residing and serving St. Joseph's Church, Oil City, Pennsylvania. The drive collected $212,000 from the people of Erie, both professional and non-professional. The new library, a handsome building with arched, expansive, leaded windows with educational symbols in stained glass, boasted a lofty reading room, but was hardly a librarian's dream. The vaulted, inefficient space of the main reading room was used for book storage only through the make-do genius of the professional librarians. Unfortunately, no trained librarians were consulted when the original building was planned.

Father Louis Lorei was named Director of the Library shortly after his ordination in 1947. An instructor in philosophy with a degree in both philosophy and library science, he did the back-breaking and herculean task of multiplying the original collection of 14,000 volumes many times over. In 1956, he was named Dean of the Division of Humanities, replacing Msgr. Nash, who was appointed acting President of the college. Father Lorei's successor as Library Director was Father Casimir J. Lubiak, who was appointed to the college faculty in June 1949, and immediately joined Father Lorei in the library. In 1954 he was awarded the M.S.L.S. degree from Western Reserve University, Cleveland, Ohio. Under Father Lubiak's steady hand and constant attention, the library continued to grow extensively so that by May 1964, it contained 57,500 volumes with 660 periodical subscriptions. Obviously, the library facilities of 1948 were very inadequate, and a number of classrooms in the mansion were commandeered to serve as additional reference rooms, periodical rooms, and storage space.

Immediately after the post-war years, Dr Wehrle had the problem of whether or not to accept women into Gannon College. Erie already had two colleges exclusively enrolling women: Villa Maria and Mercyhurst Colleges. However, many women did not wish to enroll in those colleges for a variety of reasons — either they could not obtain specialization in the area which they sought or they preferred coeducational college. Hundreds of them were leaving Erie to enroll in other colleges. Many of them sought entrance to Gannon, and ever so gradually, they were accepted. At first, in 1962, and for years, they were accepted only into afternoon and evening divisions of Gannon College. Since the administration did not want to compete with its sister institutions, Villa Maria and Mercyhurst, the college was very hesitant to confess to the presence of women once admitted. The women were incomprehensibly and outrageously referred to as "non-male-evening-students-taking-day classes." But gradually, year by year, the number of women students increased, so that in 1969, they were accepted as regular students. Today the university has almost as many women as men.

Obviously, as Gannon College grew from a two-year college to the institution it is today, the general administration became more complex. In the 40's almost the total administration was in the hands of President Wehrle. He administered the budget, had complete control of educational policies, and worked out plans for college development. It was principally this centralization of administration of the college in the Office of the President that postponed the college's accreditation the first time around in 1949. At that time, the visitation team of the Middle States Association of Colleges and Secondary Schools zeroed in principally on President Wehrle's penchant toward centralized authority and administration and deferred accrediting the young college for a few years, until 1951, when the necessary corrections were made.

As the college increased in student enrollment, and faculty were hired to teach in expanding programs, college administration was divided into three divisions — Humanities, Pure and Applied Science, and Business Administration, each division headed by a Dean directly responsible to the President.

The first Dean of Humanities was Father Wilfrid J. Nash, who served from 1948 until appointed acting President in May 1956, upon the resignation of Msgr. Wehrle. He was succeeded as Dean by Father Louis Lorei, Director of the Library. With Father Nash, Mr. Gerald R. Kraus, long-time Professor of Mathematics, served as Dean of Pure and Applied Science most capably from 1956 until his retirement in the Summer of 1972. The Business Administration Division, from its very beginning, was headed by Dr. John Waldron, who had served along with Dr. Wehrle both at Cathedral College and at Gannon School of Arts and Science since 1933, with a two year military interruption. Energetic Joseph P. Scottino, fresh from Fordham University with a doctorate in political science, was named Director of Evening and Summer

Sessions. Owen Thomas Finegan was appointed the college's first Director of Guidance and Placement in 1947. A former principal of St. Mary's High School in St. Marys, Pennsylvania, he also served as Director of Practice Teaching and later as Dean of Science and Engineering Division before an untimely death on March 7, 1974. Finegan Hall is named in his memory.

By the termination of Dr. Wehrle's presidency, there had been appointed a Registrar and Chairman of the Committee of Admissions, Director of Guidance, Treasurer, Business Manager, and Dean of Men. Miss Violet Nellis served as Registrar from 1947 to 1949, to be replaced by Father Robert J. Levis who served in that capacity until 1959. Father Frederick Nies and Father Thomas Griffin served successively as Treasurer from 1946 until 1956 when Father Norbert Wolf was appointed. Mr. John Hynes was appointed Business Manager in the Treasurer's Office during the 50's. Father Robert Barcio, former Cathedral Preparatory School teacher, in June 1956, succeeded Father Wolf as Dean of Men. The Dean of Men's Office, at that time, was responsible not only for the general conduct of the student body, but also for athletics, student housing, student activities, and discipline. It was not until 1957 that the Student Personnel Office was first formed to be an umbrella office for all non-academic services of the institution.

With Gannon College's dramatic development, a very reputable academic institution was evident in the awarding of accreditation by the Middle States Association in 1951. This process began in early March of 1949. The team that was appointed to inspect the college included the following members:

Mr. Morris Gelford, Queens College, New York, NY, Library
Dean Howard J. Leahy, Seton Hall College, Program and Instruction
President Calvert N. Ellis, Juniata College, Organization
Mr. John Reilly, Marywood College, Facilities
Dr. Roy J. Deferrari, Chairman, The Catholic University of America, Purpose and Objectives

This team made a thorough investigation of the college in both the academic and non-academic areas. Their recommendations changed the academic, organizational, and financial procedures of the entire college. For example, the following suggestions were made:

1. Revision of entrance requirements to one specific series of quantit-a-tive subject matter requirements for all degrees, and setting up of definite criteria to be followed rigidly by admissions officers.

2. Study and revision of the curricula so as to reduce the separate offerings to not more than a total of two courses of study. One curriculum could lead to the Degree of Bachelor of Arts and stress in its content courses in general education, social sciences, and the humanities. However, this A.B. Degree should be designed so that a person might attain it even in the field of biological and physical science. The second curriculum could lead to the Degree of Bachelor of Science in such fields as accounting and business administration.

3. Specific course offerings in religion for Catholic students should be designed for each semester and carry at least one credit for a total of eight units for the entire four-year program.

4. Specific course offerings in religion or character formation should be designed for non-Catholic students for at least one full year of the regular four-year program.

5. Revision of the credit requirements for each of the two proposed degrees so as not to exceed a total of 125 semester hours.

The team made the above kind of evaluation for every facet of the college.

Indeed, there were so many changes that had to be made that it seemed to be an impossible task to fulfill a substantial number of the recommendations. However, the evaluating team that visited the college on March 4-5, 1951, were amazed at what had been accomplished since its first visit in 1948, and recommended that the college be accredited by the Middle States Association of Colleges and Secondary Schools. Much of the credit for this major achievement must be given to Bishop Edward P. McManaman, Auxiliary Bishop of Erie and Secretary of the Board of Incorpora-tors and Board of Control as well as "Doc" Wehrle, the Rev. William Sullivan, a member of both boards, and the Rev. Wilfrid J. Nash, Dean of the College.

The committee work that was necessary for the evaluation was performed by several members of the Committee on Curriculum at the college. In 1950, this Committee was chaired by the Rev. Wilfrid J. Nash. Other members of the Committee included Richard Beyer, Ph.D., Professor of History; the Rev. Edward Q. Franz, Ph.D., Director of Philosophy and Religion; Alfonso

Garcia-Yglesia, LL.D., Instructor in Spanish; Wilfred J. Mathewson, M.A., Instructor in English, Berta M. Weber, Ph.D., Chairperson of the Department of Foreign Languages; James Freeman, M.S., Instructor in Mathematics; and John Susko, M.A., Instructor in Economics. Additional faculty members who aided in preparing the reports were Owen T. Finegan, Director of Guidance; Rev. Louis Lorei, Librarian; Rev. Robert J. Levis, Registrar; Mr. John Waldron, Dean of Instruction; Mr. Joseph H. Zipper, Director of Teacher Training; Joseph J. Bednarski, Instructor in Spanish; and Louis J. Tullio, Director of Physical Education and Basketball Coach.

The members of this evaluation committee which launched Gannon College on this important step toward academic recognition included the following:

> Rev. Thurston N. Davis, S.J., Dean of Fordham College, Fordham University (Program);
>
> Dean Charles J. Edgett, College of Business, Niagara University (Program in Business Administration, Admissions, Records);
>
> Assistant Controller George E. Gere, Carnegie Institute of Technology (Finance, Plant and Equipment, Military Science);
>
> Librarian James D. Mack, Lehigh University (Library);
>
> Rev. Cyril F. Meyer, C.M., Vice President, St. John's University (Organization, Student Personnel Program);
>
> Dean Henry Grattan Doyle, The George Washington University, Chairman (Purpose and Objectives; Outcomes).

When the Committee had examined the college with regard to its purpose and objectives, its organization, the academic program, its finances and facilities, and the library, it came to several conclusions in its report. In the first place it said, "it was obvious to the Committee that a determined effort had been made by the authorities of Gannon College to meet categorically all the criticisms made in the 1949 evaluation report." A committee of the Board of Control had been set up immediately after the 1949 report in which Bishop McManaman and Father William Sullivan had taken leading parts. This committee implemented most of the recommendations that had been made at frequent meetings of the

Board of Control. Outstanding progress had been made in tightening up financial controls, and the loose and chaotic business methods mentioned in the 1949 report had completely disappeared, but further improvements remained to be made as recommended by the financial inspector. "Plant and equipment were fairly satisfactory," he wrote, "given the urban setting of the college and its limited resources." Expansion of facilities was expected to continue as finances permitted.

"The financial and moral backing of the Bishop of Erie," they continued, "is vital to the financial stability of the college." They further pointed out that the Bishop was the trustee of the $500,000 protective endowment from which $10,000 annually had been received since 1944. Contributed services of priests were estimated at $51,000 annually. Also included in part of the endowment was the annual Seminarian and Catholic University Collections which yielded enough funds to establish an endowment of $1,000,000. Unrestricted gifts for 1949-50 were reported at $112,961.86, of which $50,000 was given by Bishop Gannon and $50,000 by Msgr. Thomas Downey of Franklin, Pennsylvania.

In their final paragraph on finances, the committee commented that "in view of the strong support of the Bishop of Erie, its Auxiliary Bishop, it is most unlikely that Gannon College will ever find itself in a really precarious financial position." Nevertheless, they strongly suggested that its financial position would be strengthened by setting up endowment funds under the control of its own Board. This would not affect ultimate responsibility to the Bishop as the Chancellor of the college and the ecclesiastical superior of the other board members; it would give the college a financial status and stability more broadly comparable to that of other institutions.

The strengthening of financial controls had been paralleled by similar improvements in the handling of admissions and in the general work of the Registrar's office. The Library was deemed to be well-administered and fairly adequate. Its chief long-range problem was the lack of space for expansion. The Student Personnel Program showed great improvement over the situation existing at the time of the previous evaluation. The faculty was considered to be generally good and interested in improving themselves as well as improving instruction.

The reorganization of the college into divisions had apparently been helpful. Teaching loads of the administrative staff had been reduced. But, the chief weakness of the faculty was reflected in undue proportions of high grades reported. Dean Nash promised to examine this problem and the catalogue, which was not really representative of the changes that had been made in faculty organization and in reponsibility for instruction. It was impossible to tell, for example, from the catalogue, who taught what course; whether a course was given every year or in alternate years; whether members of the instructional staff were on a full-time or part-time basis; and who were the heads of divisions and departments. In making these criticisms of the catalogue, the Committee commented that "it was aware that the 1950-51 issue was probably a 'rush job' and had high expectations of Dean Nash's work on its successor."

In their final words on the evaluation of 1951 which made Gannon College a member of the Middle States Association of Colleges and Secondary Schools, they wrote:

> In all of the problems confronting the College, the Committee is impressed by the spirit that seems to animate the Board of Control, the administrative staff, and the faculty, and particularly by the cordial appreciation expressed throughout our inspection of the benefits derived from the earlier evaluation.

Also, in the earlier part of the report, they mentioned what they considered to be definite assets of the college. They went on to say,

> The youth of the administration is striking. With the exception of Msgr. Wehrle, they are all below forty, and several of them have not yet reached their thirtieth birthday. They have the enthusiasm, the courage, and the enterprise of youth. Their *esprit de corps* is excellent. As a young institution they are not hampered by the traditions which often stagnate the waters of progress. They have the humility which is the fruit of appreciation that they still have much to learn, and they are both anxious and willing to acquire what they lack. For the most part, there is a clear definition of the limits of each one's authority, and they function smoothly as a team. They have a wonderful unifying force in the Dean of the College who is a real spark to the team. The evidence of faculty participation is most encouraging.

Thus, what seemed to be an almost impossible task after the disastrous report of 1949, became an amazing turnabout. It had taken tremendous courage on the part of the faculty and administration to attempt to implement most of the recommendations of the "report", but the intense work of the various committees over a two-year period met with unbelievable success. The college had made definite progress toward the goals of academic, administrative, and financial stability. The news passed quickly throughout the community that Gannon College had received accreditation from the Middle States Association. Consequently, increased numbers of students, not only from the Erie community, but the entire tri-state area, began to flock to its doors.

With the increasing enrollment of the college after the war, "Doc" Wehrle was hard-pressed to provide the necessary physical expansion of the college's campus. The college was situated in downtown Erie and was first envisioned primarily as a day school for residents of the city. However, because it was relatively inexpensive in comparison with other colleges within a fifty or hundred mile radius, Gannon attracted a considerable number of students outside of the city. So, student housing became an immediate priority. But property was expensive in downtown Erie and very little was available.

Indeed, students were first housed on the top floor of "Old Main" along with some members of the clergy faculty. "Doc" himself used a room on the second floor. However, in 1952, the college purchased an apartment building at 409-411-413 West Sixth Street which would house between fifty-five to sixty freshmen. These properties were later sold to the Sisters of the Divine Spirit for their convent in June 1955. In the meantime, students were living in some rather dilapidated private residences and apartments in the area. The more fortunate ones managed to find finer boarding facilities in other parts of Erie.

The only other housing provided by the college in these early years was the athletic dormitory at 137 West 19th Street — off campus by quite a distance. Railroad tracks ran past this former residence of the Drumgool family. Thomas P. Gannon, brother of Archbishop Gannon, married to Jennie Drumgool, lived there for several years until the property was acquired by Mary and Leona

Suttelle, nieces by marriage to Thomas Gannon, and heirs of the Drumgool estate. The college made use of the residence for the members of its famous football team in September 1950. The new dormitory was the responsibility of Father James Peterson, who for many years after his ordination in May 1947, was Professor, Chairman of the Theology Department, and Director of Religious Activities on the Gannon campus. Today, Father "Pete" is pastor of St. Theresa's, Union City, Pennsylvania, as well as the founder and director of a prayer house and a rehabilitation center, Martha's Farm, for some of the poor of our society.

Also during the presidency of "Doc" Wehrle, the first official residence for the clergy faculty was acquired from the Frederick C. Jarecki family at 221 West Sixth Street. It provided housing for seven priests, and later on, was named the Barr Faculty House to honor one of its priest residents.

In addition to housing for students and the clerical faculty, there was also a need for expanded classrooms. The former Franklin Elementary School Building on upper Peach Street at 26th Street was used for a short period beginning in 1946 to accommodate the burgeoning enrollment. It became, during its short tenure, the center of the college's Business Administration Division. It was purchased from the Erie School Board for $250,000 on September 5, 1946, after the sale was approved by the Court of Common Pleas. However, with the completion of the new library in the Fall of 1948, more classroom space was available on campus, and consequently the building was used only for the 1946-47 school year.

Shortly after the Library and Commons opened in 1948 for the faculty and student use, the college embarked on its second major piece of construction. Ground was broken on May 1, 1948, for what came to be known as the Gannon Auditorium. The land on which this building stands was formerly occupied by the Strong Family's servants' quarters, which first were used as offices and classrooms and even as a dormitory. The "Audi" provided space for the athletic and social activities of the students as well as those of local high schools. It also became the Civic Center for the City of Erie. The building was first used on November 13, 1949, when it hosted a Confraternity of Christian Doctrine Convention. It was officially dedicated January 20, 1950. The total cost was about $500,000.

The college now had space for its ROTC Program on campus. Before the construction of the Auditorium, the college used a parcel of land on West 26th and Pittsburgh Avenue as the ROTC Drill Field. This land had been the former site of the Erie County Poor Home. Also during the years of 1947 and 1948, a government surplus gymnasium was constructed behind St. Mark's Hall at 218 East Third Street, which had been a residence for seminarians of the Erie Diocese until 1959, when they moved into the new St. Mark's Seminary on East Grandview Boulevard. Although the gym was only a few blocks from the center of the Gannon campus, few students made use of it, instead it was appreciated more by the Erie seminarians than Gannon students. By April 1, 1962, the entire property of St. Mark's was deeded to the city and the buildings razed. Today, it is known as the Nate Levy Playground.

The third large scale construction during the Presidency of "Doc" Wehrle was the Engineering Building immediately west of Beyer Hall in January 1954. In 1972, it was renamed in memory of Father Bernard "Barney" Russell, C.S.V., who taught most of his mathematics courses in its classrooms until his unexpected death on February 27, 1969, at St. Vincent's Hospital, Erie. Father Russell was a priest of the Congregation of St. Viator and had been a close friend and adviser of "Doc" Wehrle for many years. A native of Shinglehouse, Pennsylvania, Father Russell assisted at St. George's in Erie in addition to his duties at Gannon. He was buried in Hillside, Illinois, in the cemetery of the religious community to which he belonged. Father Russell was well known for the personal help and encouragement he gave to all his students. He spent many hours in his office or his quarters with students who were having difficulties with calculus or other matters. Many a young priest likewise sought his wise counseling. His sharp wit is exemplified by notes found written in his mathematical collection in the library and archives of Gannon. For example, in many of his books he had written in large letters "Stolen from Bernard M. Russell," in reference, of course, to the many students who had borrowed books from him, but took a long time to return them, if they ever did.

Besides classrooms, Russell Hall contained offices, five laboratories, two lecture halls, and one large meeting room. Architects for the building were Gifford and Sunda.

With the completion of the construction of the new Engineering Building, engineering programs burgeoned and additional space was needed, especially for laboratories. This necessitated the purchase of a property at 714 and 715 Myrtle Street in 1955. The building on the front of the lot had been a private residence and behind the house was a large garage. At first, the house became a dormitory for faculty and students, and the garage in the rear was remodeled for the use of engineering laboratories. In the 1970's the building was converted for maintenance operations.

Also, in June 1955, a rather large building across the street from Russell Hall was purchased from James M. and Angeline Egan for approximately $100,000. It was first known as the Engineering Laboratory Annex Building. It was used as a Mechanical Engineering building and later for a variety of uses, including a coffee house for students, and a Black Cultural Center. Classes were first scheduled in the building in June 1956. In the early 1960's, part of the store front housed a book store. In later years, it was used for faculty services, a print shop, a key shop, shipping and receiving, and a post office. The building was last remodeled during 1979-1980 for several of the above-mentioned services.

By the Spring of 1956, the Gannon campus comprised of fifteen buildings, most of them clustered in the square block just west of Perry Square and south of Sixth Street in downtown Erie. From the original two buildings that once belonged to the Strong mansion, in less than twelve years, the college had grown to a fully accredited four-year institution with over 1,000 full- and part-time students. It had three modern and imposing new structures which included the Library Building and Commons, the Auditorium, and the four-story Engineering Building, Indeed, the foundation of Gannon University had been firmly established, largely through the insights and efforts of the beloved Msgr. Joseph J. Wehrle, S.T.D., its first President. It had all begun with a small group of Prep graduates who, in the Fall of 1933, desired to continue their education but did not have the necessary funds. Thus, a great university evolved essentially from the compassion and concern of the devoted priest everyone called "Doc."

Dr. Wehrle had accomplished the goal he had set in 1925. In 1956, he had given the community of Erie a growing, respected institution of higher learning for men (as well as for women), with a brilliant prospect for the future. Little did "Doc" Wehrle realize that his educational career would suddenly be terminated in 1956. His health was good, he was as active as ever, he had many plans both expressed and unexpressed for the future of the college, but it was not meant to be.

CHAPTER IV

A SECOND BEGINNING

The growing faculty of Gannon College was becoming increasingly convinced that the institution was already too complex and too diverse for the bold educational pioneer who had founded it. Dr. Wehrle's retirement was as sudden as it was personally tragic. Gannon College had received a grant of $200,000 from the Ford Foundation to be awarded to deserving faculty members. The President and the entire faculty were elated over the grant. However, Dr. Wehrle pared the faculty salaries with a massive across-the-board demotion in faculty rank and tenure. "Doc" had for years solicited the services of new faculty members by offering them a rank or two higher than that obtainable in other institutions. And so he planned that the readjustment of their salary upward would compensate for the readjustment of their rank downward. It didn't work. Immediately upon receipt of this notice, the faculty organized, sent representatives to Archbishop Gannon, the Chancellor, to demand no less than the immediate removal of Dr. Wehrle, the founding president of Gannon College. Archbishop Gannon, caught between anvil and hammer, had no alternative but to make one of his most distressing decisions. He had to let Dr. Wehrle go into retirement or lose the major part of the faculty. This he did to the shock and amazement of the entire Erie community. Dr. Wehrle, after a brief vacation, was assigned pastor of his home parish, Ss. Cosmas and Damian Church, Punxsutawney, Pennsylvania and later pastor of St. Michael's Church, Emlenton, Pennsylvania, and died in Butler Memorial Hospital on December 25, 1967. Obviously, "Doc" suffered deeply these last years of his long and fruitful life, but did reconcile it all.

Into this maelstrom of dismay and controversy, Father Wilfrid J. Nash was thrust. He had been assigned to the college since his ordination in May 1942. From the very beginning, he performed the dual roles of teacher and administrator. He had been Dean of the College since 1950 and Msgr. Wehrle's loyal and expert supporter during these early years. Bishop Gannon appointed Father Nash acting president for the first several months, but soon realized that Nash would best fill the shoes of the former president.

The new president was born September 8, 1915, in Erie, of devout Catholic parents. He first attended St. Mary's Elementary School on the lower east side when the school was staffed by the brothers of Mary, and then enrolled at Cathedral Preparatory School for Boys, which at that time was housed in the basement of St. Peter's Cathedral, with additional classroom space provided in the Downing Building on West Ninth Street. Although he was an excellent student, after his graduation in 1933, he had no funds to continue his education. It was at this time that "Doc" Wehrle decided to start Cathedral College for young men like Wilfrid Nash who deserved an opportunity for further education. After spending two years at the new college, he was sent to Catholic University on a Basselin Scholarship to prepare for the diocesan priesthood. He earned a Bachelor of Arts degree in 1937 and a Master of Arts in 1938. From the same institution in 1942, he earned a Licentiate in Sacred Theology and later pursued studies in psychology at Fordham University. Ordained a priest May 14, 1942, in St. Peter's Cathedral, he was immediately assigned to the Gannon School of Arts and Science.

Father Nash received his appointment from Bishop Gannon in March 1956. At that time President Dwight D. Eisenhower had neared the end of his first term and was preparing for a second term, despite a heart attack late in 1955. He was re-elected by soundly defeating, once again, Governor Adlai Stevenson of Illinois, in one of the most overwhelming victories since President Franklin D. Roosevelt defeated Alf Landon in 1936. For the most part, the Eisenhower years were rather peaceful except for the turmoil created by the civil rights movement which began in the middle fifties and continued until the present. However, Eisenhower did face a severe recession in late 1957 when unemployment reached its highest level since 1941. It was during these years that Gannon College was directed by the dynamic leadership of Father

Gannon College was directed by the dynamic leadership of Father Wilfrid J. Nash. He soon proved to be a very capable administrator with the personal approach and organizational abilities necessary to build the academic and non-academic programs essential for a college in its early history.

With Father Nash's appointment as president, the college immediately entered into an unprecedented period of academic development and physical expansion. Father Nash proved to be a most efficient administrator.

The first monumental task that faced President Nash was the preparation of the college for re-evaluation by the Middle States Association of Colleges and Secondary Schools. Gannon had been an accredited member of the Association since 1951. The self-review process had already begun during the presidency of Dr. Wehrle with an interim report on April 26, 1954, to Ewald B. Nyquist, Chairman of the Commission. This was followed by another report on October 8, 1955, with recommendations from F. Taylor Jones, Executive Secretary of the Association and the man on the scene during the evaluation. For more than a year, the entire administration and faculty of the college laboriously engaged in committee meetings in painstaking preparation for the team's visit from February 19-21, 1957.

Before the actual days of evaluation, Rev. Joseph G. Glose, Jesuit priest and consultant to Jesuit colleges for many years in higher education, guided the various committes and administration. His counsel and expertise was of inestimable value to the college during this period of uncertainty. Indeed, he had been on the scene to aid Gannon in its growth and development almost from the very beginning and was always a source of strength to the young administrators concerned with Gannon's well-being. In recognition of his efforts, the college granted him its first honorary degree at commencement exercises on June 3, 1957.

On May 2, 1957, Father Nash happily received a letter from Ewald B. Nyquist which informed him that Gannon's membership in the Middle Atlantic States Association had been reaffirmed.

Dear Father Nash:

It is my pleasant responsibility to report to you the official action of the Commission on Institution of High Education taken recently after serious and careful consideration of the Self-Evaluation Questionnaire you submitted to us, the Evaluation Report prepared by the Visiting Committee under the Chairmanship of F. Taylor Jones, the Executive Secretary of the Commission, and of Mr. Jones' oral analysis.

The Commission voted to reaffirm the accreditation of Gannon College as a member institution of the Middle States Association.

Several copies of the Evaluation Report will be sent to you under another cover by the Executive Secretary. You will find in this Report several indications of commendable points observed by the Visiting Committee including: your lay advisory boards, the basic required program of Liberal Studies, financial position, library administration, the religious program and, in general, the College's marked progress under your leadership. This is more extraordinary, of course, because your tenure as Chief Executive Officer has been so brief. In the Report, too, you will also find reference to other areas where the Commission felt that further improvement is warranted.

More specifically, because the Commission continues to take a deep interest in your institution and believes that it can be of further assistance to you, the Commission requests that you submit a report by no later than October 1, 1958, on (a) improvement in the academic preparation of the faculty, (b) efforts to obtain financial support in the community, and (c) other significant development since the occasion of the evaluation on which you, as President, may wish to comment.

The Commission has directed me, too, in this letter of transmittal, to caution the College at this time against further diversification of its education program and the offering of graduate work.

In closing, may I congratulate you on this action of the Commission which reaffirms the accreditation of Gannon College. If there is anything that the Executive Secretary, Mr. F. Taylor Jones, or any of the officers of the Committee can do for you now or at any time, please do not hesitate to call upon us. It would afford me a great deal of pleasure to be of personal assistance to you.

Faithfully yours,

Ewald B. Nyquist
Chairman

Father Nash had survived his first important test as president with success. The entire administration, faculty, and student body were invigorated with confidence in the College's future. The opening paragraphs of the report by the evaluators during this critical time bolstered this confidence:

The College has accomplished a great deal recently toward tightening its organization and getting things done. The minutes of the Executive Committee which functions in many respects as a Board of Trustees although it does not have final authority, show, for example, that within the past year it purchased and equipped a fine old residence as a student union, negotiated a loan and began construction of the College's first dormitory, created a Lay Advisory Board, established a committee to study long-range development, appointed a new administrative team, adopted a better salary schedule, raised tuition, and approved a re-edited catalogue.

This seems to the Evaluation Team rather spectacular accomplishment for a new president's first nine months in office. Great credit is due to him and his colleagues, and certainly to His Excellency the Archbishop of the Erie Diocese, founder of the College, Chancellor of the Board, Chairman of the Executive Committee who never misses a meeting and is constantly in communication with the president between meetings. His Excellency has been foresighted in looking to the president for initiative and administrative leadership, limiting his own activities to policy consultation and financial and plant development. Perhaps, nothing the Archbishop has created in his long and distinguished career as a builder will keep his memory as green and his people as grateful as his namesake Gannon College.

His close associate, the Auxiliary Bishop Edward P. McManaman is maintaining the same high level of policy relationship, as are the consultors of the Diocese, who function as the Board of Trustees. Gannon unites in a very special way the services of a community college and the character of a religious institution. It is an advantageous combination, though one which requires an unusual degree of objectivity and educational leadership.

The evaluators are pleased to see that Gannon College is at least ready to make effective use of that proven and important device of a clerical institution, the Lay Advisory Board. The diversified professional and religious distribution of its membership suggests strategic planning on someone's part. The visitors were impressed also with the personal qualities and informed interest of the members they met individually and in the lively meeting some of them attended. The Lay Board will be a decisive factor in this college's future, as its best means of liaison with the industrial community to which it must look for financial support.

The evaluation team for the reaffirming of accreditation, so vital for the college in February 1957, consisted of:

F. Taylor Jones, Executive Secretary of the Commission on Institutions of Higher Education, Middle States Association (Chairman);

Major General E. E. MacMorland, President of Pennsylvania Military College, Chester, Pennsylvania;

Allen B. Edwards, Treasurer and Business Manager, Allegheny College, Meadville, Pennsylvania;

Rev. Edward J. Clark, S.J., Academic Vice President, Fordham University, New York, New York;

Finn B. Jensen, Professor of Economics, Lehigh University, Bethlehem, Pennsylvania;

B. Richard Teare, Dean, College of Engineering and Science, Carnegie Institute of Technology, Pittsburgh 13, Pennsylvania;

Robert S. Burgess, Jr., Professor of Librarianship, State University of New York College for Teachers, Albany, New York;

R. Kenneth Fairman, Director of Athletics, Princeton University, Princeton, New Jersey;

Carl E. Seifert, Deputy Superintendent, Department of Public Instruction, Harrisburg, Pennsylvania.

Soon after this critical re-evaluation, Father Nash was asked to submit additional reports to the Middle States Association on progress that the college was making on recommendations made by the team in various areas, both academic and non-academic. Progress reports were sent by the President on September 25, 1958, and September 23, 1960, and accepted by the Association on November 30, 1960.

Having successfully passed this hurdle, President Nash looked to the possibility of granting graduate degrees. Again, Father Joseph Glose offered his welcome counsel. He submitted a report on February 28, 1963, which first suggested that the college's charter must be amended before graduate degrees could be awarded. In March 1964, a report on amending the charter was proposed and, in a letter dated September 14, 1964, to F. Taylor Jones, Father Nash informed him that the Pennsylvania State Board of Education had authorized the college to offer graduate degree programs in the fields of English, social studies, education, and guidance and counseling.

In 1965, the Engineering programs were professionally accredited by the Engineering Council for Professional Development.

And in November 1966, the Guidance program received the official recognition of the American Board of Counseling Services. For the second time during the presidency of Msgr. Nash, on February 12-15, 1967, an evaluation team from the Middle States Association approached the Gannon campus. While this experience is always stimulating but sometimes intimidating to the administration and faculty, evaluators actually give generously of their time to learn how a particular college has progressed and to make recommendations for improvements. Their purpose is never to be so critical that they endanger the very existence of a particular educational institution. They simply want to help and they surely do.

On this 1967 visitation, the members of the evaluation team included the following:

C. William Huntley, Professor of Psychology, Union College, Schenectady, New York, Chairman of the Team;

Bruce M. Brown, Librarian, Colgate University, Hamilton, New York;

Joseph W. Cole, Dean of Students, University of Rochester, Rochester, New York;

Brother Urban Gonnoud, O.S.F., President, St. Francis College, Brooklyn, New York;

John A. Guthrie, Chairman, Program in Counselor Education, University of Pittsburgh, Pittsburgh, Pennsylvania;

George W. Hoffman, Coordinator for State Colleges, Department of Public Instruction, Box 911, Harrisburg, Pennsylvania;

Helen M. Kleyle, Professor of Education, Coordinator for Student Teaching, Duquesne University, Pittsburgh, Pennsylvania;

Jay Luvaas, Associate Professor of History, Allegheny College, Meadville, Pennsylvania;

Ralph A. Morgan, Dean of Graduate Studies (Engineering), Stevens Institute of Technology, Hoboken, New Jersey.

On April 26, 1967, Albert E. Meder, Jr., Chairman of the Commission, informed Msgr. Nash that the Commission had again voted to reaffirm Gannon's accreditation. He also noted that the Commission planned to send an observer to the college in two years to determine to what extent the major changes recommended by the evaluating team had been accomplished. The final paragraph gave additional reassurance, "Please be assured," he said, "that the Commission, its Chairman, and its Executive Secretary stand ready to assist Gannon College by consultation or by other appropriate means at any time."

Less than two years later, F. Taylor Jones on February 5, 1969, wrote to President Nash to remind him that the observer "who was to determine to what extent the major changes recommended in the report of 1967 have been accomplished" would be Professor C. W. Huntley of Union College who had been the chairman of the team. In their correspondence, Msgr. Nash and Professor Huntley agreed on February 26, 1969, as the day for the latter's visit. In the meantime, President Nash sent the following letter which outlined to what extent the recommendations by the Team in 1967 had been accomplished.

February 18, 1969

Dr. C. William Huntley, Chairman
Department of Psychology
Union College
Schenectady, NY 12308

Dear Bill:

I have reviewed the improvements which have been made or contemplated in the areas identified by the Evaluating Committee as in need of further study. My remarks will be introductory in nature and prepare you to discuss them in more detail during your visit to Gannon College.

The Evaluating Committee recommended that a faculty constitution be created. A five member Constitution Committee has been formed; three were appointed by the Faculty Senate and two by me. The Committee has been meeting once a week for the last year and a half. A progress report has been made to the Faculty. Msgr. Lorei will arrange for you to meet with the Committee.

The Office of Admissions has been separated from the Office of Registrar. Dr. Richard Herbstritt is now the Director of the Department of Education; Mr. Al Wedzik is the Registrar; and Mr. Randy Cicen the Admissions Officer. Both the Registrar and the Admissions Officer are directly responsible to Mr. Thomas Finegan. The Admissions Officer hired two full-time recruiters. Mr. Cicen and Mr. Finegan are prepared to review the developments in the past two years.

September 1934, Bishop Gannon with newsboys for whom he founded the college.

First chapel, Gannon School of Arts and Science, located in extreme west wing of Old Main, first floor, 1941.

Parents at Departure Ceremony of students leaving Gannon School of Arts and Science, February 13, 1943. They are seated in the corridor of Old Main facing west.

Gannon Theatre, winter scene.

Gannon College, summer 1944.

Monsignor Wilfrid J. Nash, S.T.L., Litt.D., in office of the president.

Gannon School of Arts and Science students leaving February 14, 1943, for induction to military service at New Cumberland, Md.

Officers of Gannon College Building Fund, June 7, 1946: J.A. Spaeder, A.E. Keim, F.L. Nash.

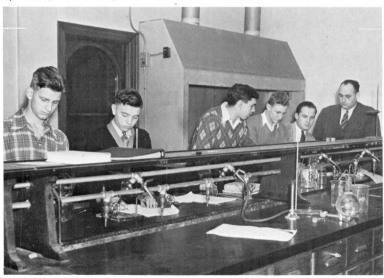

Francis Herrmann in Downey Hall chemistry lab with students, November 24, 1944.

Dr. Wehrle with G. Richard Fryling, Litt.D.

Rita Ann Nies with student, Circulation Department, Gannon
Library, May 1948.

George Hesch, Richard Fox, Dr. Richard Beyer.

William Schubert directing medical students Washabaugh, Groutt, and Teed, May 22, 1959.

Old St. Mark's Hall, East Third Street, residence for seminarians until 1960.

Gannon College Glee Club, 1960. Rev. Richard Sullivan, Director. 1st row: George McAlee, Thomas Glosick. 2nd row: William Hughey. 3rd row: Robert Evans, Charles Bonavita, Richard Pryjomski, Francis Riddle, Richard Trzeciak. 4th row: Richard Bonini, Steve Kerchansky, Joseph Wiskowski, Thomas Aiello, Carl Amann, Dave Trzeciak, Vincent Proto. Piano: Larry Spangenburg.

Ten Years awards: (front) Rev. Dr. John Schanz, Rev. Dr. Bonaventura Ciufoli, Archbishop Gannon, Rev. John Thompson, Rev. Dr. Wilfrid J. Nash. Standing: Mr. John Hynes, Dr. Melvin Carney, Dr. Charles Colvin, Dr. J. Carter Rowland, Atty. James Hanes. December 11, 1960.

New faculty members, September 23, 1960: Frank Scalise, Aloysius Dapprich, John Wallach, Clarence Schelling, Jack Peng, Rev. John Hilbert, Arthur Pitts, Thomas Miller, and Rev. Joseph Hipp.

Dean Gerald R. Kraus, 1960.

Hammermill Paper Company's $25,000 donation, July 1, 1960. President Donald S. Leslie, Rev. John Slater, Rev. Wilfrid Nash, B.E. Claridge, J.H. DeVitt, F.E. Bahrenburg.

Bishop Gannon, Bishop McManaman, Dr. Wehrle, Rev. Frederick Nies.

Beyer Hall under construction, 1961.

Rev. Louis Puscas (1964 Dean of Students, presently Rouman-
ian Bishop of Chicago), Basketball Coach James Harding, William
Latimer, John Rouch, Elmer Kohlmiller, John Susko.

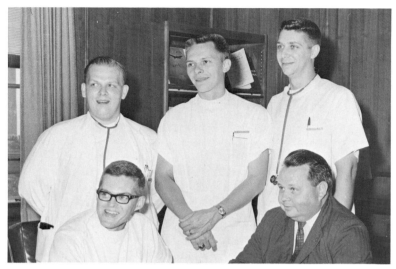

Dr. Elmer Kohlmiller confers with four Gannon graduates doing internships: David R. Jobes (seated), Forest C. Mischler, Ronald Zieziula, and William C. Wilhelm, August 1967.

Anti-Vietnam War protest, Perry Square, 1968. The late 1960's and early 70's reflected the concern of Gannon students for the Vietnam War, as shown in this peaceful demonstration.

Msgr. Wilfrid Nash, Bishop Michael J. Murphy, Dr. Joseph P.
Scottino.

Msgr. Wilfrid Nash, Mayor Louis J. Tullio, Vice President Hubert
Humphrey, Congressman Joseph Vigorito, October 7, 1968.

Owen Thomas Finegan (around 1948), Director of Guidance.

Three graduates, June 1948: Ernest L. Kuhn, John J. Latimer, Paul J. Clancey, with sons.

Dr. Joseph Scottino, at the time of the evaluation, was Director of the Afternoon and Evening Sessions and also Director of the Graduate Programs. Mr. Raymond Cicero is now the Director of Afternoon and Evening Sessions. Dr. Scottino is the Director of the Graduate Program. No new graduate program has been introduced in the last two years. However, we are currently planning to introduce a graduate program in Engineering Science. The development in this area has been triggered by the trend in engineering education. Dr. James Palmer, the Director of Engineering, and Mr. Gerald Kraus are prepared to discuss the developments in this area.

The Committee recommended that the present core curriculum be restudied. The progress made in the curriculum can best be described by the Deans.

The Evaluating Committee was concerned about our ability to hold the more promising people. We have agreed with the Faculty Senate to maintain at least a "C" rating in Average Compensation and a "B" rating in Minimum Compensation according to AAUP standards. In the year 1968-69 our rating in Average Compensation is "B" for instructors, "B" for Assistant Professors, "C" for Associate Professors, "C" for Professors. Msgr. Lorei will discuss other projections in salary planning.

The Committee's recommendation that the form of budget and annual report follow the same categories has been implemented. Father Norbert Wolf can give you further information you might need.

In the area of Research — $5,000 was budgeted for the year 1967-68; $5,000 for the year 1968-69. The awards were made to the teachers by a Committee appointed by the Faculty Senate. Father Robert Sciamanda can report the success of the program.

The new $5.5 million science building is under construction. The application for federal and state participation in the library building has been submitted. Mr. Gerald Kraus will explain the academic use of the areas in the new science building. Father Casimir Lubiak, the Librarian, will review the plans which have been finalized and submitted for funding.

Father John Slater, the Director of Development, will bring you up-to-date on the voluntary support which the College has received in the past two years. We are encouraged by the results.

We are also planning a dormitory and additional dining facilities. Father Speice, the Dean of Men, will explain the developments in student housing.

I am prepared to supply any additional information you might need in advance of your visit.

Sincerely yours,

Wilfrid J. Nash
President

On May 8, 1969, Monsignor Nash received a brief note from Frank P. Pishor, Chairman of the Middle States Association, that the Commission received and studied the report submitted by Professor Huntley. He further informed the President that the report would be retained in the files of the Commission with other records pertaining to Gannon College and further assured him that "the Commission, its Chairman, and its Executive Secretary (F. Taylor Jones) stand ready to assist Gannon College by consultation or by other appropriate means at any time."

Before the evaluation team appeared at Gannon in February 1967, the faculty and administration were again busily engaged in preparing a report which was submitted on January 5, 1967. This report, in its opening pages, serves as an excellent summary of the growth of the college in Msgr. Nash's first ten years as President.

Gannon College:

Liberal arts, sciences, engineering, business administration, Master's degree program. No off-campus instruction, enrollment, Fall 1966: 2,980 total; 1,920 full-time; 1,060 part-time; 2,633 men; 357 women.

DATA SUMMARY
Gannon College:

Located in downtown Erie, Pennsylvania; largely industrial metropolis of approximately 200,000 population. Only four year college for men in Erie. Strong community commitment. Privately controlled, affiliated with the Roman Catholic Church; sponsored by the Diocese of Erie, chartered in 1944. First baccalaureate degree awarded in 1945.

Governing Board:

Board of Trustees, Bishop of Erie is Chairman of Board, eleven elected members, clergy of the Diocese of Erie, composition of Board currently being changed subsequent to court approval of new charter.

Educational Program:

Undergraduate program divided into three divisions: Division of Humanities with degree programs in English, history, languages, and linguistics, philosophy, political science, psychology, sociology, social science; Division of Pure and Applied Science with degree programs in biology, chemistry, engineering (electrical and mechanical — four and five year programs), industrial management, general science, mathematics, physics; Division of Business Administration with degree programs in accounting, economics, finance, management, marketing, medical technology. Master's degree programs (begun in 1964) in English, social sciences, education (teaching and guidance counseling certification). Teacher certification in secondary education. Cooperative program with Mercyhurst College provides additional baccalaureate programs in business education, music education, art education, elementary education. Army ROTC required for two years. Engineering programs accredited by Engineers' Council for Professional Development. Counseling services accredited by American Board of Counseling Services.

Student Body:

Day undergraduate sessions open to men students. Afternoon, evening, summer sessions, and graduate programs open to men and women. Women allowed in day sessions in Mercyhurst Cooperative Program and in programs not available at two women's colleges in Erie.

Undergraduate enrollment: 2,795 total

Day Session: 1,926 total; 1,733 full-time; 193 part-time; 1,892 men; 34 women; 1,016 from Erie and Erie County; 910 non-local.

Afternoon and Evening Sessions: 868 total; 171 full-time; 698 part-time; 623 men; 246 women.

Graduate Programs: 185 total; 16 full-time; 169 part-time; 108 men; 77 women.

Degrees Conferred May, 1966:

Undergraduate 261; Graduate 8.

Admission Requirements:

16 high school units, rank in upper three quintiles, CEEB Scholastic Aptitude Test.

Faculty:

143 total; 119 full-time; 24 part-time (equated as 11 full-time); not including ROTC staff.

Full-time Faculty: 31.1 % have Doctorate; 65.6 % have Master's degree; 3.3 % have Bachelor's degree. Lay 89; clergy and religious 30.

Full-time teaching load: 12 semester hours.

Median salaries: (nine-month basis) Professor: $11,380; Associate: $10,400; Assistant: $8,000; Instructor: $6,500.

Fringe Benefits: Old Age and Survivors Insurance, TIAA Retirement Plan; Life Insurance; Group Insurance Protection (medical and hospitalization); major medical; disability insurance; college education for family.

Library:

67,533 volumes; 773 current periodicals; $44,261 spent on books and periodicals in 1965-66; 5,241 volumes added in 1965-66.

Finances: (1965-1966)

Total current income $2,137,980; educational and general $1,980,600 (Student fees $1,798,459; other $289,978); auxiliary enterprises $581,017; student aid (from College funds) $147,256. Gifts or appropriations for capital purposes $106,291. Total book value of endowment assets $474,335.

Buildings and Grounds:

7 acres. Total value buildings $5,170,863; land $605,090; equipment $1,544,313.

In this report, we find the well-documented description of the college at this time.

A mission statement adopted in 1964 was also included in the 1967 Middle States Report and follows:

Gannon College is a community of higher learning under Catholic auspices.

As a community of higher learning, Gannon is committed to the goal of intellectual excellence. Toward that end, both the faculty, and the students share in the continuing task of acquiring and communicating knowledge. While encouraging the student to be the primary agent of his own education and to evaluate whatever is presented to him, the College endeavors to impart to him already ascertained truths and probabilities and the help needed to develop his capacities for the perception and enjoyment of aesthetic values.

Gannon College is equally concerned with helping its students move toward mature vocational competence. Therefore, the College provides areas of specialized study in the sciences, the humanities, and in the professions. It aims to prepare its graduates for the fullest possible achievement in professional or graduate education.

In an age of constant change and rapid communication, Gannon College also attempts to nurture in its students a realistic knowledge and appreciation of the major problems, achievements, and failures of mankind, as well as a sense of history and a knowledge of the ties which link present-day institutions to those of the past. The College is also concerned that its students, as social beings, manifest a deep respect for human dignity and an active concern for the promotion of justice, charity, and peace in the whole community of man.

As a College under Catholic auspices, Gannon College dedicates itself to fostering in its student an appreciative understanding of the tenets and values of the Judaeo-Christian tradition, in a manner which encourages the student to make his own personal religious decisions, and in ways which emphasize the positive values in all religions and promote mutual understanding among religious peoples.

Gannon College is deeply concerned about the mutual relevance of revealed religion and current thought. It aims at protecting and fostering the virtue of faith and attempts to make clear that faith entails a personal commitment of God. In the College setting, particular stress is put on the fact that faith calls for intellectual honesty, the search for understanding, and the challenging responsibility of coping with complex social problems in the light of revealed truth.

The secondary objectives of Gannon College are goals which College will strive to attain in ways compatible with the attainment of the primary objectives. These goals concern the College itself and the wider community of which it is a part.

In general, student-oriented secondary objectives are implemented with a vigorous program of student personnel and religious activities.

Since Gannon College is concerned that its students be men of strong moral character, disposed to live and to act in accordance with their vision of moral values, the College seeks to provide an environment that helps them reach a high degree of personal moral integrity. A most important facet of this environment is a common liturgical life enabling the great works of God which are studied intellectually in the classroom to be experienced by active participation in the Church's sacramental life.

In order that he might be prepared to be of service to his fellow man, the student must attain a high degree of personal and social maturity. The guidance and counseling program plays a significant role in the attainment of this objective. Social maturity is fostered only through a rich program of co-curricular activities.

Recognizing the importance of student health and physical development, the college provides medical services and an intramural sports and general recreation program.

Along with its concern for student needs, the college is sincerely interested in the community and its area of influence. Located as it is in the heart of the City of Erie, Gannon College serves the area through its undergraduate and graduate programs, and also through such diversified services as cultural programs, adult education, consultation for business and industry, speakers' bureau, testing and guidance, and language translation. College alumni and faculty contribute significantly to the professional and business life of the community in which the College grows and flourishes.

Another area where the expansion of the college was evident after the first ten years of Msgr. Nash's Presidency can be observed in the organizational structure from a relatively simple one with a Board of Trustees, a President with three divisional Deans and some faculty committees, to one considerably more complex. By 1967, the Board of Trustees had full and complete responsibility for the college as a corporate entity. The Board chose the President and other principal officers, as needed, for the operation and control of the college. All such officers were directly responsible to the Board of Trustees. It exercised general supervision over the work of the administrative officers of the college and decided upon the retention or dismissal of officers.

The President was responsible for all matters which pertained to the governance of the college. This embraced the general direction of all educational affairs of the college as well as the development and executing of educational policies approved by the Board. He appointed the members of the Committee on Admissions, the Committee on Athletics, the Committee on Grants in Aid, the Library Committee, the Committee on Curriculum and Academic Policy, and the Committee on Teacher Education. The President governed the academic activities of the college through the Deans of the Divisions; financial and business activities through the Treasurer; and the student services through the Director of Student Services.

The Assistant to the President was appointed by the President with the approval of the Board of Trustees. He was directly responsible to the President and was in charge of administrative functions pertaining to development, public relations, continuing education, special psychological services, community development, and alumni relations. He was the secretary of the President's Council. Father John Slater (named Monsignor in 1970) was the first to hold this position until he was appointed Rector of St. Peter's Cathedral in 1969.

The Director of Student Personnel Services was also appointed by the President and had the general supervision of all Student Personnel Services. Father Robert Levis was the first to hold this position which superseded the office of the Dean of Men which had been responsible for this entire area. Father Levis held the position for a relatively short period of time when he left the college in June 1959, to pursue a doctorate in Religious Education at Catholic University. He was succeeded by Father Robert Barcio who had been the Dean of Men and a teacher at Cathedral Prep before he was appointed to the college in 1952. The Director of Student Personnel Services coordinated the work of the Registrar, the Dean of Students, the Director of Guidance, the Director of Psychological Services, the Director of Athletics and Physical Education, the Director of Religious Activities, the Financial Aid Officer, the Director of Health Services, the Director of Admissions, and the Committee on Athletics.

The Treasurer during the Nash administration was appointed by the President with the approval of the Board of Trustees. Father Norbert Wolf, who had been Dean of Men under the previous administration, was one of Msgr. Nash's first appointments. He held the Treasurer's post from 1956 to 1975 when he opted for parish work at St. Michael's, Emlenton. His wise decisions kept the college on a solid financial basis during these years. When difficulty did occur in the early 1970's, it was not due to poor management on his part, but to an inability to gather together a sufficiently large cash flow to cover current expenses during this rapid period of expansion. The Treasurer had the responsibility of the direct supervision of the Business Manager, the Controller, and the Personnel Director. The Treasurer was a member of the President's Council.

At this time, the college still functioned under three academic divisions on the undergraduate level — Humanities, Business Administration, and Pure and Applied Science. Each division was headed by a Dean who was appointed by the President with the approval of the Board of Trustees.

The Academic Dean had particular charge of the Division which he headed and presided at the meetings of his own teaching faculty. Msgr. Louis Lorei succeeded Msgr. Nash as Academic Dean. He had been appointed to the college shortly after his ordination on May 15, 1947, as Chief Librarian. He governed this academic area of the college with quiet deftness, concern, and efficiency. President Nash, from the very beginning of his tenure, depended upon him as his second in command. Msgr. Lorei, elevated to that rank in 1963, in recognition of his work at the college, left the scene when he was appointed pastor of St. Titus Church in Titusville in June 1976.

The governance of each department under Msgr. Nash was entrusted to a Director. The Director, appointed by the President after consultation with the respective Dean, was directly responsible to the Dean of his Division. Each academic dean was a member of the President's Council, of the Committee on Curriculum and Academic Policy, and the Committee on Admissions.

The Librarian was appointed by the President, also with the approval of the Board of Trustees. Responsible to the President for the administration of the Library, he was the Secretary of the Library Committee, a member of the President's Council and of the Committee on Curriculum and Academic Policy. Father Casimir Lubiak succeeded Father Lorei in 1956 as Library Director when the latter became Dean of Humanities. Under his leadership, the library collection was significantly increased and plans for the present Nash Library were initiated and completed. Father retired from his top post as Director in 1980.

The Director of the Afternoon, Evening, and Summer Sessions was also appointed by the President with the approval of the Board of Trustees. Responsible to the President for the supervision of the entire program pertaining to these sessions, he was a member of the President's Council. The first Director of these programs was Dr. Joseph P. Scottino, who became the third President of the college when Msgr. Nash resigned. Dr. Scottino was also the first Director of the Graduate School which was inaugurated in September 1964.

Finally, the President's Council was the principal policy-making and coordinating body of the college. The Council dealt with all matters affecting the organizational and financial welfare of the college as a whole. "Ex officio" members were all those mentioned above, plus the Business Manager, with the President as Chairman, and the Assistant to the President as Secretary. All actions of the Council were subject to the approval of the President and the Board of Trustees.

The Board of Trustees remained the legal governing body of the college after these first ten years of Msgr. Nash's presidency. In practice, the Executive Committee of the Board of Trustees exercised the authority vested in the Board of Trustees. In 1966, a candidate eligible for membership of the Board had to be a priest of the Diocese of Erie, a Diocese at this time with 270 priests and 180,000 laity. In addition, a trustee was expected to have either a background in education or administrative experience. For example, Archbishop John Mark Gannon, the first Chancellor, graduate of Clark Business College, educated in Rome and Germany, had been Superintendent of Schools of the Diocese of Erie (1908-1919). During his episcopacy he had supervised the construction and subsequent growth of an extensive diocesan education system which included grade schools, high schools, and colleges. He continued to have a dynamic interest in education up to the time of his resignation, December 14, 1966, as Bishop of Erie when he was 89 years old.

In addition to Archbishop Gannon, the Executive Committee

of the Board was comprised of Bishop Alfred M. Watson, Msgr. John Mark Gannon, Msgr. Joseph J. Cebelinski, Msgr. Paul E. Gooder, and Father Otto Pisoni. Bishop Watson at this time was Auxiliary Bishop of Erie and Secretary of the Board of Trustees. He had spent four years as Chaplain and professor at Mercyhurst College and seven years as Assistant Headmaster of Cathedral Preparatory School for Boys. He also brought with him considerable fiscal and administrative experience as Rector of St. Peter's Cathedral. Msgr. Gannon earned both his Licentiate in Sacred Theology and his Doctorate in Canon Law from the Catholic University of America. In his many years as Chancellor of the Diocese of Erie, he had administrative responsibility for supervising a diocese of more than 100 parishes and mission stations. Msgr. Cebelinski had been the pastor of Holy Trinity Church, a large Polish-American parish in Erie, and had twenty years experience as part-time teacher at Alliance College, Cambridge Springs, Pennsylvania. Msgr. Gooder was the pastor of St. Catherine's, DuBois, Pennsylvania, one of the largest parishes in Clearfield County. And Father Otto Pisoni was the pastor of St. Paul's, Erie, the largest Italian-American parish in Erie. All of these clergymen brought a wealth of administrative experience to the Committee. Such background on the part of the Trustees gave the college the leadership it needed in these gestational years. In anticipation of future expansion and consolidation, the college later enlarged the Board to include prominent representatives from the academic, professional and business world.

Indeed ten years later, the increase in Board membership reflected another period of tremendous development and expansion of the college. For example, in 1977, the Board of Trustees included: Frederick A. Blass, Chairman of the Board, Erie Brewing Company; the late Philip G. Cochran, President, Lyons Transportation Lines, Inc., an authentic hero during World War II in the Far East whose exploits were depicted in a nationally syndicated comic strip, "Terry and the Pirates"; James A. Currie, President, Erie Press Systems; Edward C. Doll, President, Erie Community Foundation; John W. English, Partner in English, Bowler, and Jenks Law Firm; G. Richard Fryling, President, Erie Resistor Company, Inc.; Tracy Griswold, President, Tracy Griswold

Company; Charles Hess, Vice President, General Telephone Company, Erie; Robert A. Keim, Vice President, Paine, Webber, Jackson and Curtis; Vincent Lechner, American Sterlizer Company, Erie; Richard C. Lyons, M.D., Department of Urology, Hamot Medical Center, Erie; Robert Merwin, Chairman of the Board, Eriez Magnetics; Hon. Samuel J. Roberts, Justice, Supreme Court of Pennsylvania, Erie; Michael J. Veshecco, Vice President, Security-Peoples Trust Company, Erie; James F. Walker, M.D., Physician, Erie. Also included on the Board at this time was the President of the Faculty Senate and the President of the Student Government Association.

Additonal clergy also attended the meetings of the Board by 1977. These members included: Rev. Msgr. William B. Hastings, Vicar General of the Diocese and Vice-Chairman of the Board; Msgr. Ennis A. Connelly, Pastor of Blessed Sacrament Parish; Rev. John Daniszewski who replaced the late Msgr. Joseph Cebelinski both as a member of the Board and as pastor of Holy Trinity Parish; Rev. Martin A. Grady, pastor of St. Bernard's, Bradford; George M. Hickey, pastor of St. Joseph Church, Warren, Pennsylvania; Msgr. Louis H. Lorei, present pastor of Our Lady of Peace, Erie; Rev. Daniel Martin, pastor, St. George's Parish, Erie; Msgr. John J. Slater, Rector, St. Peter's Cathedral; and Rev. Norbert Wolf, the present pastor of St. Boniface Church, Kersey, Pennsylvania.

Another barometer of the development of the college in the second decade of Msgr. Nash's Presidency can be viewed in the organizational chart that appeared in the Self-Study Report presented to the Middle States Association in 1977.

One of the most significant parts of this enlarged structure was the implementation of the principal objectives of the Undergraduate Academic Programs by the appointment of a Director of the Liberal Studies Program. This program is constituted of a number of courses and staff charged with the responsibility of assisting students to attain the knowledge, perspective, and skills implicit in the collective objectives of the Undergraduate Programs.

The Liberal Studies Program aspires to give each Gannon student a coherent general education in the major areas of human knowledge. It spans for four years of a conventional college curriculum and should equip a student with a competence to confront perennial issues of men and women in their various circumstances. The Liberal Studies Curriculum embodies several of the objectives of the Undergraduate Programs:

1. An understanding of the revealed message of Christ as presented in the teachings of the Church;

2. Development of the capacity to know and think about reality;

3. Development of the capacity to engage in life-long education;

4. The acquisition of a basic body of knowledge, including concepts, truths, and principles in various disciplines;

5. Experience in the application and utilization of this knowledge;

6. Development of the capacity to utilize these approaches to knowledge and these bodies of knowledge in directing one's own life and behavior;

7. Development of the capacity to respond positively to the aesthetic values of the past and present;

8. Development of the capacity to communicate effectively.

Finally at the time Msgr. Nash assumed the Presidency of the college, the members of an evaluating team cautioned the college with a Latin proverb *"Festina lente,"* which meant to move ahead with certain programs, but cautiously and thoroughly. The actual translation of the phrase of course is "hasten slowly". And, that is exactly what occurred during the twenty-one years that Msgr. Nash had served the college. The academic conspectus of the school showed accreditations by the Middle States Association of Colleges and Secondary Schools, the State Board of Education (Commonwealth of Pennsylvania), the Engineer's Council for Professional Development, National Council for Accreditation of Teacher Education, the American Council for Social Work Education, and the Law Enforcement Assistance Administration, U.S. Department of Justice. There were forty-five baccalaureate programs; seven career education (two-year) programs; and nine masters programs.

In May 1976, 381 undergraduate degrees and forty graduate degrees had been conferred by Gannon. In the Fall of 1976, the undergraduate enrollment reached 2,808 and a graduate school enrolled 740 students. Library holdings contained 125,918 bound volumes with 1,150 current periodicals. The annual budget for 1976-1977 was $6,097,000, an amount more than six times what it was when Msgr. Nash accepted the Presidency in the Spring of 1956. Also, under his careful direction and that of the Academic Deans, the faculty grew to 109 by the beginning of the 1976-1977 scholastic year. Along with Msgr. Nash, the men and women who joined the faculty and administration in these years brought great strength and vitality to the mission of the college. Indeed, they were largely responsible for laying the foundations of a great university.

CHAPTER V

GROWTH YEARS 1956-1977

While the student enrollment and academic programs increased significantly during the 21 years of Msgr. Nash's Presidency, the physical plant of the school also expanded greatly. One most pressing need in Gannon's early history was student housing, since many of the students from outside the City of Erie were enrolling. On October 9, 1956, ground was broken for Wehrle Hall, the first residence hall, named after Gannon's first President. Up to this time various private residences in the area had been used for student housing as well as one floor of the old Richford Hotel, at Sixth at State Streets, for a short period. Wehrle Hall was built on the former site of the Wallace Home. The latter was purchased in 1947 for a priests' dining hall, but instead became the quarters of the Institute of Social Action conducted by the Mission Helpers of the Sacred Heart for catechetics and non-credit adult religious education programs. Wehrle Hall houses approximately 240 students and their resident advisors. The building, financed by a 40-year government loan, cost between $675,000 and $750,000. Gannon's first college dormitory was filled to capacity with students on every class level when dedicated on September 8, 1957. Eventually it became a residence for freshmen only.

South Hall was a residence for upper class students. It had been converted from the former Lawrence Hotel Annex at 21 West Ninth Street. Purchased December 19, 1961, from the Lawrence Hotel Corporation for $345,000, the college spent several thousand dollars renovating the building in the Spring and Summer of 1962 for student use. It housed about 160 students including some faculty members. South Hall was sold on September 30, 1976, to the National Development Corporation. It is now known as Tullio Towers, a home for the elderly.

When Gannon became co-educational the school urgently needed to provide housing for women. In April 1970, a building on West Ninth at Chestnut Streets was purchased and was to be remodeled to accommodate thirty-six women. The building was to be named after the late Father Russell. September arrived but no renovation took place, so the young ladies were housed in the Hamot Nursing School Dormitory, at Second and State Streets. The college leased this space for one year and it became known as North Hall, a solution less than ideal.

Since the building of Wehrle Hall, the only other dormitory that has been constructed with government aid was Finegan Hall, with ground breaking taking place on December 19, 1970.

Finegan Hall was named in memory of Owen T. Finegan who died March 8, 1974. He had been at Gannon from its earliest days and certainly is considered one of its most cherished benefactors.

Owen Finegan, born September 16, 1915, was the father of four sons and two daughters. His wife, Anna, served as college librarian for many years. He resided on Station Road in Harborcreek and was very proud of his Concord grape vineyards which often were the focus of his conversations, especially during the growth and harvesting seasons. His educational background included a B.S. Degree from Duquesne University and a Master's Degree from the University of Pittsburgh. He was the Principal of St. Mary's High School in St. Marys, Pennsylvania before it became a regional school and changed its name to Elk County Christian. During World War II, Finegan served as Lieutenant in the United States Coast Guard.

A steady guiding force, he began his Gannon career in 1948 in the Education Department and later became its Chairman. Subsequently, he served as Director of Guidance and Placement, Vice President of Student Personnel Services, and Dean of the Division of Pure and Applied Science. He had served first as Acting Dean of that Division in 1972, upon the retirement of Dean Gerald Kraus. In August 1973, he received his full appointment as Dean.

Nationally known as a pioneer in job placement in colleges of the Middle States region, Dean Finegan was also one of the Founders of the Northwestern Pennsylvania Personnel and Guidance Association and served as one of its presidents. He was also one of the chief founders and coordinators of the Faculty Scholarship Fund.

Before Wehrle and Finegan Halls were constructed, most of the students were housed in various private residences and apartments in the downtown area, most of them very inadequate. But as early as 1952, the college attempted to improve this situation by purchasing an apartment building at 409-411-413 West Sixth Street. According to a news item in the school paper, *The Gannon Knight,* on October 24, 1952, the newly acquired dormitory was expected to house between fifty-five and sixty freshmen. These properties were eventually sold to the Sisters of the Divine Spirit for their convent in June 1955.

Again in 1970, a building at 164 West Fifth Street was leased from Ramwin Ltd. on September 1. Six years later it became a dormitory for Gannon's basketball players. The structure provided space for fifteen people.

In addition to student housing, the college was pressed to provide living space for several members of the clergy, a notable part of the administration and faculty from the very beginning. Adequate clergy housing was a perennial problem. The top floors of Old Main provided some space soon after its purchase in 1941. The same was true of many other buildings that were designated principally for other purposes, but a clergyman or two was usually to be found carving out quarters in some part of the building. Eventually a number of private homes were purchased and converted into private apartments for priests assigned to the college.

First among these was the Barr Faculty House at 221 West Sixth Street. It was purchased by the college in 1950 from the Frederick C. Jarecki Family and provided living quarters for clergy, most of whom were members of the Gannon faculty. It was the residence of Msgr. Bonaventure M. Ciufoli, Rev. Alphonse F. Crispo, Msgr. Homer DeWalt, Msgr. Nash, Rev. John P. Schanz, and Rev. Robert G. Barcio. Msgr. Ciufoli taught art and music for several years before his retirement, September 30, 1966. He returned to Italy to his ancestral home in Marino near Rome. Father Crispo taught philosphy and ancient history and headed the philosophy department for several years until his retirement in 1977, when he moved to East Rochester, New York. He died January 7, 1985.

Msgr. DeWalt, Superintendent of Diocesan Schools until 1982, still resides at the Barr Faculty House and has been appointed as a liaison officer for education between the university and the Catholic Diocese of Erie. Msgr. Nash lived there until he became co-pastor of Blessed Sacrament Church, Erie, in the Fall of 1981. Rev. John P. Schanz, Professor of theology, with longest tenure and author of successful theological texts, still resides there. It was also the residence of Rev. Robert G. Barcio who served the college as Dean of Men, Director of Student Personnel Services, and eventually as Professor of history and Chairman of the history department. In January 1974, he was appointed pastor of St. Francis Church in Clearfield, Pennsylvania.

For several years, the Barr Faculty House was simply dubbed "221," but in 1972 it officially memorialized Rev. Joseph J. Barr who resided there during most of his years at the college. Father Barr joined the Gannon faculty in 1950. Chairman of the social sciences, 1951-1956, and Director of the political science department, 1956-1968, he initiated the Gannon College Model United Nations and worked feverishly to make it the success that it became. Every late winter and early spring Father "Joe" would "hit the road" (as he would express it) to visit various high schools throughout the entire Diocese of Erie as well as area schools in Ohio and New York and invite them to send representatives. Model U.N. Day continues today to be a fruitful and popular learning experience for high school students. Father Barr left the college in 1968 to become the pastor of St. Joseph's Church in DuBois, Pennsylvania. His untimely death precipitated by an auto accident on an icy hill in DuBois. He died in a Pittsburgh hospital February 2, 1970. A gentle and priestly man who never raised his voice no matter how volatile the situation, he was beloved by students and faculty alike.

In 1952, the college acquired another residence for its clergy faculty on the corner of Sassafras Street at Sixth. It was known as Suttelle Hall in honor of the Suttelle Family which was most generous to the college. It was razed for construction of the Learning Resource Center in 1973, named Msgr. Wilfrid J. Nash Learning Resource Center on May 21, 1977. Another property was leased for clergy use in 1971 from Ramwin, Inc. at 136-138 West

Fifth Street next to Finegan Hall. Purchased in 1979, this residence was named in memory of Rev. Joseph E. Hipp who died as the result of a tragic auto accident on February 19, 1967. He was the Financial Aid Officer at the time of his death at the age of 42. A member of the Gannon faculty since his ordination at St. Peter's Cathedral on May 26, 1960, Fr. Hipp was a veteran of World War II and had participated in many of the major battles of the European theatre. A graduate of the University of Notre Dame, as Financial Aid Officer of the college, Father Hipp greatly expanded the program of scholarships, student loans, government loans, and student employment for nearly 600 students each semester.

In delivering the sermon at the Mass of Resurrection for Father Hipp, Msgr. Nash eulogized:

> Everything he did for us has value this morning because by it he expressed his commitment to God. We know the number of students he interviewed, the sleepless nights he spent trying to determine where and how he could get money to help them — all these things he did to serve the God he loved. The only way he knew how to serve his God was through you.

Besides living space for its students, faculty, and administrators it was necessary to provide the necessary academic, social, and athletic facilities for an increasing college enrollment. Of course, the most important of all academic facilities on any campus is a library. In the early 1970's, Gannon broke ground at 619 Sassafras Street for its library. Heidt-Evans Partnership Incorporated supplied the architects, Hardner-Doyle the contractors, and Father Lubiak much of the design. It is perhaps the most attractive building on the Gannon campus and contains all the necessary materials for a modern library: the Schuster Art Gallery dedicated to William and Frances Schuster, December 18, 1979, displaying Gus Pulakos' Greek and Egyptian Antiquities, and the Founder's Room in memory of Archbishop John Mark Gannon. Costing $4.2 million, the building contains 82,181 square feet of space. The college underwrote the building with a grant from the U.S. Department of Education and a loan from the Pennsylvania Higher Education Facilities Authority. On September 5, 1973, the new library was dedicated as the Learning Resource Center, and on May 21, 1977, was renamed the Nash Learning Resource Center in honor of

Msgr. Nash who retired as President at that time. Today it is more familiarly called the Nash Library.

To make room for the new library, a number of buildings had to be razed. Among them were Suttelle Hall, a group of apartments along Sassafras Street, and the Employment Service Building, 144 West Seventh Street, which had been purchased as early as 1962 by the college.

Next in importance to the Nash Library, the Zurn Science Center at 143 West Seventh Street and 136 West Eighth Street was constructed and dedicated on October 17, 1970. Gannon's largest building, it contains offices, laboratories, lecture halls, computers, and classrooms. Some of the funds for this building came from the Zurn Foundation under the direction of Melvin A. Zurn (1901-1970). One of its lecture halls was named the Hammermill Auditorium in gratitude for the financial aid given by the Hammermill Paper Company of Erie. In recognition of a substantial gift to the Investment in Excellence Program on November 24, 1981, by Mr. and Mrs. Joseph Spiteri, Sr., a portion of the third floor was designated the Spiteri Engineering Center. The Language Laboratory was named in memory of Hans Funk, Director of the laboratory and an instructor of language until his death in 1970. The total cost of the Center was close to $5.5 million.

Other buildings mushrooming on the Gannon campus during the presidency of Msgr. Nash were the Student Union (1956), Dale Hall (1960), Beyer Hall (1962), the Gannon Theatre (1963), and the Walker-Reklaw Buildings (1964). Some of these buildings were used for student services and others for both academic purposes and recreational services. The Julius G. Siegel Mansion, Gannon's first Student Union, at 459 West Sixth Street, was the first building almost exclusively set aside for student activities. Two clergy resided there as supervisors, and for some time the dining room was used for the evening meal for Gannon clergy. The large garage and maintenance shop in the rear of the home became, for a time, an experimental theatre for the college. The building was furnished by proceeds from the first Christmas Carnival in 1956. This first student effort of its kind at Gannon was organized by Rev. Robert Barcio, Dean of Men, and William Garvey, later to become President of Mercyhurst College. The mansion was purchased for about $35,000. It was sold to the Erie County Department of Human Services in January 1974. The building is presently used by the Office of Mental Health and Mental Retardation and the Office of Drug and Alcohol Abuse.

Dale Hall was purchased from Perry Square Corporation in 1959. The building had been the garage of the Appel automobile dealership. It housed the ROTC (Reserve Officer Training Corps) which had grown significantly from its early beginnings in 1947. The Gannon ROTC Drill Team engaged in national competition and its trophies abound Gannon. The ROTC quarters were named in honor of John N. Dale, who graduated in June 1950, commissioned a Second Lieutenant in the Military Police Corps. He was listed as "missing in action" during the Korean War on December 12, 1950. This hero was the first Gannon ROTC graduate to receive the Silver Star. Dale Hall opened in 1959 but was sold to the City of Erie in 1976. The building is now the Erie Senior Citizens Center and is used by the Steady Strivers of Erie, Erie Civic Ballet School, Senior Citizens Center, and Health Care.

Prior to 1959, the ROTC was housed in Aquinas Hall at 209 West Sixth Street, east of Wehrle Hall. Built by Thomas Carter, a steamboat operator, it became the home of M. and C. Shannon according to the 1939 City Directory, before it was purchased by the college in 1947. In 1962 it became a faculty residence and small chapel. It was converted to a Health Center in the later 60's and early 70's where the students were treated for minor ailments. The Florence Nightingale of the Center for several years was the late Mary Hilbert, loved and honored as "Mother" by all students who lived on campus. Dr. Edward Heibel served long and loyally as the college's first physician.

On November 29, 1960 a ground breaking ceremony was held for the construction of a multi-purpose building named Beyer Hall. This building was the first large scale construction in the first decade of Msgr. Nash's presidency. It contained classrooms, offices, cafeteria, greenhouse, snack bar, laboratories, and lounges. It was attached to the Gannon Auditorium (now Hammermill Auditorium) and added space for 1,500 guests for banquets and other functions. The snack bar in the basement became a haven especially for commuter students. Not only was food available at reasonable prices, but it was a rendezvous for meeting friends and having a few hands of pinochle. During the 1970's, the basement room became known as the "Scrounge," and even after it was remodeled, the name remained.

Beyer Hall was constructed on the site of the former Fisher Hotel which, prior to its purchase by the college in October 1948, served as a landmark hotel and restaurant. The former hotel had been used to augment the college's housing and cafeteria needs both before and after its purchase. The purchase price was estimated at $110,000.

Dedication ceremonies for Beyer Hall took place on April 29, 1962. The estimated cost of the building was around $1 million. It became Beyer Hall in 1972 in memory of Dr. Richard L. Beyer, Chairman of the history department for many years until his untimely death on August 7, 1966.

Scholarly, able to hold students spellbound with his lectures, "Doc," Beyer was born April 27, 1905, the son of Richard H. and Mary Feichtner Beyer, prominent local jewelers. He graduated from Academy High School and attended Allegheny College in Meadville while working as a newspaper reporter during his undergraduate days. He earned a doctorate in Colonial American History from the University of Iowa in 1929 and subsequently taught and became the Chairman of the history department at Southern Illinois University at Carbondale. In 1945, he returned to Erie and soon joined the faculty of Gannon College which was beginning to recover from the disaster of World War II. He quickly became a key member of the faculty and was well known throughout the city as broadcast moderator of the Gannon College Roundtable during its fifteen years on radio and television. He cheerfully spoke wherever invited in Erie and Western Pennsylvania to the delight of civic and historical groups. An annual lecture is scheduled through the history department at Gannon in his memory.

In 1983, a considerable part of Beyer Hall was named the Dahlkemper School of Business Administration. Joseph B. Dahlkemper, a prominent local businessman, contributed $2,000,000 to the Investment in Excellence Program inaugurated by President Joseph P. Scottino.

One year after Beyer Hall was dedicated, the college purchased the Erie Civic Theatre, 128 West Seventh Street. Exactly what price the college paid for the building when it was purchased in March 1963 is unknown, but it probably sold for $75,000. It was renamed the Gannon Theatre shortly thereafter.

Following the purchase of the Gannon Theatre, the Walker and Reklaw Buildings were acquired by the college for $200,000 from James F. and Mary Walker in 1964. They were a complex of three buildings at 703-705 Peach Street and 23-27 West Seventh Street. The Walker Building and Book Store Building for the first several years housed the book store, faculty services, the development office, faculty offices, the *Gannon Knight* and *Lance* offices, the print shop, and the post office. The latter, along with faculty services and the print shop, were removed to the newly remodeled Service Center in 1980. Also by 1981, the Walker complex housed the Erie Metropolitan College, now termed University College, and the Diocesan Communications Office. The Reklaw Building on Seventh Street (Walker spelled backwards), has been used largely for faculty residence.

During the second decade of the Nash Presidency, the Pontifical Center was established with its Director, Rev. Robert J. Levis, Ph.D., in June 1972. Space was first allotted to the Center in the Walker Building, but in 1979 it was housed at the Sacred Heart House, 554 West Tenth Street. In August 1981, the Center moved to the recently remodeled Student Services Center, at Fifth and Peach Streets. The latter site had formerly been the First Presbyterian Church and Education Buildings, 502 Peach Street, and 109 and 111 West Fifth Street. The building complex is actually three connected structures, the Selden Chapel (1897), the Church proper (1947), and the Education Center (1965). The First Presbyterian Church no longer needed these facilities after it merged with the Church of the Covenant Congregation, 247 West Sixth Street. Gannon purchased this needed space for $510,000 in March 1981. Today this property houses the University Chapel, the Pontifical Center for Catechetical Studies, administrative offices, Student Activities, Student Government, Freshman Services, Religious Activities, Guidance and Placement, Testing Services, and classrooms.

While expansion was considerable in most areas of the college during Msgr. Nash's presidency, very little progress was made in providing sufficient physical education and athletic facilities for the growing student body. The only building on the campus for such activities was the Gannon Auditorium constructed in 1948 during the presidency of "Doc" Wehrle. As far back as 1957, the Middle States Association pointed out that the lack of sufficient facilities for physical education and limited activity in the varsity sports was a serious deficiency in the college's facilities. This weakness at last was corrected with the construction of a Student Recreation Center, December 1984. The auditorium is now known as the Hammermill Center of Gannon University through a $600,000 contribution made by the Hammermill Foundation on December 14, 1981, to the Investment in Excellence Program of the University.

Despite meager athletic facilities, Gannon's sports program blossomed during the presidency of Msgr. Nash. It began in the late Fall of 1944 at a typical after-class "bull session", when the notion was proposed that the college should have an intercollegiate basketball team. In a few short months Naz Servidio was hired as the first player coach for the 1944-45 season. "Naz" played at Erie Academy High School where he excelled in both football and basketball. A letter was sent to every institution located within a 150-mile radius of Erie in an effort to schedule games. Due to the late organization of the program, many schedules had already been completed, but eventually, thirteen games were contracted. This first year squad surprised everyone with a 10-3 record which included victories over established programs such as St. Bonaventure's, Kent State, and Niagara University.

At the conclusion of this inaugural season, the college newspaper, *The Mansion,* recognized Father Nash's role by

> paying tribute to the generous, kindly, and untiring guidance and assistance which Father Wilfrid Nash had given to the newly inaugurated athletic program at Gannon, particularly the basketball team. He was the moving spirit in its beginning and its strong support and inspiration in a highly successful season. With such a good beginning, the collegiate program of sports at Gannon will move to great athletic heights. Our congratulations to you, Father Nash.

But for a brief interlude in the late 40's, basektball became the principal varsity sport. Gannon fielded a football team in 1949-1950 and 1950-1951 that gained national attention. During the first season, the team was undefeated and it also produced a winning record the following year. The team was coached by "Lou" Tullio, a former Cathedral Prep and Holy Cross football star, and the present Mayor of Erie for the fifth four-year term. He was assisted by the late "Jack" Komora who was a successful local high school coach. In spite of its initial success, the college was forced to drop varsity football after two years. The program had operated under a considerable deficit which was rumored to be in the vicinity of $50,000 over a two-year period. This was too much in those early days of the college, struggling to keep itself financially afloat.

Soon after his appointment as president, Father Nash indicated his continued interest in an athletic program for the students of the college when Milt Simon became Gannon's first full-time Athletic Director and Basketball Coach in 1956. "Milt", a native of Erie and star in basketball at Penn State University, had served with the U.S. Navy at Pearl Harbor from 1943-1945. He had been Basketball and Golf Coach at Behrend Center from 1954-1956. Under Simon, the Golden Knights posted a .500 record for the next five seasons prior to his resignation in 1961.

Soon after Milt's resignation, Father Nash and the Athletic Committee signed up the legendary Ed McCluskey of Farrell High School, one of the most successful high school coaches in the nation. However, after recruiting one of the most talented groups of freshmen in the history of Gannon University, McCluskey resigned his post in mid-July without ever coaching a game.

He was succeded by George Hesch, star player of the team during 1951-1955 and former assistant to Milt Simon. Hesch led the young Knights to a 16-9 record and the first NCAA tournament appearance. Hesch coached one more season before returning to devote full-time to his teaching position in the chemistry department of the college.

One of the most successful coaches in the history of the college was George Hesch's successor, Jim Harding. Born in 1929 in Clinton, Iowa, Jim attended the University of Iowa where he earned his B.S. and M.S. degrees. He was a strict disciplinarian which caused some of the members of the administration and faculty to question his methods. In three seasons at Gannon, 1963-1966, his teams won 57 and lost 14 games. After two consecutive bids to the NAIA playoffs, the controversial Harding resigned in 1966 when the college declined to accept a post-season playoff invitation to the divisional playoffs despite a 20-3 season. Following his tenure at Gannon, he was signed as head basketball coach at La Salle University in Philadelphia.

It was at this time that Msgr. Nash made the determination that the dual position of Basketball Coach-Athletic Director should be divided, and Howard (Bud) Elwell, who had been Intramural Director and Assistant Basketball Coach under both Harding and Hesch, was promoted to the position of Athletic Director. Elwell turned to the College of Steubenville, one of the Knights' biggest rivals and signed John (Denny) Bayer to a four-year pact. Bayer continued Gannon's winning ways when he produced a record of 79-30 before departing for the University of Nevada-Las Vegas. Bayer was able to recruit some of the better players in Gannon roundball history including All-American Glen Summors, Al Chrisman, and Larry Daly, who led the Knights to their only NAIA District 18 Championship in 1969. That squad went all the way to the National Quarter finals in Kansas City before bowing out with a 24-6 record. Bayer's teams earned three post-season playoff bids in his four years at the helm.

Dave Markey followed during the 1970-1974 period, and the former Canisius College Assistant was also a winner with a 62-41 overall record and a spot in the 1972 NCAA playoffs.

Ed Sparling followed with 76-34 results over the next four seasons that included two East Region NCAA invitations and one Regional Championship. Sparling was the second Gannon mentor who honed his coaching skills at Steubenville College. Sparling's first season (1974-1975) proved to be one of the best in Gannon history when he directed the Knights to the NCAA East Region Championship and a berth in the National finals at Evansville. All-American Gerry Walker was the mainstay of that club which also included Al Farmer, Neal and Dave Stoczynski, and the dimunitive Willie Wade, MVP of the East Regional Tournament.

During the Nash presidency, six coaches headed the basketball program. All had the same winning experience as the Knights, with a .644 winning percentage on a 336-170 record during this period. A complete picture of thirty-eight years of Gannon basketball are included in the *Gannon University Media Guide* for 1983-1984, and reproduced on the following page.

While basketball has admittedly been the most visible sport in Gannon athletics, dynamic growth also occurred in other areas of the program. Cross country running was started in the Fall of 1962 when Gannon joined the NCAA in order to fulfill the requirement that a member institution sponsor a varsity sport in the Fall, Winter, and Spring seasons. After a 0-10 start in the initial season (1962), the team steadily improved to a point where it won the NAIA District 18 Championship in 1967 and advanced to the National Championship in Omaha, Nebraska. At the end of the 1968-69 year, the team had achieved a 70-33 record despite its dismal start, and the team established itself as a respectful opponent under Coach Elwell.

Wrestling first became a part of the Intercollegiate Program in 1968-1969 after several years of informal practice among the students under Louis Marciani, Intramural Director. Marciani, a native of New Jersey, also organized the college's first soccer team in the Fall of 1968.

The success of the golf team has paralleled that of the basketball squad. After the initiation of the College Division Championship in the Spring of 1970, Gannon was presented at the National Golf Tournament either by a team or an individual seven straight years through 1976, including four team entries (1970, 1971, 1973, 1975). Harry Boback, Jr., had All-American seasons in both the NCAA (1972) and NAIA (1973) and Gene George (1973-74 teams) received national recognition by earning his professional tour card. The Golden Knights, as a team, finished fourth in the nation at the NAIA National Championship in Bemidji, Minnesota, in 1959.

It is probably not common knowledge that the Gannon Bowling Team was the class team of the area during the decade 1962-1972, but the Knights' only National Championship was achieved by the 1962 Keglers. Under the direction of Rev. John (Tex) Hilbert,

88 THE STORY OF GANNON UNIVERSITY

38 YEARS OF BASKETBALL

Opponnent	W	L	Last Year Played
Pitt-Johnstown	1	0	80-81
Providence	0	1	66-67
Quincy College	1	0	67-68
Rio Grande	1	0	65-66
Rochester	3	0	58-59
St. Bonaventure	5	22	76-77
St. John Fisher	5	0	82-83
St. Francis (NY)	6	2	77-78
St. Francis (PA)	1	9	71-72
St. Vincent	15	8	71-72
Saginaw Valley	0	1	81-82
Sampson AFB	2	2	55-56
San Diego U.	0	1	70-71
San Francisco State	8	0	73-74
Scranton	1	1	74-75
Shaw	1	0	74-75
Siena	1	1	74-75
Slippery Rock	8	2	82-83
S. California State	1	0	74-75
Southern Illinois	1	0	62-63
Southampton	0	1	82-83
S. W. Missouri State	1	0	65-66
Steubenville	30	24	80-81
Steward AFB	1	1	69-70
Taylor U.	0	1	58-59
Tenn.-Chattanooga	0	1	73-74
Tennessee State	5	9	73-74
Tennessee Tech	0	1	76-77
Texas Southern	1	1	66-67
Thiel	18	2	61-62
Thomas More	6	0	75-76
Tiffin	5	2	50-51
Toronto	1	0	68-69
Vermont	0	1	70-71
Union	1	0	75-76
U. of Dist. of Col.	0	1	82-83
Walsh	5	0	75-76
Washington & Jefferson	3	4	64-65
Waynesburg	6	0	61-62
W. New England	2	1	71-72
Western Reserve	2	0	52-53
West Liberty	3	0	74-75
Western Ontario	1	0	62-63
Westminster	3	10	68-69
Wheeling	3	0	80-81
Wilberforce	1	0	77-78
Wisc./Green Bay	1	0	79-80
Wittenberg	0	1	61-62
Wright State	0	2	82-83
Xavier	0	2	62-63
Youngstown	25	39	82-83

Year	W	L	Pct.	Coach
1982-83	17	12	.571	Dick Fox
1981-82	17	9	.653	Dick Fox
1980-81	17	10	.630	Dick Fox
1979-80	20	9	.689	Dick Fox
1978-79	18	9	.666	Dick Fox
1977-78	15	11	.577	Ed Sparling
1976-77	20	8	.714	Ed Sparling
1975-76	16	11	.592	Ed Sparling
1974-75	25	4	.862	Ed Sparling
1973-74	15	11	.576	Dave Markey
1972-73	17	9	.853	Dave Markey
1971-72	19	7	.730	Dave Markey
1970-71	11	14	.440	Dave Markey
1969-79	18	7	.720	John Bayer
1968-69	24	6	.800	John Bayer
1967-68	19	8	.703	John Bayer
1966-67	18	9	.667	John Bayer
1965-66	20	3	.870	Jim Harding
1964-65	20	4	.833	Jim Harding
1963-64	17	7	.708	Jim Harding
1962-63	13	12	.520	George Hesch
1961-62	16	9	.640	George Hesch
1960-61	12	9	.571	Milt Simon
1959-60	8	9	.471	Milt Simon
1958-59	10	9	.526	Milt Simon
1957-58	9	8	.592	Milt Simon
1956-57	9	14	.391	Milt Simon
1955-56	11	12	.478	Lou Tullio
1954-55	12	8	.600	Lou Tullio
1953-54	16	7	.696	Lou Tullio
1952-53	17	10	.629	Lou Tullio
1951-52	12	13	.480	Lou Tullio
1950-51	12	13	.480	Al Hook
1949-50	14	12	.538	Gene Powers & Lou Tullio
1948-49	10	16	.385	Gene Powers
1947-48	8	14	.364	Joe Niland & Gene Powers
1946-47	2	16	.111	Naz Servidio
1945-46	5	9	.375	Ziggy Markowitz
1944-45	10	3	.768	Naz Servidio
Totals	568	371	.605	

the Gannon squad of Al Kendziora, Tom Kirk, Dick Dowling, Joe Nieratko, and Rick Sambuchino traveled to Kansas City to win the national title. District 18 NCIA crowns also came in 1967, 1969, and 1972, and the Bowling Knights received additional national honors with a third place finish at the National Championship rolloff in 1967.

Shooting was another lesser known intercollegiate sport of this period although it sported a strong program. Competing in the Lake Erie Intercollegiate Rifle Conference, the Knight shooters went through the league unbeaten (11-0) and won the Conference title under Captain Jim Quisenberry in 1971.

The college sponsored fencing at the intercollegiate level in the late 1950's under the direction of Laszlo Doemeny, who also served as Intramural Director. He had been a Hungarian freedom fighter before coming to Gannon as a physical education instructor.

Dick Detzel, Dick Fox, and Ivan George have managed the fortunes of the Gannon baseball program over these years with better than average success. Steve Grilli, a native of Long Island, New York, who pitched for the Knights during the 1968-1970 years, made his way from Gannon all the way to the Major Leagues with the Detroit Tigers.

In addition to basketball and golf, tennis is another sport which has survived the test of time on the Gannon campus. The program reached its peak in the mid-1960's under Coach Udo Zaenglein, former professional at the Kahkwa Club, with standout players Rich Herbel, Tom Pacansky, Bill Root, Dave Rudy, and John Stine.

Responding to the needs of the influx of women to the Gannon campus in the early 1970's, the college instituted a women's athletic program in 1974 with intercollegiate competition in basketball and volleyball. Softball was added to the program in 1975 and tennis a year later. Karen Morris, a graduate of Syracuse University and Coach at Cazenovia College in New York, was the first women's athletic director. She became a full-time employee of the college in 1976.

Msgr. Nash will be remembered and recognized for his tremendous interest and support of intercollegiate athletics in the formative years at Gannon, and as a quiet contributor to the competitive spirit of student athletes.

Besides an expanded sports program, the students' needs for recreation and fellowship were met during the Nash presidency by a growing, balanced, and controlled social program. Traditional events of the social calendar included major dances in the Fall and Spring, the concert program, the Winter Carnival, college-wide forums, and the varied events of the campus student organizations, fraternities, and clubs.

The college's clubs provided a good co-curricular or extra-curricular involvement for the student in his major field. Practical application of classroom knowledge was the main objective of his or her participation. By the end of the Nash presidency, the college catalogue listed the following clubs and their advisers:

American Institute of Biological Sciences
    Adviser: Dr. Elmer F. Kohlmiller
American Institute of Physics
    Adviser: Dr. Paul B. Griesacker
American Marketing Association
Chemistry Club
    Adviser: Dr. George Hesch
Commuter Organization
    Adviser: Fr. Casimir Wozniak
Criminal Justice Club
    Adviser: Thomas Seiverling
German Club
    Adviser: Dr. Berta Weber
The Historical Society of Gannon College
    Adviser: Dr. Robert Allshouse
The Institute of Electrical and Electronic Engineers (I.E.E.E.)
    Adviser: Frank W. Groszkiewicz
Law Club
    Adviser: Dr. Gregor Reinhard
Gannon College Section of the American Society of Mechanical Engineers
    Adviser: Dr. Halit M. Kosar
Omicron Delta Epsilon
Honor Society in Economics
    Adviser: Ernest C. Wright
Political Science Club
    Adviser: Dr. Gregor Reinhard

Psychology Club
    Adviser: Dr. John Duda
Ski Club
    Adviser: Rev. Stephen Minkiel
Spanish Club
    Adviser: Dr. Eron de Leon Soto
Sociology Club
    Adviser: William Murphy
Social Work Club
    Adviser: Charles M. Murphy
Student Investment Trust
    Adviser: Ernest C. Wright
Student Pennsylvania State Education Association (Education Club)
    Adviser: Dr. Robert A. Wehrer
Who's Who in American Colleges and Universities
(Honorary for Junior and Senior Campus Leaders)
    Adviser: Louis J. Agnese, Jr.

Membership in a campus military organization was and remains a rewarding involvement. Programs sponsored by the Department of Military Science served as an enrichment to the degree programs offered at the college. Military science courses and the military organizations were open to all students, male and female, whether or not they were enrolled in the ROTC Program. Some of the organizations in the military science department were the Pershing Rifles (a national society), the Scabbard and Blade (an honorary society), and the Raiders (a social organization).

Since their inception in 1953, fraternities at Gannon University have been an integral part of the educational process and an influence on the development of Gannon College and University. During the latter part of the Nash era when many fraternities were frowned upon and decreasing because of economic and social pressures, the system at Gannon managed not only to survive but began to thrive in a spirit of service to Gannon and the community. The fraternity system broadened its scope to give new meaning to the term "social fraternities". While social activities were still a major part of the fraternity program, much greater emphasis was placed on scholarship, athletics, leadership, and community service. Because Gannon felt that fraternity houses had at that time a definite role in college life and that their group discipline and educational atmosphere was important to the individual, Gannon has permitted the social fraternities to operate individual houses.

For several years, they have aided in solving the student housing problems. A 1971 *Gannon Catalog* lists the following fraternities and their advisers at that time:

Alpha Gamma Delta - Social
   Adviser: Marianne Bock
Alpha Kappa PSI - Professional Business
   Adviser: Joseph L. Bressan, C.P.A.
Alpha Phi Delta - Social
   Adviser: Ernest Wright
Alpha Psi Omega - Dramatic Honorary
   Adviser: Michael Morris
Beta Beta Beta - Honorary Biology
   Adviser: Stanley J. Zagorski
Blue Key National Honor Fraternity
Cardinal Key National Honor Society
   Adviser: Mary Pat Carney
Delta Chi - Social
   Adviser: Rev. Lawrence T. Speice
Delta Signa Phi - Social
   Adviser: Mario Bagnoni
Gamma Sigma Mu - Veteran's Fraternity
   Adviser: Dr. Robert H. Allshouse
Interfraternity Council
   Adviser: Louis Agnese
Alpha Phi Omega - Service
   Adviser: Dr. Austin O'Toole
Pi Gamma Mu National Social Science - Honor Society
   Adviser: Dr. Gregor Reinhard
Pi Kappa Alpha - Social
   Adviser: John Alberstadt
Tau Kappa Epsilon - Social
Adviser: Ward McCracken
Pi Sigma Epsilon - Professional Business
   Adviser: Joseph L. Brennan, C.P.A.
Sigma Pi Sigma - Physics Honor Society
   Adviser: Dr. Paul Griesacker
Shiek - Social
   Adviser: Fr. Robert Susa

Student publications, the *Gannon Knight*, student newspaper, and *The Lance*, the student yearbook, have existed on the Gannon campus almost since the foundation of the college and continued through the years of the Nash administration. The *Gannonite* (sic) first appeared July 26, 1946, and the *Lance* in 1952. The Student Government Association, by the end of the Nash term, was the elected representative body on campus charged with the responsibility of the general welfare of the student body. In the middle 50's and through the 60's, it was known as the Student Council. Its function was to enhance the Gannon student intellectually, culturally, socially, and religiously through diversified programs throughout the year.

With the purchase of the Erie Playhouse in 1963, the Gannon College Theatre gave the opportunity for practical experience in acting and other theatre skills for anyone associated with the college who gained membership in the Drama Department's Talisman Players. Those who showed outstanding achievements and ability in the theatre arts were eligible for election to the Kappa Beta Chapter of the national dramatic honor fraternity, Alpha Psi Omega. Each year, the players have presented a variety of classic and modern plays, including musicals. The Drama Department developed rapidly in the early 1970's under the direction of Father Thomas McSweeney, a Gannon alumnus. Shirley Levin preceded him as Director of the drama program in 1972.

It goes without saying that Msgr. Nash had provided dynamic and effective leadership during his tenure as president. Evidence of this in the academic area has already been discussed. But outside the classroom, vigorous expansion of the Gannon campus and student services also took place. Additions to the physical plant included two dormitories for students, one faculty residence, a new library, science center, and two buildings devoted exclusively to offices, a theatre, and various student facilities. The campus has more than doubled its facilities since the beginning of the Nash presidency.

The value of the land, buildings, and equipment, according to a self-study report to the Middle States Association in 1977, was $20,243,738. These facilities and the academic equipment and resources they included represented a major investment in excellence that was to provide the foundation for the eventual movement toward university status.

Indeed, Msgr. Nash could look back with justified pride over the considerable progess of the institution he loved so dearly. At the time he assumed the presidency of the college in 1956, the members of the evaluating team cautioned the college with a Latin proverb *festina lente.* That is exactly what occured during twenty-one years of Msgr. Nash's service. The school had been accredited by the Middle States Association of Colleges and Secondary Schools, the State Board of Education (Commonwealth of Pennsylvania), the Engineer's Council for Professional Development, National Council for Accreditation of Teacher Education, the American Council for Social Work Education, and the Law Enforcement Assistant Administration, U.S. Department of Justice. There were forty-five baccalaureate programs, seven career education (two year) programs, and nine masters programs.

In May of 1976, 381 undergraduate degrees were conferred and forty graduate degrees. In the Fall of 1976, the undergraduate enrollment reached 2,808 and graduate programs enrolled 740 students. Library holdings contained 125,198 bound volumes with 1,150 current periodicals. The annual budget for 1976-1977 was $6,097,000 an amount more than six times what it was when Msgr. Nash accepted the presidency in the late Spring of 1956. Also, under his careful direction and that of the Deans, the faculty grew to 109 by the beginning of the 1976-1977 scholastic year.

It must have been a difficult hour while Msgr. Nash contemplated terminating his tenure as President in the Spring of 1976. His entire career after his ordination on May 14, 1942, revolved around the college. By virtue of his Christian faith, his love and concern for all who joined the Gannon community, and the strength of his conviction about the contributions which Gannon could make in the lives of its students, faculty, and the community at large, he made an indelible impression. The door to the presidential office was always open to anyone who might need his wise advice and friendly counsel. After twenty-one years of faithful and fruitful service as president, of the thirty-nine years he served at Gannon, Msgr. Nash won the gratitude and appreciation of his colleagues and many friends as well as the Gannon students and alumni. He notified the Trustees of his wish on October 28, 1976, and officially retired on July 1, 1977. He was designated an Honorary Alumnus, President Emeritus, and remains a Trustee. The new library at Gannon was renamed the Wilfrid J. Nash Learning Resource Center. Also, the Monsignor Nash Christian Service Award was established by Gannon College in May 1977 to be presented to an apostolic graduating senior who displayed outstanding service to others both on and off the campus.

In addition to the honors bestowed upon him by the institution he served so well, he also received them from his church, other colleges and universities, and the local community. He had already been named a domestic prelate with the title of Right Reverend Monsignor by Pope John XXIII on February 12, 1961; and, on May 21, 1977, Pope Paul VI elevated him to the rank of Prothonatory Apostolic. He also received Honorary Doctorates from Fordham University, New York; the Hahnemann Medical College, Philadelphia; and Allegheny College, Meadville, Pennsylvania. In 1962, he was awarded the Distinguished Citizen Award by the City of Erie; in 1968, the Service Award by the United Fund of Erie; in 1969, the Liberty Bell Award of the Erie County Bar Association; in 1977, the Notre Dame Man of the Year by the Notre Dame Club of Erie; the Medallion Award of Behrend College; and the Certificate of Merit by Edinboro State College. But the honor that Msgr. Nash appreciated more than any other was the one that was bestowed to the college when he became a priest *secundum ordinem Melchisedech.* Whatever he might have accomplished in his priestly career, or any recognition he might have received paled in his eyes, compared to the priesthood that was conferred upon him over forty years ago. Anyone who has ever had even a slight acquaintance with Msgr. Nash realizes that he is a priest first, last, and always, despite a life and a career that has been filled with such diverse and illustrious achievements.

CHAPTER VI
FROM COLLEGE TO UNIVERSITY

The year 1977 marked the period of full maturity of Gannon College. Under the able leadership of Monsignor Nash, the institution had achieved the respect of the Erie community, broad diversity of academic programs and fiscal stability. Upon his retirement from the presidency on July 1, 1977, Monsignor Nash, was succeeded in that office by Dr. Joseph P. Scottino.

The presidency of Dr. Scottino inaugurated a new phase in Gannon's institutional growth, culminating in university status.

Dr. Scottino had been part of the Gannon community for over thirty years as a student, faculty member and adminstrator. Following his baccalaureate degree in political science from Gannon College, he obtained his Master's and Doctorate in Political Philosophy from Fordham University. He joined the Gannon faculty in 1955 in the department of political science. In recognition of his demonstrated administrative talent, Dr. Scottino was appointed Director of the Evening School and the Summer Sessions in 1962 and Director of the Graduate School in 1964. In 1972 he was appointed to the newly created position of Vice President for Academic Affairs and Provost.

In a tenure marked by innovation and energy, the outstanding accomplishment of Dr. Scottino's term as Vice President for Academic Affairs was his obtaining a grant from the W.K. Kellogg Foundation in the amount of $2 million, the largest in the history of the institution.

Ths grant founded two of the most distinctive academic programs of the institution, the Physician's Assistant Program and the Family Medicine Program presented in affiliation with Hahnemann Medical College of Philadelphia.

Upon assuming the presidency of Gannon College, Dr. Scottino began formulating a design for its future growth including advancement to university status. The concept of becoming a university was not new. Early in the history of the college, the founder, Archbishop John Mark Gannon, had cherished that dream. He publicly proclaimed in an address that if the community were to organize fund raising efforts necessary for its attainment, he would designate his school as the University of Erie. A major deterrent to the realization of Archbishop Gannon's vision of a university was the provision in the Pennsylvania School Code governing private universities, Section 43.2: "The second unit (after the undergraduate program) shall provide advanced degree programs through the doctorate in the arts and sciences, with an adequate number of majors in the various disciplines."

Since Gannon College graduate programs extended through the Master's level only, the requirement of the doctorate stipulated in the school code effectively blocked aspirations for university status.

The awaited breakthrough came in 1978 with the release of the Master Plan for Higher Education in Pennsylvania. This document noted that employment opportunities for Ph.D. graduates in Pennsylvania would diminish in the future. In consequence the Master Plan proposed no new programs in the projected reorganization of the state college and university system. Although this repeal of the doctoral program requirement as a condition of university designation had been intended initially to benefit the public institutions of the Commonwealth under the aegis of the Keystone State University System, it was the private sector which first seized the opportunity it offered. St. Joseph's College of Philadelphia and then Widener College applied for and were granted designation as universities under the new regulations.

In May of 1978 the Board of Trustees authorized Dr. Scottino to apply under the new dispensation to the Pennsylvania Department of Education for designation as a university. At the same time, a Committee on University Status was organized to prepare the college's case statement in support of the application.

The *Application for University Status* drafted by the committee was submitted to the Department of Education in November 1978 after six months of intensive effort. The preface of that document contains the following declaration:

"Gannon has been developing in accordance with the principle of university structure in academic administration in order to attain excellence in the presentation of its many and diverse academic programs."

"University status is essentially a confirmation of the academic quality that has been achieved at Gannon in presenting a broad spectrum of undergraduate, graduate and professional education programs."

"Gannon possesses the characteristics of a Catholic liberal arts university. Designation as a university would be appropriate to Gannon's mission, objectives and size, and to the educational programs and services which it is committed to the people and communities that Gannon serves."

In response to the application for university designation, the Pennsylvania Department of Education assigned a visitation team to evaluate the merits of Gannon's petition. The team of eight members under the chairmanship of Dr. Howard B. Maxwell, Vice President for Administration of the Commission for Independent Colleges and Universities, visited the Gannon campus on April 8, 1979. After four days of intensive study on campus and throughout the community, the Visitation Team conducted an exit briefing at the Hilton Hotel on April 11, 1979. The comments were encouraging. In addition to their finding of community support for Gannon's goal of university designation, the team indicated that it has perceived a broad-based willingness to contribute to the financial support of its attainment.

In anticipation of a favorable recommendation from the visitation team, the Gannon community under the leadership of Dr. Scottino set to work on a plan for the implementation of university structure. The resulting document entitled *Gannon College - University Transition Program* was published on October 19, 1979.

A list of the chapter headings indicates the nature of the transition strategy proposed:

1. Long Range Planning.
2. Academic Organization.
3. Affirmative Action.
4. Institutional Governance.
5. Board of Trustees.

6. The Relationship of Gannon College to the Catholic Diocese of Erie.

7. Academic Rank, Tenure and Freedom.

8. Research.

These efforts of the Gannon community proved successful. On December 19, 1979, Governor Richard Thornburgh came to the campus to proclaim in person that Gannon College was forthwith to be designated Gannon University.

The bestowal of university status on Gannon was greeted with widespread rejoicing by the entire community of Erie. Plans were immediately undertaken to celebrate the event with appropriate ceremonies. The first of these was scheduled for Sunday, April 20, 1980. This was the Liturgy of Dedication and Recommitment held in St. Peter's Cathedral. The highlight of the event was the homily by Msgr. Wilfrid J. Nash, past president of Gannon College, in which he reviewed the aspirations for the establishment of a university in Erie on the part of the institutional founder, Archbishop John Mark Gannon, and the events which led to the realization of that vision. Presiding prelates at the liturgy were Most Reverend Alfred Michael Watson, Bishop of Erie, and his Coadjutor Bishop, Most Reverend Michael J. Murphy.

Following the liturgy at St. Peter's Cathedral, the faculty and staff of the university convened in the Gannon Auditorium to recognize faculty members who had contributed twenty-five years or more of service to the institution. Members so honored included: Arthur H. Cook, Dr. Eron deLeon Soto, Rev. Robert G. Fin, Dr. John J. Fleming, Wiliam N. Latimer, Rev. Robert J. Levis, Rev. Casimir J. Lubiak, Rev. Msgr. Wilfrid J. Nash, Rita Ann Nies, Dr. Paul W. Peterson, Rev. John P. Schanz, Jerry A. Selvaggi, Dr. John P. Susko, Dr. Berta M. Weber, Ernest C. Wright and Rev. Addison Yehl. The climax of the academic convocation was the presentation of honorary doctoral degrees to Dr. Gerald R. Kraus, Sr., emeritus Dean of Science and Engineering and Dr. John E. Waldron, deceased former Dean of Business Administration.

The concluding event of the celebration of university status was in academic convocation in honor of Gannon's nieghboring colleges in Erie. At the event held on Thursday, April 24, 1980, each of the presidents of these colleges was awarded an honorary degree of Doctors of Laws.

Recipients were:

> Sister M. Lawreace Antoun, S.S.J., President, Villa Maria College
> Irvin H. Kochel, President, Behrend College
> Marion Leo Shane, President, Mercyhurst College

A fourth doctorate was conferred upon Dr. J. W. Peltason, president of the American Council on Education, who delivered the principal address.

The formal designation of the institution as Gannon University launched the implementation phase of the University Transition Plan in early 1980. The first phase was the establishment of the Office of Institutional Planning and Development under the direction of Rev. Francis W. Haas. Assisting him was the Technical Committee charged with the compilation of statistical data on regional economic and demographic trends on which to base the projections necessary for institutional planning.

An upgrade in the quality of institutional planning has been recognized as a priority need by Dr. Scottino from the outset of his presidency. Within one month of his inauguration in 1977, he had contracted with Dr. Edward D. Jordan of Catholic University of America to conduct training workshops on the Gannon campus. The sessions began on the evening of February 13, 1978 and continued every Monday evening through the spring. All administrators and several faculty participated in the design of the institutional planning format under the direction of Dr. Jordan.

A significant step in the transition from college to university was the reorganization of the administrative structure of the University in early 1978. The existing academic divisions were converted to colleges; i.e., the Colleges of Business Administration, Humanities, Science and Engineering, the School of Graduate Studies and the Erie Metropolitan College, the latter being the agency responsible for the Evening College, Summer Sessions, the Open University and outreach programs. The newly formed colleges were granted a higher degree of autonomy in pursuing their respective missions than had been the case with the academic divisions of Gannon College. Their specific expanded jurisdiction included the following provisions:

1. The faculty of each college, with the concurrence of the Dean,

could establish standards for student admission to the college that might vary from those set by the Admission Committee for admission to the institution.

2. Academic degree requirements, other than the Liberal Studies Program requirements, could be defined by the faculty of a college with concurrence of the Dean.

3. New courses and modifications in the syllabi of existing courses presented by each college would be approved by the faculty of that college with the concurrence of the Dean.

4. The general level of faculty salaries in one college might be higher than that of the other colleges in relation to the institutional faculty salary scale, as a consequence of variances in the circumstances impacting on the appointment of qualified faculty members.

5. The budget of the institution would include funds for each college in each of the following accounts: salaries, travel, supplies, and equipment. Funds within the travel, supplies and equipment accounts in the budget of a college might be reallocated with the approval of the Dean.

The dispersion of authority entailed in the greater level of autonomy accorded to the colleges of the university contained the risk of factionalism within the academic community resulting from competition for funds and facilities. To insure coordination of the efforts of the colleges, a Deans' Council was organized pursuant to the provisions of the University Transition Plan, Element 2: Academic Organization. This Council comprised of the five academic deans began to meet weekly under the chairmanship of the Vice President for Academic Affairs to coordinate the objectives of the several colleges and to negotiate budget and resource allocation. In 1981 membership was expanded to include the Director of the Liberal Studies Program, Director of the Educational Opportunity Programs and Director of the Library.

From the earliest stages of planning for university status, it had been apparent that the enhancement in institutional quality implied in such status would require major financial resources. Accordingly the planning process for University Transition was paralleled by a study of the strategies for producing the required funding. The professional development consulting firm of Goettler

Associates, Incorporated of Columbus, Ohio was engaged in January 1980 to conduct a feasibility study for a capital fund campaign and to advise the administration on the details of conducting the campaign.

A preliminary report of the Goettler firm was released to the community on the occasion of the University Dedication Program in April of 1980 in the form of a brochure entitled "Gannon University Committed to Excellence."

The summer of 1980 was devoted to detailing the outlines of the projected capital campaign. The completed plan was presented to the Board of Trustees at the meeting of September 25, 1980. The campaign was to be designated the *Investment in Excellence Program*. The preface to the plan contained the statement: "Continuing Gannon's commitment to excellence and unfolding the developments that are inherent in the designation of Gannon as a University require greater support from the alumni, friends and benefactors of Gannon within the framework of the Investment in Excellence Program that has been adopted at Gannon University."

The campaign goal was the acquisition of funding in the amount of 21 million dollars over the period 1981-1991. Expenditure allocations designated include:

1. Centers of Excellence $9,000,000
   For improvements in Business Administration, Engineering, Erie Metropolitan College, Health Sciences, Humanities, Graduate School, Liberal Studies, Library and Natural Sciences.
2. Faculty Development $2,000,000
3. Endowments - Student Scholarships $2,000,000
4. Campus Development - Renovation 3,000,000
5. Campus Development - New Facilities 4,000,000

The implementation phase of the capital campaign was approved by the Board of Trustees on May 20, 1981 with the designation of Donald S. Leslie, Jr. and James Currie as co-chairmen. The solicitation period stipulated was August 1981 through June 1984. The community response was most gratifying, spearheaded by the pledge of $1.6 million by the trustees, faculty and staff of the University. By August 1983, the end of the second year of the campaign receipts of 19 million dollars were recorded and the full campaign quota of 21 million dollars was realized by the deadline date of June 1984.

The availability of the funding achieved through the Investment in Excellence Program and the generous community support which it reflects provided major impetus to Gannon University to pursue the goal of excellence.

The dynamism which had characterized Gannon College from its earliest era continued strong in the Scottino era. The strong commitment to health education initiated in the 1970's was maintained. Programs include the accelerated Family Medicine Program presented in cooperation with the Hahnemann Medical College of Philadelphia and the unique Physician's Assistant Program. The Associate Degree Program in Radiological Technology was certified by the Pennsylvania Department of Education in April 1978. The year 1979 saw the inauguration of Master of Education degree in Elementary Education presented cooperatively by Gannon, Mercyhurst and Villa Maria College. Major equipment acquisitions included a Prime 500 minicomputer to serve both the academic and the administrative needs of the college; and a Westinghouse Electron Scanning Microscope for study and research in the life sciences. Two additional associate degree programs were certified: Medical Assistant and Lawyer's Assistant Programs. In December 1979, a baccalaureate program in Computer Science was initiated under the direction of Ralph J. Miller. An important supplement to Gannon's research capability was the establishment on October 29, 1979 of the Engineering Research Institute devoted to responding to research and development needs of area industry.

Significant achievements of 1980 centered on the implementation of the University Transition Program and planning for the Investment in Excellence campaign. A new graduate program, the Master of Science Program in Public Administration, was approved in June, followed by a program for Reading Specialists in November. On December 15, the archives of the Erie Catholic Diocese were housed in the Nash Library under the direction of Sister Gertrude Marie, S.S.J.

The year 1981 is marked by major facilities acquisitions. The Student Activities Center converted from the former First Presbyterian Church was dedicated on June 29. This facility houses the chapel and all offices of the Division of Student Personnel Services, and the Pontifical Center. Student Housing facilities were expanded by the purchase of the Kenilworth and the Wickford apartments with a combined capacity for 300 students.

In 1982 the first major expenditure of the Investment in Excellence Program was the renovation and redesignation of the Gannon Auditorium as the Hammermill Auditorium in acknowledging the outstanding contribution of Hammermill Paper Company to the capital fund campaign. New academic programs approved were the associate degree programs in Medical Laboratory Technology and Respiratory Therapy. Baccalaureate programs inaugurated were International Business and International Studies under the direction of Dr. Berta M. Weber.

The year 1983 marked the 50th Anniversary of Gannon, dating from the founding of its precessor institution, Cathedral College in 1933. The inaugural celebration was a liturgy of Thanksgiving on January 23 at St. Peter's Cathedral featuring a homily by Bishop Michael J. Murphy followed by a banquet at Hilton Hotel with an address by Msgr. Wilfrid J. Nash.

On April 21, the first annual Founder's Day was celebrated in remembrance of Archbishop John Mark Gannon. Msgr. Nash delivered a moving account of the early formative days of the institution as recalled from his personal experience.

The ROTC Reunion held to celebrate the 50th Anniversary was held on March 4, 1983. The featured speaker was General Edward C. Meyer of the Joint Chiefs of Staff.

In April approval was granted by the Board of Trustees for the establishment of a College of Education in cooperation with Villa Maria College. Designated Dean was Dr. Richard L. Herbstritt of Gannon with Dr. Mary Jo Cherry of Villa Maria College serving as Associate Dean.

On October 1, agreements were concluded for the purchase of the Christian Science Church located on Sassafras Street opposite the Nash Library. November 7 marked the groundbreaking ceremony for the long awaited Student Recreation Center.

The significant events of 1984 included the appointment of Dr. Norris H. Barbre as Director of the Advanced Technology and Productivity Center followed by inauguration of the Metalliding Institute under the direction of Robert K. Jordan. The metalliding process is a revolutionary metalliding process for improved bonding of ultra-thin layers of special feature metals and alloys to base metal substrates. The technique was developed by Dr. Newell C. Cook for the General Electric Company. Through the solicitation of Mr. Jordan, General Electric transferred the process with its fifteen patents to Gannon University.

Gannon moved into the age of satellite communication on July 19 with the installation of a satellite receiving station adjacent to Finegan Hall. The dish has been successfully used in presenting a variety of teleconference programs.

On November 28, a victory banquet was held to mark the successful completion of the Investment in Excellence campaign.

In September, Dr. Howard C. Smith had joined the staff as Dean of the Erie Metropolitan College. The college was renamed on December 17 as University College.

At the conclusion of a half century of growth Gannon University stands confident and committed to greater endeavors toward excellence. As a Catholic university it joins in the pursuit of the goals enunciated by Pope John Paul II during his visit to the United States in 1979.

1. To make specific contribution to the Church and to society through high quality scientific research, indepth study of problems and a just sense of history, together with the commitment to show the full meaning of the human person regenerated in Christ, thus favoring the complete development of the person;

2. To train young men and women of outstanding knowledge, who have made a personal synthesis between faith and culture, will be capable and willing to assume tasks in the service of the community and society in general, and to bear witness to their faith before the world;

3. To set up, among its faculty and students, a real community which bears witness to a living and operative Christianity, a community where sincere commitment to scientific research and study goes together with a deep commitment to authentic Christian living.

Implicit in these aims of a Catholic university and of Gannon University is the ecumenical dimension expressed by Bishop Murphy at the opening Liturgy celebrating the 50th Anniversary of the Founding of Gannon University: "The campus is not intended for proselytizing. The religious sensitivities and true conscientious convictions of students and faculty must be respected. The insights of other religious traditions, non-Christian as well as Christian, must be appreciated and the talents of professors and instructors of other religious convictions must be enlisted."

Dr. Scottino, in bringing the college up to university status, is most aptly fulfilling all the countless responsibilities inherent in that excellence to which he has committed both the institution as well as himself.

CHAPTER VII

PILLARS OF THE UNIVERSITY

Gannon University is an exquisitely complex set of relationships between individuals some of whom teach, most of whom learn. William Stringfellow once wrote that a university is constituted when a teacher on one end of a log speaks to a student seated on the other end. Gannon University has completed, hopefully, its simple days of beginning and now is well launched into modern complexities of contemporary education. But the personal relationships between teacher and student have always been an especial characteristic of this great educational endeavor, and God willing, this will always be so.

It would be both foolhardy and impossible to single out all those individuals at Gannon University who have through the years carved out deep relationships with students, who have given birth to thousands of careers in all branches of knowledge and service, who have reproduced themselves in graduates serving throughout the world. What follows are vignettes of those men and women who have served Gannon for at least thirty years with deepest apologies to the hundreds whose story must remain untold in these few pages.

ARTHUR H. COOK

Quiet, slim, always the gentleman, neat and composed, Arthur H. Cook served Gannon College for thirty-five years, from the Summer of 1946 to August 1981. Married to the former Annagrace E. Molnar, the Cooks' bore two sons, Gary, a Doctor of Opthalmology, with a specialty in retina surgery, and Kevin, a civilian hydrologist, with the Army Corps of Engineers.

Born in Erie, "Art" attending high school both in Wesleyville and North East; he was graduated from California State College in Pennsylvania with a B.S. in Education and post-graduate studies at Pennsylvania State College and the University of Pittsburgh. "Art" still retains his inveterate interest in sports, all sports, but especially basketball and football. Down through the years, "Art" rarely missed a Gannon home basketball game. He played basketball and football in both high school and at California State. In fact, he regularly mentioned his 5 a.m. college rising habit to his students who were late for an 8 a.m. engineering drawing class, much to their embarrassment.

"Art" Cook taught about 6,000 students during his time at Gannon, most of whom gave him great personal satisfaction, since so many have proven themselves in varous industrial and technological and scientific services in America, Canada and, in fact, all over the world. He started teaching engineering drawing on the fourth floor of the former Strong mansion which he intimately referred to as "the pigeon loft." He generally offered three years of drawing; i.e. two years of engineering drawing and one year of descriptive geometry to satisfy E.C.P.D. accreditation. Gannon in the early 50's was tied into the University of Detroit system as a member college on their cooperative plan. This lasted about six years until Dr. Wehrle realized the possibility of Gannon's conducting its own engineering program.

"Art" likes to think of how rewarding his long experience at Gannon has been in watching young men (and later, women) change so radically from inexperienced, angular freshmen to quiet, mature, responsible technicians and engineers. When asked if he could remember any unpleasantries in his professional life, he paused for a moment and offered, "No, no, I really don't have any sad memories of my time at Gannon. Oh naturally, I had the normal frustrations of operating with limited facilities and a small budget, but it was all up-beat."

An Assistant Professor in the Science division, he was named Director of the Industrial Management Program in 1965 and held that post until his retirement in 1981. When asked how the digital computer has changed the teaching of engineering drawing, Mr. Cook first enumerated the undeniable benefits this technical wonder has affected. First, there is the rapidity in producing a design in two or three dimensions. Next, there is the recall capacity for study and alteration. This is certainly better than the old Ozilid copier that had to be fired up thirty minutes before using. He liked the memory in the machines and their elimination of tedious repetition. But then he saw the limits of the computer; that only a computer with built-in refinements for drawing can compete with the artistry of a draftsman or an engineer. He concluded that the computer is no better than the software inserted into it, and that depends exclusively on the genius, the creativity, and the imagination of the expert. Today he fears that the student without courses in drawing might be functioning with an embarrassing lack of knowledge of the historical development behind design and formularies. "If you don't know where you have been, you don't know where you are," he said.

Mr. Cook recalls the cyclical changes in the student population during his long tenure. His first students, all men, were 25 years old, and on the whole, veterans, mature, married and fathers; they knew exactly what they wanted and did their work without need of stimulation. Today's students are necessarily much younger and without experience, more immature, but yet, with unlimited reaches, imagination, and spirit. "They will make their mark, these young men and women, in their own way, in their own time."

"Art" looks back at the immeasurable contributions which Gannon College has made to industry and engineering in the tri-state area as well as all over the country. He observes,

> We must not be compared to speialized engineering colleges conducted by a, let's say, MIT and Rochester Institute of Technology or a Rensselaer Polytechnic Institute. We are a great university with a general program for engineers and for our size and the amount of specialized resources, I think we have done an excellent job in preparing our students for their pursuit in their chosen career.

REV. ALPHONSE F. CRISPO

Born in Benevento, Italy, in 1912, educated in Rome with a Doctorate in Philosophy from the Gregorian University and another in literature from the State University of Rome, Fr. Crispo arrived at Gannon College in 1948 to pursue an outstanding teaching career at the university. Together with Msgr. Bonaventura Ciufoli, he gave a cultural depth and intellectual maturity to a faculty and administration which was notably young and inexperienced.

At his Month's Mind Mass on February 7, 1985, one of his students, now an experienced Professor of Philosophy himself, the Rev. Gilio Dipre, described his intellectual awakening in 1948 as a young student under Fr. Crispo.

> It was one of the most remarkable intellectual experiences of my life. Plato's cave myth became a reality for me. I truly experienced the journey from darkness into the light of understanding and reasoning. Within one year of Greek study we are able to read the New Testament in Greek, and translate it into English. I learned more from Father in one year than six years of Latin from other language teachers.

Another student said that Fr. Cispo's descriptions of the ancient battles between Greeks and Persians were so vivid he felt as though he were there himself fighting. Fr. Crispo taught history as an encounter with another time and another culture, never as embalmed facts and museum pieces.

Students were amazed at his incredible memory. He never used notes. Father would walk into class with his role book only. In the early 50's he taught in five different departments: history, theology, philosophy, languages and literature. Father had the habit of ending his lecture precisely at the bell, even if it meant stopping in the middle of a sentence. He would complete the sentence at the beginning of the next class. His new students would deliberately check this anecdote to see if it were true.

It was always heart-warming to walk into his apartment. It was like walking into an art gallery, or Carnegie Hall, or the Metropolitan Opera House. In the early mornings and late afternoons, his room resembled a library or poustinia, a place for study and quiet contemplative prayer.

Fr. Crispo was no sentimental romantic. He was *not* in love with abstractions. His love was directed towards individuals. It made no difference whether the person was a university professor, student, altar boy, or simple old Italian lady.

As Director of the Philosophy Department, he defended and fought for his colleagues. He forever enjoyed a good argument and took especial delight in winning a point with one of the college administrators. He never held a grudge. Forever friendly and kind, never vindictive, he remained a manly priest and a priestly man. Fr. Crispo possessed an extensive private collection of books, the envy of many, as well as an exquisite audio tape library in classical music. Whether he taught theology, history, Italian, Latin, or Greek, he did it with verve and gusto, determination and originality, but most especially with enthusiasm.

He retired in 1977 to join his large family in East Rochester, New York, and died suddenly on January 7, 1985.

REV. ROBERT G. FIN

In the years following the Second World War, many Europeans arrived in the United States having been displaced by the ravages of war. Since Gannon was a rapidly developing institution of higher learning at that time, many Europeans with academic backgrounds found teaching positions here.

Father Fin was born in Hungary. After completing his seminary studies in Hungary, Czechoslovakia, and Italy, he was ordained in Czechoslovakia on March 21, 1943.

With the disruption of Eastern Europe during and following the Second World War, he traveled extensively in that area and eventually earned three degrees from the Gregorian University, Rome, Italy, and an additional degree from Middlebury College, Middlebury, Vermont. Finally, from 1963 to 1966, he undertook post-doctoral studies at Case-Western Reserve University, Cleveland, Ohio.

He was able to obtain an immigration visa in Italy in 1951, and left there at that time with twenty-five Italian orphans whom he accompanied to the United States under the sponsorship of the International Refugee Organization. These orphans were entrusted to his care until they were adopted by residents of the New York City area.

Following his arrival in the United States in 1951, he taught for two years in Michigan, and then joined the faculty of Gannon University in 1953. During the 1950's he taught courses in three different departments at the university: education, languages, and theology.

Father Fin continues to teach Russian, and is a member of the university's Translation Bureau and the National Slavic Honor Society. Thanks to Fr. Fin's academic preparation and linguistic skills, the Gannon students are able to take twelve Russian courses, for a total of forty-two credits.

In addition to his regular assignments, Fr. Fin presented a lecture series at the University's Institute of Continuing Education, under the direction of Rev. Dr. John P. Schanz, from the Fall of 1964 to Spring 1967. His topics included: "The Russia of Contradictions"; "The History and Analysis of Revolutions in Russia"; "The Fatal Mistakes of the Czars"; "Women in Russian History"; "Will the Russians Bury Us?!"; "Capitalism: The Soviet Worker's Dream"; "Is God Dead in the USSR?"; and related topics.

When the Language Department grew, and new language laboratories were needed, he assisted Dr. Paul W. Peterson, Vice-President for Academic Affairs, in the installation of the two language laboratories located in the Zurn Science Center. Since that time, he has been supervising the maintenance of these facilities and is preparing study-aids for all the languages taught by the Department.

Fr. Fin was incardinated into the Diocese of Erie on December 15, 1960, and, in addition to his work at the university, he became a Pro-Synodal Judge of the Diocesan Tribunal. As such, he is responsible for reviewing and rendering decisions in marriage annulment cases. His service to the diocese also includes weekend assistance at various parishes.

JOHN J. FLEMING

When the University appointed Dr. John Fleming as permanent secretary of the university, it honored a faculty member whom most colleagues consider paradigmatic. His scholarly manner of speaking, his studied approach to all questions, his cultured balance, even his tweed coat — these express the character of one who has influenced most profoundly and significantly thousands since his arrival in 1952.

"Doc" Wehrle hired Dr. Fleming with a fresh M.A. from Fordham University in February 1952, to set up a Department of Psychology at Gannon. This he did, and he looks back with great satisfaction at achievements wrought in that department through the early difficult years. He recalls that Dr. Raymond Francis, Clinical Psychologist practicing in DuBois, Pennsylvania; Dr. Robert Dowling, Psychologist at Edinboro University; Dr. David Reynolds, Vice-Commissioner for Mental Health of Erie County in Buffalo; and Mr. Daniel Hatton, former Director of Mental Health and Mental Retardation of Erie County, are Gannon men who got their start in his young department.

Married to the former Mary Catherine Gallagher, Dr. Fleming boasts of three children. Through the years these three were ready examples of child development in the countless talks John delivered at area service clubs, PTA's, educational meetings, as well as classes. Dr. Fleming served for more than ten years as Clinical Psychologist at the Erie (Child) Guidance Center.

He judges that students of twenty years ago were more highly motivated than contemporary students who unfortunately look at their years in college as a *sine qua non* requirement for financial success. Of new students, he observes,

> Our women students have actually saved us. They have given dignity to the University, they provide a cultured and restrained scholarly atmosphere that we didn't have years ago. God knows most of them are quality students. Look at the recipients of graduation awards. Seventy-five percent are women.

Dr. Fleming observes also that the administration of the university today is much more complex and sophisticated than formerly when processes were simple and more casual. In spite of this, yesterday's administration wielded far more power, say, under "Doc" Wehrle than it does today under Dr. Scottino. "Gannon faculty has much more freedom of expression and determination today than it ever had in the past, although I must admit constitutional change did that years ago."

Dr. Fleming received his Ph.D. from the University of Ottawa in Canada in the area of clinical psychology. His dissertation centered on response probabilities in mental association. Gannon University honored him not only by designating him permanent Secretary of the University, but also by designating him, last year, as Distinguished Faculty Member along with Dr. Richard Beyer and Mr. James Freeman. This was the first time any faculty was ever so designated.

Sigmund Freud, the creative pioneer of modern psychology, remains a hero to Dr. Fleming. Erikson, Maslow, Fromm simply develop what Freud created. All of them present possible theories or models, or frameworks to work in, unfinished answers to human conduct. Dr. Fleming has presented them in his career at Gannon University as spinners of "methodological fiction," some of whom might provide remedies to pathological cases. None of them present the whole story of man.

What is the future of psychology at Gannon University? Dr. Fleming looks to the University's granting a doctorate in Industrial Psychology. The university, he opines, has always been closely tied-in with the community's commerce and industrial interests, and so, a professional but practical degree in Industrial Psychology is a distinct possibility, and Dr. Fleming looks forward to its inception.

REV. EDWARD QUINLISK FRANZ

"Doc" Wehrle put the bright young seminarian, Ed Franz, to work teaching philosophy and psychology at Gannon College several years before his ordination to the priesthood, May 10, 1945. This athletic, dedicated, and intense teacher was a pivotal professor in the fledgling college from its second decade on even to the present. Father Ed had received his Master of Arts Degree as a student of the Basselin Foundation at the Catholic University of America in Washington, D.C., even before he started studying Theology. He continued his philosophical pursuits from that time on. He was awarded his Ph.D. from that same university in 1950 with a dissertation entitled *Thomistic Doctrine on the Possible Intellect.* He served as Associate Editor for *The New Scholasticism,* 1953-1955, a national honor and distinction for the young professor.

Father Franz was named Professor of Philosophy by "Doc" Wehrle upon ordination and assignment to the college and also appointed Chairman of the Division of Philosophy and Religion.

Father Franz held this position until 1955 when Philosophy and Theology were separated as departments, and Rev. Dr. Alphonse Crispo was appointed Chairman of Philosophy, and the Rev. James Peterson, Chairman of the Department of Theology.

Father Franz served as Professor of Philosophy from 1962 to 1964 at the College of St. Mary of the Plains, Dodge City, Kansas, and then took a series of pastorates: Sacred Heart Church in Genesee; Holy Cross Church in Brandy Camp; Immaculate Conception Church in Clarion; and Our Lady of the Lake Church in Edinboro — all four churches in the Diocese of Erie. Father Ed was also distinguished by being named Director of the Continuing Education of the Clergy in 1976 and served through 1979.

Presently, Father Franz serves as senior member of the Theology Department where he integrates his profound philosophical insights with new readings in the theology of Vatican II.

Father looks back with legitimate nostalgia to the closely knit relations of faculty, administration, and student body of Cathedral College in its earliest days. He notes that the smallness of its operation was not necessarily a deficiency since each student knew each faculty member intimately — his principles, his biases, his preferences. Father Ed observes that contemporary students have far more factual information than former students, they lack somewhat the power of tight discursive reasoning of former students. Otherwise, Father observes little differences between student generations. He concurs with the prsence of women at the university and notes that women bring with them a cultural grace which the college never enjoyed when peopled only by men. Father guesses he has taught around 5,000 students in his career at Gannon. While his specialty is the Philosophy of Man, which used to be called Rational Psychology, he has also offered his share of courses in Educational and Abnormal Pyschology.

Father Franz is an inveterate proponent of Liberal Studies at Gannon University. The Liberal Arts Program makes contemporary education contiguous both with the historical past as well as with the future, and complements training in the complicated skills necessary today in earning a living, he observes. He insists that no student has the background to elevate his/her own life without knowledge of the arts, science, philosophy, theology, and religion (and the last two are not identical).

Father Franz confesses that theology is more important than philosophy, science and art because it transcends not only reason, but also involves the realm of faith and revelation. There is no dichotomy between faith and reason, and in the Liberal Education Program at Gannon University, the total integration is attempted within the parameters of the faith. Father Franz believes that the future success of the Gannon University lies in being open, being ready, and being prepared to handle any and all new challenges and opportunities. He hopes that the university will be closely interwoven with the ministries of the Diocese of Erie as is being envisioned with the commercial television station, Channel 66, the joint responsibility of the university and the diocese.

Does the diocesan priest fill a needed role at the University? Absolutely! Father Franz insists. The priest-teacher performs a specialized intellectual, social and religious role at the university and any religious body is blessed to have such a cooperating university, especially one with priest-teachers. The layman performs his/her own role in furthering the Kingdom of God on earth, but that role is not as focused as that of the priest in education. The tendency for the layman is to develop temporalities, and this is excellent and necessary, according to Father Franz. However, the priest brings to his work at the university a further consciousness of spiritually, of faith, and of the divine dimension of the Kingdom. Father Franz exemplifies, most perfectly, the priest-teacher at Gannon University who has served God as Truth and who has introduced with relish this Truth, this Ultimate Reality, to thousands of students in whom he takes legitimate and immeasurable delight.

JAMES J. FREEMAN

On rare occasions an individual will shine forth among his peers who in his person so embodies the aspiration of an Institution that his name becomes synonymous with it. We have found such a man, and today we rejoice to honor him.

In this way, on May 21, 1978, Gannon University paid tribute to James J. Freeman by awarding him a Doctor of Laws degree, a unique event inasmuch as the university had never previously so honored a faculty member while still in service.

Jim Freeman started to work for "Doc" Wehrle as a math teacher in 1934 at the Cathedral Prep School and at Cathedral College in 1939. With only one slight interruption (1944-1946), Jim taught at both the Gannon School of Arts and Science and at Gannon College and University almost until the day of his death on January 12, 1980.

While being a full professor in the Department of Mathematics, he also chaired the Division of Natural Science from 1952-1955 and directed the Physics Department from 1958-1964.

He was a familiar presence on major committees of the college: Committee on Rank, Tenure and Salary (1950-1955), Committee on Curriculum (1952-1955), Faculty Senate (1957-1959, 1972-1974), Committee on Teacher Education (1962-1980), Committee on Student Conduct (1972-1973).

Dr. Freeman taught math. This is his achievement — he taught math. He taught it long and he taught it well. He taught an estimated 12,000 students, if one counted his pre-college students in the Upward Bound Program and his students at the Erie Veterans School (1949-1960). This is not to speak of the tens of thousands of hours he "squandered" in special tutorial sessions here at the college, in his home, almost anywhere a table or blackboard could be found.

Jerry Kraus rates him as one of America's finest teachers of mathematics, although in fact not a mathematical theoretician. Fr. James McCullough, a lifelong colleague and friend of Jim, dubs him, "the finest math teacher I have ever known". Jim Freeman loved teaching. He often remarked with a kind of perplexity. "I don't know," he quipped, "I like teaching, I've always liked teaching. I don't know, but I'm happiest when I'm teaching. And to think I'm getting paid for it!"

He was always quick; talked loud and fast; limped along slightly, burdened with about 100 pounds excess weight, with pants in need of pressing and shirt liberally floured with chalk dust.

"Look at the board and I'll run through it again!"

"Be pacifio, young man, east or west, shape up or ship out."

"Whose money are you wasting, your parent's or yours? I hope it's yours because you deserve to lose it."

Jim was one of those profs, those unpolished diamonds who knew who he was and what he wanted to do with students. And he did it. And he did it with a twinkle in his eye and a happy lilt in his whole being.

Impatient of loafers whom he called "woafers," he pushed students to produce far beyond what they deemed their potential. At times he seemed curt, but only when he judged that a student was either lazy or deceptive. He loved the student who might be slow to learn math as much as the student bright in the field. Jim was a simple man who couldn't countenance duplicity at any time. To him the essence of the college experience was in the classroom, in a meeting between a hard working teacher and attentive student.

Fr. McCullough also reports the following incident during one of the rare meetings of the Department of Mathematics. The priest apparently presented a point of view with which Dr. Freeman disagreed. Freeman called for a show of hands. The department, to a man, voted against him. Champing his unlit cigar, he suddently stood up, announced, "I'm tabling the motion," and stormed out of the room.

Dr. Freeman was never happier at old Cathedral College than when tossing a beat-up football with the boys on the grassless lawn to the west of the Downing Building, or in beating some unsuspecting student in ping-pong, in which he delightedly excelled. Many of his table tennis victims, in charity, should now forgive his carelessnes in scorekeeping when he occasionally cheated a tad (in his own favor, of course.)

His students never, if ever, were sentimental over their mathematical "Mr. Chips," but universally respected and appreciated him. During the 60's, one black student asked another, "Does Mr. Freeman hate blacks?" The answer came back, "Don't worry about him; he hates everyone equally."

The accepted opinion was that "if Jim Freeman could not teach one mathematics, then no one could." "The multitudes from this community and from throughout the world who has benefited from his wisdom and from his quiet strength are far beyond measure." So, his doctoral citation summarizes the work of this great man. If Gannon University has many pillars, Dr. James Freeman supported its main arch.

GERALD A. KRAUS

"Doc" Wehrle met Jerry Kraus in the lobby of a conference building on the Penn State campus in 1937 where Jerry had just delivered a paper for the American Mathematics Society, actually the mathematical solution for a problem for which Carnegie Tech had awarded him an M.S. degree. "Doc" wanted a good man in mathematics and the president of Mount Mercy College in Pittsburgh had given him Jerry Kraus' name as one who was quite able as a math teacher. He had already left Mount Mercy College for employment at the Union Carbon and Carbide Company. "Doc's" pitch was direct: "Young man, come to Cathedral College and I will give you $5.00 more than Union C & C." Kraus accepted.

On arriving in Erie during the Summer of 1937, Jerry had a hard time finding Cathedral College. He drove by the Downing Building back and forth several times. He saw the Erie Business College (a sign designated that). Some youngster finally brought him into the old gray building and presented him to "Doc," who introduced him to Jimmy Freeman, whose mother had an empty room where it was decided Jerry would stay. This was the beginning of a most effectual team, Kraus-Freeman.

Three years later, Fr. Leo Kraus of Pittsburgh, Jerry's brother, witnessed the marriage of Jerry to Beatrice L. McCabe and eventually the Krauses bore five children and seven grandchildren.

Mr. Kraus taught both mathematics and physics at Cathedral College until the war years when he temporarily left to establish his own manufacturing firm in the area. He was called back persistently by "Doc" through the good offices of Father "Barney" Russell, who, in 1954, painted such an urgent picture of the college's need, "it was a proposition I couldn't refuse." He came back as Dean of the college's Division of Science and Engineering where he eventually introduced electrical engineering, mechanical engineering, industrial management, engineering technology, and the general science programs. With a familiar chuckle, Mr. Kraus sums up his achievements at Gannon very humbly. "I wanted Gannon to progress, to move ahead in science. Thank

God, we had some little measure of success."

His philosophy of science education was equally humble. As a teacher, he presenteed his material as clearly as he could and repeated it patiently until the students understood it. "If you can read English and know the meaning of mathematical symbols, what can stop you? You teach the student to understand and he/she can do anything."

Kraus made a brilliant, competent, articulate and insightful Dean. He had a stabilizing effect on his faculty not only because he knew science as well as any of them, but also because of his practical industrial experience. He feels this was one of his strengths, that he knew the industrial application of mathematics. He was firm in his convictions, and in committee voiced his own opinion though it be the only contrary opinion of the group. For this integrity he is remembered. In this period of rapid expansion of the college, Jerry Kraus with his sound judgment, intelligence, and quality leadership was an inestimable boon. Science courses at the university today are but his lengthened shadow.

In 1973, hearing that there were Federal monies available for science buildings, Jerry went to work, laying out on his dining room floor, what eventually was to become the Zurn Science Building. He wrote an initial proposal, he recounts, revised it with departmental chairmen, sold Gannon's need to representatives in Harrisburg, and "luckily," to quote him:

> Gannon College ended up on the top of the list. We over-built, since we were all sick and tired of buildings which were overstuffed the day architects presented the keys to the building. But I think now the building is about the right size.

Mr. Kraus recalls, with satisfaction, his role in bringing one of the first electronic data processing machines to Erie. It was built by the Leberscope General Precision Company which built the computer for the first manned space craft, Friendship 7, piloted by astronaut John Glenn in February 1962. At the time, it sold for $80,000, but Mr. Kraus and "Doc" Wehrle finagled the machine for royalty costs, $8,000. Then Mr. Kraus went to Chicago for two weeks to learn how to operate it. The IBM Corporation, for the next several years, hired Gannon College graduates most consistently because of their experience on this very data processing machine.

Never a remote and academic theoretician, Mr. Kraus consistently worked with local industry and personnel to coordinate activities at Gannon College with their needs and resources. For example, Martin Grotjehon, Manager of General Electric Apprentice Training and of the General Electric Night School, worked hand-in-hand with Kraus to further the science education of local students. For several years, Jerry Kraus arranged that Gannon present the basic courses in mathematics and engineering for these students.

"I have been most fortunate all my life," Kraus gratefully remembers. "My life has been one uninterrupted blessing from God. I have always had time to do things. And somehow things always work out." His wife, "Bea," describes him as "the most contented person I ever knew."

As to the future of Gannon University, Mr. Kraus believes that the $21,000,000 for Centers of Excellence should never be touched. It's a trust fund, an endowment we have never had and always needed. We should stash it away and only use its interest, and industry should be invited to add to it, to support activities of the University. But Kraus ruefully, wisely, and wryly knows that money is already being targeted for current pressing needs.

The traditions that Jerry Kraus painfully forged at Gannon College are being perfected by his son, Gerald A. Kraus, present chairman of the Department of Mathematics. A granddaughter, Virginia von Hoene, is currently a freshman resident in Finegan Hall, but she has broken the Kraus tradition. She is majoring in Accounting.

WILLIAM NORTON LATIMER

"Someone else will be hired to teach Bill's accounting courses, but he or she will not take Bill's place at Gannon. He is irreplaceable." So eulogized Msgr. Nash at Bill (Willian Norton) Latimer's funeral liturgy in St. Jude's Church, Erie, October 2, 1984.

He married Elizabeth Ann Babbitt of Cleveland who bore him three sons and three daughters. At Western Reserve University, Latimer was called back to Gannon by "Doc" Wehrle in 1949 with, "Come on back here, Bill, we need you in accounting!" He didn't need to be asked twice. He returned to his *alma mater* in 1949 to serve until his death in 1984, with but a three-year interruption (1955-1958), when he worked at the General Electric Company.

Mr. Latimer was named Chairman of the Management Department in 1964, first Director of the MBA Program in 1970, and Chairman of Accounting in 1971. After Dean Waldron succumbed, he took over as Acting Dean of the University's Business Division. He held two CPA certificates — one from the District of Columbia, the other from Pennsylvania.

While he dutifully served the university in these several administrative posts, his abiding personal satisfaction remained in teaching accounting to his students. This was always his delight.

In fact, he preferred his freshmen students to all others, since these students most called on his teaching reserves. A just teacher, his wife remembers how often he agonized over final grades, but once he made them, recourse was futile.

Along with Dean Waldron and especially after his death, Bill Latimer served as a pillar of all business programs, a calming and steadying force, especially for the younger faculty. Dean Ron Volpe compares him to a kind of Supreme Court Justice, a grey eminence whose practical judgment and experience was so often called upon to mediate and reconcile differences of judgment among colleagues. In issue after issue, it was Mr. Latimer's compromise that finally was accepted by peers who respected him for his predictable fairness and wise perspective. He exercised a kind of fatherly statesmanship in all business programs at Gannon so that he still remains the measure of all teachers of business.

He could predictably be found at two regular events of the college. First, he always attended home basketball games. Never a player himself, he loved to support the Golden Knights with his presence. For years, he served on the Athletic Committee with its unending battle of finding, hiring, and replacing coaches.

The Thursday 11:00 a.m. liturgy was the other event at the university where Bill Latimer could generally be found. As a matter of fact, the last Mass he participated in was the Thursday Community Mass. He died two days later on a Saturday. The brother of Msgr. Edward Latimer, he remained a most fervent Catholic all of his life. This devotion revealed a rock-like faith which served both as consolation and stimulus to him. He took great joy in realizing he was serving his God as he taught his students the principles of justice, of fair management, of equitable distribution in the business world. He actually grieved over whatever changes were made at the university which he deemed an erosion of Gannon University's basic Catholic and Christian commitment. More than once, he quietly questioned members of the clergy faculty at the university to inquire why certain things not to his liking were taking place. He loved the university and all it stood for, most especially its commitment to Christ.

REV. ROBERT J. LEVIS

Fr. Robert J. Levis has been "where the action is" since he was assigned to Gannon in June 1949, a year after his ordination. Starting as Registrar and Director of the Admissions Committee, his duties increased as the college administered to the returning servicemen who were interested in college education.

Since that initial appointment, his entire priestly career has been Gannon-centered. He covered the positions of Director of Student Personnel Services, Chairman of the Theology Department, Director of the Pontifical Center for Catechetical Studies, and Director of the Liberal Studies, with a three-year sabbatical interruption to attain his doctorate at Catholic University.

In 1965, the closing year of Vatican Council II, Father was appointed Chairman of the Theology Department and filled the post for twelve years, during a time of post-Vatican change and turmoil. In 1972, he was appointed the first Director of the Pontifical Center for Catechetical Studies by President Nash as well as by the Prefect of the Sacred Congregation of the Clergy, the Vatican congregation immediately responsible for catechetics world-wide. He still holds that post, together with the Directorship of the Liberal Studies Program.

The Pontifical Center, Fr. Levis says, has anchored the University solidly with the Holy See of Rome and has proved most beneficial in maintaining the university's Catholic and Christian tradition in these last few years of radical change. The Center, since 1972, has sent out hundreds of catechists to all parts of the eastern United States and Canada, (and even Africa, Singapore, and the Philippines), all well-equipped to present the Faith.

He looks at himself as a stubborn Irishman who feels that the university is still the finest bastion to fire off shots against the secular and positivistic forces that are taking over American culture. He sees himself as a tiny voice against the noisy, strident roar raised against religious values which institutions like Gannon University have always presented. In the last decade, Father has written numerous articles mostly on the topic, "American culture and religion" (for magazines and periodicals). He is a regular columnist in the diocesan newspaper, *The Lake Shore Visitor* and *The Catholic Register* of Toronto, Canada. He attempts to encourage people to keep a tight grip on the heritage of their own spiritual and intellectual traditions. As he looks back over thirty-six years of service, he simply says,

> I stay at Gannon to do what I can to maintain the university's fidelity to Christ. After all, He is the center of the whole place. He is the teacher in every classroom, the chairman of every department, the director of every program, the coach of every team, the chef of every meal.

When he arrived on campus along with Fr. Casimir Lubiak in June 1949, he felt it was a temporary assignment. He stayed one year at a time and regularly expected each year to be his last. "I suppose the Bishop kept me here where I can do the least amount of harm," Fr. Levis remarks. Of late he sees the university as one of several national centers of excellence, one of a few fairly large Catholic and Christian educational centers in which both the nation and the church take pride. As a Catholic priest, he judges that he could serve mankind no better in any other station than that of aiding young men and women of the university to be formed in the light of the Gospel and for the betterment of the world.

> The chances of presenting what I love best and whom I love best, Christ, is here on this asphalt campus. I don't think any life could be better spent than with these beautiful people to teach, to counsel, to correct, to direct, to encourage.

As he mounts his banged-up, blue Schwinn bicycle, which he swiftly pedals on and off campus, he also says, "I also try to give them something to laugh at."

MSGR. LOUIS LOREI

Actually "Doc" Wehrle assigned Fr. Louis Lorei as Head of the Library in 1944, long before his ordination to the priesthood in May 1947. "Doc" had eyed the bright seminarian early on and had advised him to take a degree in Library Science at the Catholic University of America where he was studying. When he finished the course, "Doc" didn't wait, he appointed him Head Librarian immediately.

In May 1947, Father Lorei took up his duties in the library just in time to prepare, with Miss Rita Nies, for the college's initial accreditation by a Middle States team. One can only imagine the professional work that had to be done so immediately. At that time, the college had boasted of fewer than 6,000 books and less than 30 periodical subscriptions. Msgr. Lorei still looks back to those days of failing to meet Middle States standards as one of the most discouraging periods of the college. When the first library building and Commons was built in 1948, it fell on the shoulders of the young priest to fill it with books. This he did, but periodically braked by "Doc" when the bills were received. At one time, Fr. Lorei was cacheing away personal money to pay book bills which he feared "Doc" would not honor. However, this fortunately proved to be overly cautious.

Fr. Lorei was appointed Dean of Humanities in 1956 and served for over twenty years in that capacity. During most of the time, Dean John Waldron served in the Business Administration Division and Dean Gerald Kraus in Science and Engineering. Dean Lorei was the immediate adjutant of Msgr. Nash and enjoyed the deepest academic confidences of the President. Fr. Lorei exercised both intelligence and tenacity in this demanding post. There was no program, no concept generated in humanities which he did not nurture and support. And there was no problem which he avoided.

During lean financial years, Dean Lorei is said to have stalled effective teachers in their bid for a raise in salary with, "But you haven't published!" And to writing faculty he offered, "But how effective is your teaching?"

It was Dean Lorei who conceived the idea of graduate studies in 1965 and pushed them to completion against articulate opposition. He also originated the drive for N.C.A.T. Accreditation (National Council for Accreditation of Teacher Education) which the University still enjoys. Msgr. Lorei takes some pride in his initiative in these two matters.

He survived the racial disturbances of the 60's, when he recalls persons not part of the university community organized dissent and campus rebellion. One day they physically escorted the Dean to Dale Hall where he was confronted with an angry mob which demanded explanation for R.O.T.C. on campus. Less seriously, Dean Lorei also recalls the flap when Fr. Eldon Somers, Dean of Men, refused the Basketball Coach, Jim Harding, and the Vice President for Student Personnel Services, Fr. Louis Puscus (now Romanian Bishop in Chicago), to permit the basketball team to play in the 1966 play-offs of the N.C.A.A. in Kansas City. Erie T.V. sports announcer, Bill Knupp, made some interesting observations about Fr. Somers and the college which still bemuse Fr. Lorei.

He observes that the City of Erie had developed through the past fifty years to give birth to its own university, and it was providential that "Doc" initiated the institution precisely when he did.

Msgr. Lorei looks on Msgr. Wilfrid Nash as the one person more dedicated to Gannon University than anyone else he knows. "He even has a bird everytime the Golden Knights lose a game!" He looks on President Scottino as "one of the best things that could ever have happened to Gannon. He has maintained the Catholic and Christian integrity of Gannon most consistently at a time when American sister colleges are secularizing." The former Dean observes that Dr. Scottino was elected Secretary-Treasurer of the National Fellowship of Catholic Scholars, a national honor and indication of his leadership role in Christian education in America.

Msgr. Lorei, both while pastor, first, of St. Titus Church in Titusville and later of the prestigious Our Lady of Peace Church in Erie, has served actively on the University Board of Trustees. From that vantage rock he modestly observes,

> While there are some good segments in some Catholic colleges and universities in America today, I have no hesitancy in saying that Gannon University is the best possible Catholic institution in America, with a future bright and promising.

REV. CASIMIR J. LUBIAK

When Fr. Casimir J. Lubiak was studying designs for the present Nash Learning Resource Center, one concept that evolved included permanent pillars that would support the structure and walls that could be moved according to the changing needs of the library. Perhaps this is analagous to Gannon University, whose pillars are reinforced by the lives of those who have been, and are, the strength of the institution.

Fr. Lubiak joined the Gannon College faculty in 1949, and was Director of the Library from 1956 until 1980, when he became Director of Acquisitions. The library at 115 West Sixth Street was moved to the new Learning Resource Center in the Summer of 1973, culminating Fr. Lubiak's efforts in planning the new building. Foresight in this planning is one of Fr. Lubiak's greatest contributions to the university: the gardens at the lower level, a media center, a microform room, an archives. The gardens have proven to be delightful areas for receptions, student orientation groups, and other festivities; the media center has adapted easily to include computers; the microform room can accomodate a growing periodicals collection; the archives is the richer because of his acquisition of the Carney and Costello collection, and the preservation of Fr. Lubiak's personal files.

His philosophy of the library's place in the university was expressed in the 1981 *Lance:* "Everybody here is to provide services to the students. That's the whole reason for the existence of the building."

Fr. Lubiak has given the mark of professionalism to the mission of this library, and he determined the needs of the curriculum and the institution as he supervised the building of the library collection. As an administrator he possessed the facility of being aware of the activities of each department, yet not interrupting, unless necessary, the flow of productivity.

In recent years, he has been tributed by many of his friends and colleagues. When he marked the fortieth anniversary of his ordination, the curriculum library at Nash Learning Resource Center was designated as the Lubiak Room. He was the subject of the first Gannon University "roast" in January 1983, and on that occasion stated, "I work at the library to be of service to students and because I enjoy overcoming the frustrations of the job." In December 1984, the library at Blessed Sacrament Church was designated as the Lubiak Library. On that occasion, Bishop Michael Murphy pointed out that Fr. Lubiak, as other priests, is like an iceberg where we only see a part. (He has been on extra service at Blessed Sacrament since 1949.)

When Fr. Lubiak retired from his position as Library Director, Fr. Lawrence Speice made this tribute:

> "The University community extends its sincere 'thanks' to Fr. Lubiak for this thirty-one years of dedicated labors, first, as Director of the College Library and, more recently, as Director of the University's Nash Library. This unique man's quiet, total and constant dedication has given the best gift that can be given — the gift of himself, to Gannon University. To have served the infant Gannon College in its early 60's, to have fostered its blusterous growth through adolescence into the 70's, and to have labored for its emerging adulthood as Gannon University, must bring a deep sense of accomplishment to this priest who is first of all a servant. That sense of accomplishment is his personal treasure . . . and we will not hear of it from him. That is the kind of man he is.

Fr. Lubiak passed on to his eternal reward on March 19, 1985.

R. JOSEPH LUCKEY

When you've been in every nook and cranny of the campus, you get to know a lot about Gannon College and Gannon University. You get to know a lot of people too. Joe Luckey thinks that he gets to know about two-thirds of the students, residents and day-hops.

He knows the campus too. "I watched the buildings go up so I'd know where things were." Watching Joe in action, we see that it works.

Robert Joseph Luckey came to Gannon as a freshman in the Fall of 1952. The next year he was on Student Council, but instead of staying with the Class of '56, Joe stayed with Gannon. At first, he did minor repairs in maintenance,for there were no tools for the bigger, specialized jobs which they farmed out. He liked to take things apart and put them together again.

That's how he learned so much about organs. It's the reason he and John Mitchell could take a 1920 vintage theater organ, originally made as a church organ by the Tellers Organ Company, and build it into an instrument for recitals. In 1968, about ninety Tekes muscled the organ out of its original location in Shea's Theater. It is now housed in the Commons, after moves to South Hall, to the Student Union carriage house at Sixth and Walnut, and to Dale Hall. The many parts and work on the organ and its toy counter (the theatrical attachments) have stories of their own, from the auto horn found on the street to the good friend and present co-worker, Harry Justka, whom he met when he needed help on an electric motor.

The organ is not Joe's only extra-curricular activity. This year he made twenty-four appearances as Santa Claus, wearing a professional costume that he bought at the Boston Store twenty years ago.

Joe Luckey is a favorite subject for feature stories because of his varied interests, and one of the annual awards made at commencement each year is the Joe Luckey Service Award, aptly described as being awarded for "outstanding dedication and service to Gannon University."

Of course, Joe Luckey has many recollections of campus events, but the "Audi" — now Hammermill Center — was to him the early civic center of Erie. He recalls that the floor in the gym was asphalt tile until a wooden floor was installed when Beyer Hall was built in 1962. More lively memories of the "Audi" happenings are: the circus that included elephants; an ice show; a water show; helping Bill Garvey (now President of Mercyhurst) build booths for the first Christmas Carnival (later called Winter Carnival) in 1956; and making false ceilings of crepe paper for dances.

Joe's present leisure time project is expanding the organ from ten to fourteen ranks of pipes, revamping the organ so it will be more of a theater organ, and adding a player piano to its capabilities. He belongs to three organ societies, from Western Reserve, Pittsburgh, and Niagara Frontier, but another of his goals is to form a local theater organ society. He would like to do a videotape of an organ concert, too, to record Fr. William Biebel's (Cathedral Prep) talented playing of the organ.

Joe has resided at nine different places on campus. He states that he has always liked the atmosphere and the people. "I knew I'd never get rich, but I never really wanted to get rich" is his explanation for being content here.

In his humble, self-effacing life of service to all at Gannon University, we know Joe Luckey is a rich man indeed.

RITA ANN NIES

It has often been said that the library is the heart of an academic institution. Those who work in the library provide research and course work assistance to thousands of students and professors. As the Reference Librarian since the early 1950's, Miss Rita Ann Nies has graciously and efficiently provided such assistance, often unheralded, but sorely missed when one walked into the reference room and did not find her.

After graduation from Villa Maria College, she worked for a year in the Circulation and Reference Departments of the Erie Public Library. This was followed by attendance at the Library School of Western Reserve University, now known as Case Western Reserve, where she received a degree in Library Science.

While home for her Christmas vacation during that academic year, Dr. Wehrle called her and asked her to work as a librarian at Gannon. She informed Dr.Wehrle that she would be graduating in June and would be happy to discuss his offer if she was still needed at the time. However, after she obtained her degree, she returned to Erie and accepted a position in the Reference Department of the Erie Public Library.

Several months passed and Dr. Wehrle called her again and said, "Now that you have your degree, maybe we can talk business." She talked to him and started working at Gannon on September 15, 1946. This long career has not yet ended, and Miss Nies is still

Joseph P. Scottino, Ph.D., President.

Bishop Michael J. Murphy

Student Council, 1956-57. First row: Norman Stark, David Buckel, Albert Rossi, William Garvey (President, Mercyhurst College), Joseph Cavanaugh, and Francis Kloecker. Standing: Donald Zbieranowski, Richard Martin, Robert Nash, Joseph Sarvardi, John Fries, Charles Sellars.

Gannon College Chess Club, 1957.

Faculty members, December 1958. First row, left to right: Revs. Homer DeWalt, Gilio Dipre, John Burke, Howard Niebling. Back row: Eldon Somers, John Bicsey, Addison Yehl, Richard Sullivan, Robert Sciamanda.

helping Gannon students and professors with their reference concerns and problems.

It has been the library staff which has provided continuity over the many years, since the library itself was located in a number of buildings before moving to its present location. In 1946 the library was located in what had been the ballroom of the Strong mansion. As Miss Nies remembers it, "The room contained some stacks, very few books, a desk and a few chairs. I started my work by arranging the books on the shelves and then cataloging them." From these humble beginnings came out a process of development culminated in the opening of the Nash Library and Resource Center with its expanding collection of books and non-print media.

Here are some of the major steps of this development. The newly ordained Rev. Louis Lorei, who went on to obtain his Library Science degree from the Catholic University of America, was named the first Librarian. In 1948, the first library building was built adjacent to the Strong mansion and served the needs of the growing institution for more than twenty years. The book collection was located on the second floor with offices on the first floor. At that time Miss Nies was the Circulation and Periodicals Librarian. She remembers fondly the seriousness of the many veterans who began their education at Gannon in the post-war years.

Meanwhile, Fr. Lorei began cataloging, and in 1949 was joined by Fr. Casimir Lubiak in the Cataloging Department. Concerning some of the other librarians, Miss Nies recalls that Bertille Warner, a graduate of Seton Hill College, now Mrs. Ray Stanovich of Uxbridge, Massachusetts, managed the circulation desk, while Miss Nies' activities involved the reference area. In the early 1950's, she took over two rooms on the first floor of the library building, and these became the Reference Department with her as Reference Librarian.

Fr. Casimir J. Lubiak became the Director of the Library in 1956, and it was he who mostly planned and designed the present library building, the Nash Learning Resource Center. The move to the new building occurred in June 1973, and as Miss Nies recalls it, "We were well-organized for the fall semester." However, she neglected to point out that one of her goals, to have a distinct reference room with adequate space, was accomplished with this move. Fr. Lubiak retired as Director in 1980, and was replaced as Director by Fr. L. Thomas Snyderwine, the third Director for whom she has served as Reference Librarian.

Taking note of the increased student enrollment, she recalled that the first inventory of the entire library prepared by her numbered 11,000 volumes and that has increased to over 216,000 volumes in the library today.

In summing up her many years at Gannon, she responded as an authentic Librarian, "During my years at Gannon I have thoroughly enjoyed the individualized teaching I was able to give the students and teachers by showing them how to use the library reference sources."

Miss Nies retired on September 10, 1985.

PAUL W. PETERSON

Paul W. Peterson was born in Erie on August 5, 1920, the eldest of six children of Cornelius J. Peterson and Gertrude Ward Peterson. He completed elementary schooling at St. John's Parochial School and graduated from Academy High School. During his senior year, he won first place in a Foreign Language Contest sponsored by the University of Pittsburgh and was awarded a scholarship. Following graduation from the University of Pittsburgh, he enlisted in the U.S. Navy. His duty assignment was the U.S.S. Eaton, a destroyer on station in the Pacific Theater during World War II. During his four years of service, he held a variety of assignments culminating in his appointment as Executive Officer. While still in the service he married the former Jaqueline Anderson in 1946. The children of the marriage are Paul Geoffrey, Karen Marie and Susan Mary. All three have become teachers. After the death of Jacqueline, he married his present wife, the former Mary Warteer in 1959.

Upon discharge from the service in August 1946, he approached Msgr. Joseph J. Wehrle, then President of Gannon College, for a letter of recommendation for admission to the Graduate School of International Relations at Yale University. Dr. Wehrle had been a friend of long-standing and his tutor in Latin. In that summer of 1946, returning veterans were inundating college campuses under the benefits of the Veteran's Education Act, the G.I. Bill. The influx exceeded valuable faculty resources, and college administrators were scrambling to recruit additional staff, sometimes of marginal qualifications. In that environment, Dr. Wehrle persuaded Mr. Peterson to defer his graduate study for one year during which he could teach at Gannon College.

During that tumultuous first year, the enrollment at Gannon increased by over 1,000%, and crowded classes and heavy teaching schedules were the norm.

In the year 1946, Mr. Peterson's contract called for a schedule of six days a week, for a twelve month year at a salary of $3,000. The first semester course load was twenty-nine hours including a variety of courses in Latin, Greek, English Composition, and Ancient History. The average class size was seventy-five students.

This regimen, however incredible in retrospect, did not seem extraordinary after the rigors of four years in combat, and Mr. Peterson thrived. His glaring academic deficiencies (he held only a bachelor's degree) were partially offset by the fine rapport which soon developed between him and the students, all of whom were fellow veterans. In any event, he decided that college teaching was the career for which he was suited, and he decided to procure the graduate education necessary to sustain that career.

In 1947, he enrolled at the Graduate School of New York University in the Department of Classics. During his studies, he taught a full schedule of undergraduate courses in Classics and in German. Following award of his M.A. in 1948, he enrolled in the Ph.D. program in Indo-European Linguistics. Requirements of this curriculum required study of languages in each of the major language families descended from the Indo-European mother tongue, and not all the required courses were available at New York University. He therefore cross-enrolled at Columbia University for courses in Sanskrit and Old Church Slavonic. Following acceptance of his dissertion on the dialects of Anglo-Saxon (published in *Studies in Philology*, October 1953), he was awarded the Doctorate in Philosophy, *summa cum laude*, in June 1950.

He resumed his teaching at Gannon College in September 1950, as an instructor in Classical Language under the chairmanship of Dr. Berta Weber. One year later, Dr. Weber took maternity leave and Dr. Peterson assumed the chairmanship of the Department of Foreign Languages and Cultures, a post which he held until 1977.

During the early 1950's, all classes and faculty offices in foreign languages and linguistics were held on the fourth floor of Old Main. In response to innovations in the methodology of foreign language teaching pioneered by the intensive language training program conducted by the United States Army, Gannon became a pioneer in the design and operation of language laboratories. In this effort, Dr. Peterson consulted at Georgetown University with Dr. Leon Dostert who had designed the multi-language simultaneous interpretation system used at the Nuremberg Trials of Nazi war criminals. His advice and consultation was widely sought in the design and construction of language labs. It was he who pioneered the use of the rear-projection screen to supply the visual dimension in laboratory exercises and later adapted to the design of Zurn 101 and 104 and similar facilities at Villa Maria College.

During the entire Summer of 1960, Dr. Peterson resumed graduate study at the Summer Institute of the Linguistic Society of American at the University of Texas at Austin. His studies were primarily in American Indian languages and the recent linguistic theories of Noam Chomsky in Transformational Grammar. His teachers included Chomsky and other world-renowned scholars assembled from American campuses and from several European universities.

In 1964, Gannon was awarded the first of three consecutive contracts for conducting Summer Institutes for high school teachers of Spanish, sponsored by the National Defense Education Act. Dr. Peterson designed and directed the programs. In connection with recruiting efforts for these projects, he became associated with the Pennsylvania State Modern Language Association and served as its president for the year 1966. In 1975, he was named by the governor of the state as an outstanding foreign language educator of the year.

Following his term as president of the Pennsylvania State Modern Language Association, he was appointed as delegate to the National Federation of Modern Language Teachers. He served as president of that organization in the year 1973. Following his term, he assumed the position of Secretary-Treasurer which he still holds. The National Federation is the publisher of the prestigious *The Modern Language Journal*. Dr. Peterson also serves on the Executive Committee of the Joint National Council for Languages, a policy-making consortium of twenty-seven foreign language teaching associations.

As a linguist, Dr. Peterson has been sought out by area industry for translation services for more than thirty years. He is certified by the American Translators Association and has done professional translations in fifteen languages.

One of his students in linguistics, later to become Dr. Charles Emmons, received a Woodrow Wilson Fellowship in linguistics in 1965. This is the only student to receive this award in the history of Gannon University.

In 1977, Dr. Peterson, at the request of then-President Msgr. Wilfrid J. Nash, assumed the chairmanship of the Self-Study Report for the regional accreditation by the Middle States Association of Colleges and Schools. This experience provided Dr. Peterson with a detailed familiarity with all aspects of institutional operation.

In this context, when Dr. Joseph P. Scottino vacated the post of Vice President for Academic Affairs to assume the presidency, Msgr. Nash, as retiring president, asked Dr. Peterson to apply for the position of Vice President. Now in his thirty-ninth year of service at Gannon, Dr. Peterson still holds that position.

In reflecting upon his life at Gannon, Dr. Peterson indicated that he believes that the motto emblazoned on the episcopal coat of arms of Archbishop John Mark Gannon continues to be the informing principle of the institution which perpetuates his name. "Ut diligatis invicem", he selected from the Gospel of John. The Archbishop lived by that mandate, "Love one another". He has passed it on his major legacy to us. So long as we honor this creed among all members of the Gannon community, we shall prosper in His service.

REV. JOHN P. SCHANZ

Theology is an exciting field! Couple enthusiasm with the desire to be a teacher, and one can understand why the Rev. Dr. John P. Schanz has helped shape Gannon University and has led a fulfilling life as a priest-teacher.

Fr. Schanz' first contact with Gannon was as a student for three months at the Gannon School of Arts and Science before he entered the seminary. Several years later, when he became part of the faculty, he taught theology and German. As the institution grew, he taught only theology. Notes from these classes led to the publishing of his first book, *The Sacraments of Life and Worship*, in 1966. The success of that publication and of his two later books in 1977 and 1983, has contributed to the stature of the Theology Department and Gannon University.

One of Fr. Schanz' earlier responsibilities was that of Director of the Gannon College Institute of Continuing Education. The non-credit courses began as Friday evening classes in the mid-fifties, under Msgr. Wehrle's administration, and ended with the Fall 1970 program. Erie area leaders and Gannon faculty taught a variety of subjects — such as O. Carlyle Brock on his travels to Africa and Asia; Robert Keim on "Investments and Securities"; Elmer Kohlmiller on "Why You Are You"; James Sample on "Adventures in Music"; Peter Smaltz on "Your Personality Impact". All were very well received in the community.

He has seen changes in the institution: the beginning struggles; the challenge of the radical upsurge in the 60's; the physical and academic growth of the fledgling college to a full-scale university. But most impressive of all, he notes, has been the enduring, long-standing faculty and administrators, whose stabilizing influence has not failed to influence succeeding ranks of both educators and students.

Commenting on Msgr. Wehrle's administration, Fr. Schanz attributes the survival of the early years to Msgr. Wehrle's determination and vision — and his total commitment to education. As far as supervision of classroom work, "You were master in your own classroom," says Fr. Schanz, explaining that even though Msgr. Wehrle could step in and teach practically any subject, he did not interfere with a teacher's class.

Identifying with his students is important to Fr. Schanz: "You must reach out and find where the students are, be cognizant of their problems, and start where they are." He enjoys relating to young people: "It keeps me young" he says. And if occasionally enjoying rock music is part of that relationship, he sees participation as a way to single out values from it, and build on that common value. "What better thing" he asks "than to plant values in the young?"

An outreach from campus life since 1965 is his weekend commitment at Holy Cross parish in Fairview, where he finds the opportunity for pastoral ministry, including participation in youth and adult education.

ERON DE LEON SOTO

There can be no doubt that Dr. Soto's earliest association with Gannon proved to be the turning point of his life. Actually, his association dates back to his student days from 1946 to 1950, by which time he obtained a degree and a certificate to teach Spanish in secondary schools. Even though his original intention had been to work in international trade, his future took another turn when Msgr. Nash, then Vice-President of Gannon, offered him a part-time position teaching Spanish. He began teaching here in September 1950, and with the exception of a few years of graduate work in Buffalo and in Mexico, has done that for the past thirty-four years.

Thinking back on these many years of association with Gannon, he recalls fondly both the circumstances of institutional development and the many students and colleagues he has known. He recalls the two buildings and the mostly veteran student body of 1946, and in addition to the small city atmosphere of Erie, he was much impressed with the character of Gannon as a Catholic institution, something which, in his own words, "fitted perfectly the most intimate part of my life and that of my family."

The Christian charity of many of his teachers and the personal help extended to him by many of his classmates encouraged him to continue his studies at Gannon in spite of a language handicap which forced him to memorize the subject matter of his courses for at least the first two years. He recalls especially the help extended to him, in his struggle to master the intricacies of English pronunciation by Fr. Edward Franz and Fr. Robert Levis as they struggled to point out the difference between "fool" and "full" and "these" and "this". Also vivid in his memory are professors such as Dr. Beyer and his history classes, Dr. Susko and his accounting classes, and "Doc" Wehrle who substituted in more than ten different subjects when other professors were absent.

As a teacher, however, it was Dr. Paul Peterson who made the greatest impact on Dr. Soto, and he recalls how Dr. Peterson's role in the development of the Language Department also contributed to his professional development as a language teacher. As so many teachers, Dr. Soto fondly remembers many of his former students, espcially those who became well known, such as Ambassador Charles Martinsen, or those who became his colleagues, such as Fr. James McCullough, Fr. Larry Speice, Richard Dunford, Kevin Quinn, Dennis Steele, Dr. Ken Gamble, "Bud" Elwell, and many others. Also among his most cherished memories was his role in helping Archbishop Gannon practice his Spanish in preparation for his visit to Mexico for the 400th anniversary of the apparition of the Virgin of Guadalupe.

There can be little doubt that Dr. Soto's life was intimately tied to the development of Gannon University. The depth of this relationship can best be felt from his words,

> I have seen and lived the historical growth of Gannon University from the main building where we used to make holes in the bathroom walls to hide bottles to sip in between classes, to the present enrollment of more than 4,500 students, with thirty-five buildings, the writings and inventions of Gannon researchers and professors, and the universal recognition of Gannon University.

In his written memoirs, Dr. Soto mentioned numerous names, too many to list here, not wanting to miss anyone who has been a part of his life at Gannon. In his words, once again,

> Gannon's history has been a part of my own history, and now approaching the sunset of my life at Gannon, I can look back and be especially proud that Gannon's life is a part of my own life and that whan I am now I owe to Gannon College and to Gannon University.

This is indeed a fitting tribute to a man who has spent much of his life working and living with this institution.

JOHN P. SUSKO

Dr. John P. Susko was always anxious to teach in a Catholic college, and so in 1948 he arrived at Gannon College. He recalls that there was then no official Business Administration program. Dr. Wehrle preferred that the emphasis would be on accounting. As a consequence, many Gannon graduates had majors in accounting, a strength which has provided a substantial number of productive careers in this field. As the college developed, the early years of a general business course led to more specific majors in marketing, management, economics, and finance.

Now a Professor Emeritus teaching one course in basic Economics, Dr. Susko can remember when his office was in the old frame building on the northwest corner of Seventh and Peach, the credit load for a professor was eighteen hours, and the students were all male. One of the economics programs was a program for the public school teachers, a project financed by ACES (Americans for the Competitive Enterprise System).

When Dr. Susko was awarded the honorary degree of Doctor of Laws at the 1980 Commencement, his citation read in part:

> . . . The wellsprings of his distinguished career as a superior and gifted teacher have been his love of students and of his discipline. A deeply religious man, Dr. Susko sees in each of his students that reflection of our Creator that commands our respect and affection. His moral and spiritual integrity have also caused him to part company with those who view economics as an academic discipline which is divorced from considerations of morality. Accordingly, he turned to the economic and social teachings of the Church as expressed in the great Papal Encyclicals for the guiding principles by which our understanding of the issues of modern economic life can be illuminated . . . An able administrator, Dr. Susko served for many years as Chairman of the Department of Economics, and he is primarily responsible for the selection of the faculty of that Department which has developed the programs of undergraduate and graduate studies that it presents . . . Dr. Susko continues to serve Gannon and our students as a distinguished teacher and a strong, clear voice for Catholic and liberal education.

JOHN E. WALDRON

If there ever was a Renaissance Man among that cadre of laymen supporting "Doc" Wehrle's earliest efforts to root a college for men in the Erie area, it was Dr. John E. Waldron. There was no learning, no segment of culture of which he was ignorant nor in which he was disinterested. This quiet man totally dedicated his whole life, his profound intelligence, his total concern to the establishment and development of culture and learning in northwestern Pennsylvania. The *Lance*, 1959, tributed him,

> . . . he has combined his superlative background with the rarer qualities of interest and enthusiasm to emerge as an inspiration to both co-workers and students . . . . he is a constant reminder that talent, preparation, and devotion to the highest of ideals can merit the recognition of a sometimes too materialistic world.

John Waldron, born in Erie on July 11, 1911, was a 1929 graduate of Cathedral Prep. He was awarded a Basselin Foundation scholarship to the Catholic University of America in Washington, D.C., which granted him an M.A. in Philosophy in 1934. He married the former Violet Scolio of a prominent Erie family, who bore him three children, and they remained the quiet pride of his very private family life.

John Waldron never taught for "Doc" Wehrle on a regular basis at Cathedral Prep School, but instead began his teaching career at Cathedral College in 1936, the third year of its operation. While he was to be chief developer of business and economic programs at Gannon College, he began by teaching the classics and social science at Cathedral College. He made the move to the Gannon School of Arts and Science in 1941 but stayed only that year. He took a position as Senior Inspector with the U.S. Department of Labor for two years until 1944, at which time he served in the United States Army in the Philippines and Japan until 1946. He returned to Gannon College that year and was named Professor of Education. In 1951, "Doc" Wehrle named him Dean of Instruction, under which title he bore the sole responsibility of supervising the entire faculty. Dr. Donahue had preceded him in this post, and Dr. Maurice Hartmann was to follow. Later on, a tripartite division would be created with a separate dean in charge of Business Administration, the Humanities, and the Natural Sciences.

In fact, Dr. Waldron was named the Dean of the Business Administration division in 1955, and he held that post until retirement in 1974. During this long tenure as Dean, John Waldron either created or cooperated in the creation of the finance, economics, management, marketing, and accounting departments.

He had been given a sabbatical and returned to study at the University of Pittsburgh where he earned a Ph.D. degree in economics in 1955. His doctoral thesis was entitled, *Academic Origins of Economics in the U.S.* Dr. Waldron must be given credit for the splendid flowering of all business programs which still claim the interest of so many thousands of Gannon students. As Dean, he effectively was "Mr. Business" in northwestern Pennsylvania; he literally was the sole monopolist of business growth in the area and was constantly on call in service to its economic health.

Besides his endless tasks at the college, he regularly served as a labor relations consultant and labor arbitrator of the U.S. Mediation and Conciliation Service. In 1962, he was selected as participating arbitrator for the Western New York Arbitration Development Program, an appointment made by the Office of the General Council of Federal Mediation and Conciliation Service in Washington. Since 1951, he served as arbitrator and member of the American Arbitration Association.

Dr. Waldron was a charter member and past president of the Serra Club in Erie; a member of the board of incorporators and finance committee of St. Vincent's Hospital; past president of the Greater Erie Chamber of Commerce; vice-chairman of the USO Committee of Erie County; and member of the board of directors of Educational Television of Erie. In addition, he was a member of the Sales and Marketing Executives International; the American Management Association; Pennsylvania Conference of Economics; the Catholic Business Education Association; the Middle Atlantic Association of College of Business Administration; Blue Key; and Phi Delta Kappa fraternities.

While Dr. Waldron was frequently feted and honored in widely disparate ways, the award he received in 1963 by Pope John XXIII, the *Pro Ecclesia et Pontifice* (For Church and Pontiff), was probably his most appreciated honor. Upon being congratulated for the honor, Dr. Waldron noted: "It's only Gannon College and its dedicated lay faculty that the Pope is honoring. I feel very embarrassed myself to represent them all."

Dr. John Waldron was a "gentleman's gentleman", not in the sense that he was servile, but rather because of his delicate sensitivity. He never wished to offend anyone, whether faculty, student, litigants in arbitration, salesman, or supplicants. He was a gentle man who saw only good in everyone he met. While seated at his desk, he never would refuse to rise when another person, student or faculty, especially young clergy, would enter his office. He was the very personification of gentleness and sensitivity.

As Dean, he was always in favor of giving a failing student another academic chance. He was the one, for example, in a budgeting session, to volunteer to give up something so that peace might result. His advice to younger colleagues was frequently, "Remember, charity before justice."

He always asked himself the question, "What's best for Gannon College," not, "What's best for economics, or for business administration," but, "What's for the best of the general college, for everyone at Gannon." For example, when one of his up-and-coming teachers was tapped to be Admissions Director by Msgr. Nash, Dr. Waldron didn't resist, but rather surrendered him with congratulations and best wishes.

John Waldron represented the rich, spiritual, and intellectual traditions of the Catholic faith which he was prepared always to uphold in his professional university work. He saw himself as giving the young entrusted to his charge the full compass of their Christian intellectual heritage and responsibilities. He served his God, his country, and his church driven by a faith that was bright, clear, articulate, and rooted in a religious culture for which he was most unapologetic. No easy optimist nor intellectual adventurer, no accommodator with secularity, Dr. Waldron served Gannon College long and remains a shining star, leading all others to truth.

BERTA WEBER

Dr. Berta Weber has been a pillar of the university since 1947, and she had come to represent German language and culture on this campus. As a consequence of her efforts for more than thirty-five years, numerous students have mastered the German language and a somewhat smaller number have become teachers and advanced students of German civilization and culture. Her efforts pre-dated the era of the internationalization of education. In addition to her efforts in the teaching of the German language, she has also contributed to the development of the language laboratories, helping to develop what is today one of the most outstanding laboratories in the region.

Looking back on her career at Gannon, Dr. Weber recalls how she was hired to teach at Gannon in June 1947. The process of hiring was much less formalized than now and Dr. Weber recalls that her husband-to-be, Gerald Weber (now Judge Weber of the Federal bench), received a phone call from Father Wehrle inquiring whether it was true that he had brought "a German girl back with him from the war." The conversation went something like this:

> Can you speak English?
> Yes, sir.
> I know you speak German, but can you teach it?
> Yes, sir.
> You got any qualifications, papers?
> Yes, sir! I hold a State Teachers Certificate and a Ph.D. from the University of Vienna.
> You want a job?
> Yes, sir!
> You got one. Come and see me some time.

As she recalls it, the personal interview was equally brief, and she neglected to ask the questions usually asked on such occasions, such as what the teaching load, salary, or fringe benefits would be; nor was there an opportunity to ask, as Dr. Wehrle was obviously a very busy man.

Since the campus was only in the process of being acquired or built, she soon found out that her classroom was located on the fourth floor of the Strong mansion and while climbing four flights of stairs was no problem for a transplanted European, fighting with a flock of pigeons each morning who liked the room when it was cold outside was another matter.

Even though most of her students were older (this was the time when many veterans returned for an education) and taller than she, this caused no problems, since she could speak German, and they wished to learn the language. Teaching became easier after she learned to relax and adapted to the patterns and folkways of higher education in the United States and Erie.

Among these early memories she recalls one day, well into the first month of teaching, when Joe Luckey knocked at the classroom door and handed her a check, saying, "That's your pay, Doc." She wonders whether he remembers that scene as vividly as she does.

Looking back on this and many other such events, Dr. Weber reminisces,

> Well, we have come a long way since those crazy early days when women were a novelty around here, when students actually wanted to learn, when faculty and administration were not at sword's point as a matter of principle, when the worst thing that happened was that Bishop Gannon's bust sported spectacles one day and ended up on the fourth floor supervising the language lab another day.

Today, a vastly larger university still builds upon traditions which can be recalled by those who were a part of Gannon during its formative years. Today, one's former students, including many doctors, lawyers, teachers, businessmen and many others, inquire about the progress of their sons and daughters. As she listens to their comments and observations, Dr. Weber begins thinking about retirement before she is confronted with the grandchildren of her first students.

ERNEST C. WRIGHT, SR.

Ernest C. Wright, who served Gannon from 1950 to 1981, doesn't know whether his greatest achievements are Kevin Quinn, Richard Dunford, Father Robert Susa, Rosalie McBride, or Ronald Volpe — all brilliant luminaries at the present time at the university, or a couple of C.P.A.'s, like Roger Geier, past Treasurer of the American Sterilizer Company, or Larry Barger, senior partner of his own public accounting firm. As proud of these people as he remains, he reminisces with ostensible pride over the 5,000 students to whom he taught finance and accounting from 1950 until retirement in 1981. Dr. Volpe, Dean of the Dahlkemper School of Business, says,

> While retired, he has not resigned. A fortnight never goes by that Ernie is on the horn advising, counseling, cajoling, directing, (and) in short, loving the faculty and students who still make up the Finance Program which he initiated and literally lived for all his time at the university.

Mr. Wright, born in 1916, married the former Cornelia T. Kwiatowski who bore four children, who, in turn, have presented him with seven grandchildren. He worked himself up from the ranks in the United States Army Infantry to the level of Captain. In 1944, he led 121 men (114 of whom were injured in 30 minutes) in a counter-attack during the Battle of the Bulge. Hit by an 88mm shell and paralyzed on his entire left side, he spent the next eighteen months in Ashford General Hospital, West Virginia. There the U.S. Army conferred him a Purple Heart. It was then he decided on more education, and it was "Doc" Wehrle who gave him his chance.

It took him only twenty-seven months, under PL#16 to receive his degree from Gannon College with a major in both English and math, and a heavy minor in philosophy. He was on the Dean's List most of the time. He lists Dr. John Susko and Mr. Conrad Spangler as his most memorable teachers, along with "Doc" Wehrle, "the greatest guy I ever met!"

Ernie always knew what he wanted, and when a senior, he didn't want to take Art and Music Appreciation. Registrar Violet Nellis insisted. Into "Doc's" office he stormed with his request. The president obligingly excused him when Ernie suggested that a course in Integral Calculus would be more beneficial. With an honors transcript, he applied to the Graduate School of the University of Chicago, where Hutchins presided. He had applied to no other graduate schools. He insisted he wanted to go to the University of Chicago. He was an excellent student, why would they not accept him? They did, and he went. He was awarded an M.B.A. in Accounting in record time in 1951, and then returned to Gannon.

"It's the greatest college in the U.S.A.," Mr. Wright volunteered when asked what he thought of Gannon. He obviously did his best and deeply loved his work. He initiated the Finance Department which still remains the only undergraduate Finance Department within a 100-mile radius of northwestern Pennsylvania. He solicited $2,500 a year for five years from Mr. Edward Lamb, as base capital for the Student Investment Trust Fund for which he served as faculty advisor for twenty-eight years. In spite of monies frequently donated to the college, the present fund is worth about $40,000.

Those who know Ernie will smile as they recall his frequent introduction to some point he was preparing to make, "You're an intelligent person and so you will agree with me," was his customary preface to a point of logic from which there was no reasonable retreat.

Mr. Wright enjoys the gratitude of a host of students. The 1981 *Lance* featured him with a 2-page spread as one of those unforgettable professors who worked profound change in their student life.

In 1981, his retirement year, Mr. Wright was listed in the *Marquis Who's Who in the East*. When told about the recent computerization of the business programs at Gannon University, he agreed that this was absolutely necessary, but that "the basics" were even more necessary. He looked back at the dropping of a required course in logic as a depressing day for the college. In explaining this, he recalled the commendation several of his graduate professors at the University of Chicago gave him on well-ordered class presentations. He in turn thanked the logic course as well as philosophy courses which he had to take in his undergraduate days. "All these are necessary for a student to see all the dimensions of life, and also English literature. Don't forget English literature!"

"I have no black thoughts about Gannon, none whatsoever. I always thought it was the greatest college in America. No kidding. That sounds like an exaggeration, but it isn't."

REV. ADDISON YEHL

Fr. Addison Yehl was born and reared in Olean, New York. He earned Bachelor and Master of Science degrees from St. Bonaventure University and was ordained priest at Christ the King Seminary. He assumed the responsibility of the Gannon Chemistry Department from 1951, the year he arrived at Gannon, until 1976, and has remained a professor in that department since then.

When he first came to Gannon his office was in the back of Downey Hall. At that time all three science departments and the psychology department were located in that former carriage house. Two other chemistry faculty members, Dr. Herbert Holtzen and Mr. Brown, split the area, later known as the "Rook", into two labs, one for organic and one for analytical, by extending a clothesline down the middle of the room, a simple solution indeed!

The late Jim Freeman was a colleague on whom Fr. Yehl reflects fondly. He describes him as one of the ten best math teachers in the country. He observed that his Bachelor degree was in Chemistry and his Master in Education.

Fr. Yehl remembers that "Bud" Elwell and Dr. George Hesch came to Gannon the same year he arrived. Also in 1951, Msgr. Nash was Dean of the College. Things were unsophisticated then. Mere survival of the institution was a constant and worrisome concern. During the 1953-54 academic year, Msgr. Wehrle decided Gannon needed an Engineering Program. At that time, the Chemistry Departments annual budget was $2,000. After asking a few people for their opinions, most if not all of which were negative, he fired up engineering. Fr. Yehl recalls the occasion clearly. He could not imagine how it could be pulled off. Dean Gerald Kraus eventually assumed direction, and, "voila", it was done. Freshmen enrollment doubled almost overnight, and Fr. Yehl judges that the undemocratic decision by Msgr. Wehrle probably kept Gannon from succumbing to academic competition. Science enrollment became almost coterminous with engineering.

Fr. Yehl sees Gannon's science programs as having become outstanding in northwestern Pennsylvania since those early days although he considers their future precarious. Enrollment will be the key. Fr. Yehl notes that there are more chemistry majors today than ever before. Many transfer in from other majors like biology, and family medicine, in addition to those recruited as freshmen. He sees the practical, job-related advantage of majoring in chemistry and the other sciences as a strength, but in competing with other colleges, no matter how good the science programs really are, it will be the marketplace perception of them by future freshmen and their parents that will determine their success or failure at Gannon. To some extent that outcome is beyond the control of science departments.

On the other hand, Fr. Yehl observes that good science programs bring good students. Strong science programs are apt to enhance the University's overall enrollment. Specifically, he favors strengthening earth and environmental sciences, and others for which there is a clear market demand.

Fr. Yehl entertains some interesting, though controversial, thoughts on the humanities. Liberal Studies courses by nature do not relate to modernity, he says, and student enrollment could not be maintained if the university depended mainly on them to attract students. He does not see Gannon as the Liberal Arts college it once was.

Fr. Yehl observes a significant change in the administrative atmosphere from the early days. Msgr. Wehrle's solo style led to many independent decisions and fairly swift action on issues. Meetings of the faculty senate (called by his friend, Mr. Freeman) back in those days were infrequent and productive. Today everyone has to have an input. Involvement of larger numbers of faculty and administrators on multiple committees is much more complicated and time consuming. What began as a struggle for existence has evolved into a struggle for effectiveness as the institution has grown larger and more diverse.

CURRENT FACULTY

The following listing of current faculty members makes no pretention to completeness but represents only those on whom information is available

NAME: Adams, Paul K.   BIRTHPLACE: Jacksonville, Ohio

MARRIED: Yes   CHILDREN: 2

EDUCATION: B.S., Edinboro State College; M.E.d., Kent State University; Ph.D., Kent State University; Study in Social Science, University of Rochester; Study in Psychology, Case Western Reserve

CAREER AT GANNON: Assistant Professor of Education, 1965-66
Assistant Professor of History, 1966-1975
Association Professor of Education, 1975-present
Director Student Teaching, 1974-present
Director of Social Science Programs, 1980-present

AWARDS AND HONORS: Koppleman Prize in English, Edinboro State; National Defense College Teaching Doctoral Fellowship, Kent State

AFFILIATIONS: AAUP, Association of Teacher Educators, NEA, PSEA, Pennsylvania Council for Social Studies

PUBLICATIONS: "Col. Henry Bouquet's Ohio Expedition in 1764." *Pennsylvania History* (April 1973); "James P. Wickersham on Education and Crime in Nineteenth Century Pennsylvania." *Pennsylvania Magazine of History and Biography* (October 1980); "General Edward Braddock's Expedition Against Ft. Duquesne;" *The Pennsylvania Social Studies Journal (Spring 1984)*.

——————————————

NAME: Aggarwal, Mahesh C.   BIRTHPLACE: U.P., India

MARRIED: Yes   CHILDREN: 2

EDUCATION: B. Tech, I.I.T., Kampur, India; M.Sc., Marquette University, Ph.D., University of Michigan

CAREER AT GANNON: Associate Professor, September 1978-present

AWARDS AND HONORS: District and Merit Scholarship, TIC, India; Merit Cum Means Scholarship, ITT, India

AFFILIATIONS: American Society of Mechanical Engineers, Northwest Inventors Council, International Society of Solar Energy

PUBLICATIONS: Numerous articles in scientific journals.

NAME: Ablamowicz, Rafal F.   BIRTHPLACE: Bytom, Poland
MARRIED: Yes   CHILDREN: 1
EDUCATION: A.B., M.S. University of Wroclaw, Poland; Ph.D., Southern Illinois University

CAREER AT GANNON: Assistant Professor, Mathematics, 1984-present

AWARDS AND HONORS: President Award, Military Technical Academy, Poland; President Award for Outstanding Grades, University of Wroclaw; President Award, Silesian University, Poland.

AFFILIATIONS: American Mathematical Society, International Association of Mathematical Physicists.

PUBLICATIONS: (J. Mozrzymas, Z. Oziewicz and J. Rzewuski). "Spinor space." *Rep. Math. Phys* 14 (1978):89. (Z. Oziewicz and J. Rzewuski). "On the projection of spinor space on the Minkowski Space." *Bull. Pol. Acad. Sci.* XXVII (1979): 201-203. (Z. Oziewicz and J. Rzewuski-et al.) "Clifford algebra approach to twistors." *J. Math Phys.* 23 (1982): 231-242.

———

NAME: Acri, Michael J.   BIRTHPLACE: Youngstown, Ohio
MARRIED: Yes   CHILDREN: 4
EDUCATION: B.A., Youngstown University, 1964; M.A., Duquesne University, 1966

CAREER AT GANNON: Professor, Philosophy Department, 1966-present

AWARDS AND HONORS: Penn State Certificate on Death and Dying; Grant from National Endowment for Humanities; International Phenomological Society, Perugia, Italy

AFFILIATIONS: American Philosophical Association, Society for Phenomenological Philosophy, Husserl Circle, Heldegger Circle

PUBLICATIONS: *Death: A Bibliographical Guide*

———

NAME: Allison, Michael Patrick   BIRTHPLACE: Erie, Pennsylvania
MARRIED: No
EDUCATION: B.A., Gannon University; Graduate Studies, Gannon University

CAREER AT GANNON: Director of Development Research, 1984-present

AWARDS AND HONORS: Certificate of Appreciation, Gannon University Center for Economic Education

———

NAME: Allshouse, Robert H.   BIRTHPLACE: Erie, Pennsylvania
MARRIED: Yes   CHILDREN: 3
EDUCATION: B.B.A., The Cleveland State University; M.A., Western Reserve University; Ph.D., Case Western Reserve University; Slavic Studies, University of Illinois, Urbana; Military History, United States Military Academy

CAREER AT GANNON: Assistant Professor of History, 1970-1977
Associate Professor of History, 1977-1981
Director of Graduate Social Studies, 1977-present
Professor/Chairman, History, 1981-present

AWARDS AND HONORS: Cereno Peck Fenn Scholar, Cleveland State University, NDEA Fellow, CIC Slavic Institute, NDEA Grantee, U.S. Army Military History Scholar, USMA, Phi Alpha Theta, Pi Gamma Mu, Merit Award, Photographic Society of New York

AFFILIATIONS: Greater Erie Chamber of Commerce, American Assoc. of University Professors, American Historical Assoc., American Assoc. for the Advancement of Slavic Studies, Midwest Slavic Studies Assoc., Organization of American Historians, Society for History Education, Assoc. of College, University and Community Arts Administrators, Ft. LeBoeuf Historical Society, Middle States Historical Assoc. of Catholic College & Universities

PUBLICATIONS: *Aleksander Izvolskii and Russian Foreign Policy, 1910-1914*. University Microfilms, 1977. *A Select Bibliography of Military History since 1715*. Erie, PA: Gannon University Press, 1977. *Photographs for the Tsar: The Pioneering Photography of S.M. Prokudin-Gorskii*. Dial Press, 1980.

––––––––––––

NAME: Angotti, Frank F.   BIRTHPLACE: Rome, New York
MARRIED: Yes   CHILDREN: 2
EDUCATION: B.S., LeMoyne College; M.A., Ph.D., St. John's University

CAREER AT GANNON: Assistant Professor, History, 1967-1971
Associate Professor/Chairman, History, 1971-1978
Professor, Liberal Studies, 1980-Present
Director, Open University, 1980-1982

AWARDS AND HONORS: New York State Regents Scholarship, Research Grant from the Italian Government

AFFILIATIONS: AAUP

PUBLICATIONS: Article in *Filosofia e Storia* (1969). "The Teaching of History: A Re-evaluation," *The History Teacher* (1978). Twenty-one articles in: *Dictionary of Modern Italian History*. Greenwood Press, 1983.

––––––––––––

NAME: Austin, Leona L.   BIRTHPLACE: Pittsburgh, Pennsylvania
MARRIED: No
EDUCATION: B.A., Capital University; M.A., The Ohio State University

CAREER AT GANNON: Coordinator and Coach, Women's Athletics, 1980-present
Director, Student Recreation Center, 1984-present

––––––––––––

NAME: Bagnoni, Mario S.   BIRTHPLACE: Italy
MARRIED: Yes   CHILDREN: 6

EDUCATION: Attended University of Pittsburgh, University of Wisconsin, Penn State, Gannon and Mercyhurst; Graduate of FBI Academy

CAREER AT GANNON: Director of Security, 1971-Present

AWARDS AND HONORS: NAAPC Award; Red Cross Man of the Year; Outstanding Achievement Award; Humanitarian Award from United Cerebral Palsy; Certificate of Honor from Erie Clowns; Contribution Award to Youth from Big Brothers and Sisters; Certificate of Appreciation from PA Commission on Crime

AFFILIATIONS: Delegate to AFL-CIO, Life Member Musician's Union, Member United Labor Leaders, Retired Police Assoc., Fraternal Order of Police

———————————

NAME: Baker, Thomas A.   BIRTHPLACE: Chicago, Illinois
MARRIED: No

EDUCATION: B.A., Loyola University; M.A., Ph.D., Marquette University

CAREER AT GANNON: Assistant Professor, Philosophy Department, 1984-Present

AWARDS AND HONORS: Scholarships and Fellowships from Marquette University

———————————

NAME: Bargielski, Mary (Crane)   BIRTHPLACE: Kankakee, Illinois
MARRIED: Yes   CHILDREN: 4

EDUCATION: B.A., University of Washington; M.B.A., Gannon College

CAREER AT GANNON: Teacher, Management and Marketing, 1979-present

AFFILIATIONS: Co-Advisor for Gannon Chapter, Alpha Kappa PSI

———————————

NAME: Bates, Paul S.   BIRTHPLACE: New York City, New York
MARRIED: Yes   CHILDREN: 2

EDUCATION: B.A., Penn State; M.B.A., University of Chicago

CAREER AT GANNON: Assistant Professor of Finance

AFFILIATIONS: Pennsylvania Institute of CPAs, American Institute of CPAs

———————————

NAME: Beck-Gensheimer, Mary Carol   BIRTHPLACE: Erie, Pennsylvania

EDUCATION: B.S., Communication Education, Clarion State College; M.S., Communications, Clarion University

CAREER AT GANNON: Director, Media Center, 1982-present

———————————

NAME: Blake, James K.   BIRTHPLACE: Norristown, Pennsylvania
MARRIED: Yes   CHILDREN: 2

EDUCATION: B.A., Swarthmore College; M.A., University of Pennsylvania

CAREER AT GANNON: Director of Public Relations

AWARDS AND HONORS: Four national awards for excellence in Public Relations from Council for Advancement and Support of Higher Education; "Silver Anvil Award" for total program excellence from the Public Relations Society of America

AFFILIATIONS: Council for Advancement and Support of Higher Education

————————————

NAME: Bock, Marianne (Thomas)　　　　BIRTHPLACE: Akron, Ohio

MARRIED: Yes　　　　　　　　　　　　　　CHILDREN: 2

EDUCATION: B.S., Florida Southern College; M.Ed., Gannon University

CAREER AT GANNON: Resident Director, Finegan Hall, 1974-1976
　　　　　　　　　　Assistant Director, Student Living and
　　　　　　　　　　Director, Student Activities, 1976-1978
　　　　　　　　　　Assistant Director, Guidance and Placement, 1978-
　　　　　　　　　　Present

AWARDS AND HONORS: Outstanding Young Woman of America

AFFILIATIONS: American Association for Counseling and Development

————————————

NAME: Bohen, Stephen E.　　　　BIRTHPLACE: Erie, Pennsylvania

MARRIED: Yes

EDUCATION: B.A., Gannon College; M.A., The Ohio State University

CAREER AT GANNON: Instructor, Theatre & Communication Arts, 1982-present

AWARDS AND HONORS: Outstanding Student from Gannon College Department of Theatre and Communication Arts

AFFILIATIONS: American Federation of TV/Radio Announcers, Alpha Epsilon Rho (honorary broadcasting fraternity)

————————————

NAME: Bonalewicz, Richard M.　　BIRTHPLACE: Fall River, Massachusetts

MARRIED: Yes　　　　　　　　　　　　　　CHILDREN: 3

EDUCATION: B.A., Colby College; M.A., California State University, Ph.D., University of Oregon

CAREER AT GANNON: Department Head, Health, Physical Education and Recreation, 1984-present

AWARDS AND HONORS: Distinguished Flying Cross, Air Medals (1964-65); Football, All American 1963; Baseball, Most Valuable Player, 1963

AFFILIATIONS: American Assoc. of Baseball Coaches; American Assoc. of Health, Phys. Ed., Recreation, and Dance; American College of Sports Medicine; Penn State Assoc. of Health, Physical Education, Recreation and Dance; Reserve Officer's Assoc., Phi Epsilon Kappa

PUBLICATIONS: "Cardiovascular Training for Pitchers," *Athletic Journal*; "A Standard Unit of Measure to Aid in Conditioning Pitchers," *Coaching Clinic*; numerous articles in *AACB Baseball Digest*; "Exercise Dilemma," *New York State Association of Health, Physical Ed. and Recreation.*

NAME: Booker, Bonita K.   BIRTHPLACE: Erie, Pennsylvania
                                    CHILDREN: 2
EDUCATION: B.S., Edinboro State College; M.Ed., Gannon University
CAREER AT GANNON: Director, CAAP Counseling Services, 1974-1975
                  Assistant Director, EOP/CAAP 1975-Present
AFFILIATIONS: Junior League of Erie

————————————

NAME: Bozza, John A.   BIRTHPLACE: Rochester, New York
MARRIED: Yes   CHILDREN: 3
EDUCATION: B.A., National College of Ed.; M.A., State Univ. of New York at
    Albany; J.D., (with honor) DePaul University
CAREER AT GANNON: Associate Professor/Director of Criminal Justice Pro-
                  gram, 1979-Present
AWARDS AND HONORS: American Jurisprudence Award (Criminal Law &
    Proc.) by Lawyers Co-op Pub.
AFFILIATIONS: American Trial Lawyers Assoc., Pa Trial Lawyers Assoc., Pa
    Bar Assoc., Erie City Bar Assoc., Academy of Criminal Justice Sciences

————————————

NAME: Bressan, Joseph L.   BIRTHPLACE: Crosby, Pennsylvania
MARRIED: Yes   CHILDREN: 6
EDUCATION: B.S., Gannon College; CPA, Pennsylvania
CAREER AT GANNON: Professor, Accounting Department, 1958-present
AWARDS AND HONORS: Fellowship in Business by Foundation of Economic
    Education, Achievement Award by Explorers Group
AFFILIATIONS: PICPA State Vice President, PICPA Erie Chapter President
PUBLICATIONS: "Special Reports," *Spokesman*, PICPA

————————————

NAME: Brinkle, Lydle F.   BIRTHPLACE: Osceola, Arkansas
MARRIED: Yes   CHILDREN: 3
EDUCATION: B.S., Southeast Missouri State College; M.A., Memphis State
    University
CAREER AT GANNON: Director of Geography, 1970-present
AFFILIATIONS: Pennsylvania Academy of Science, Pennsylvania Geographical
    Society
PUBLICATIONS: "Geography and Genetics," *Proceedings of the Pennsylvania
    Academy of Science.* (Spring 1985); (Lydle Brinkle & Carolyn Brinkle)
    Health and Disease. Erie, PA: Gannon University Press, 1983 et al. *Applied
    Climatology Manual.* Erie, PA: Gannon University Press, 1981

————————————

NAME: Brooker, Robert   BIRTHPLACE: Los Angeles, California
MARRIED: Yes   CHILDREN: 1

EDUCATION: A.A., Pierce College; B.A., University of South Florida; Ph.D., North Carolina State University

CAREER AT GANNON: Assistant Professor, Economics

AWARDS AND HONORS: Faculty Research Grant from Gannon University Faculty Senate

AFFILIATIONS: American Agricultural Economics Assoc., American Economics Assoc.

PUBLICATIONS: "Multiple-Component Pricing of Milk" *Proceedings of PA Conference of Economists 1983.*

―――――――――

NAME: Brown, Stephen J.   BIRTHPLACE: Oil City, Pennsylvania

MARRIED: Yes   CHILDREN: 1

EDUCATION: B.S., M.Ed., Gannon University

CAREER AT GANNON: Assistant Professor, Computer Science, 1983-Present

―――――――――

NAME: Bucholtz, Michael L.   BIRTHPLACE: Greenville, Ohio

MARRIED: Yes   CHILDREN: 2

EDUCATION: A.B., Manchester College; Ph.D., Florida State

CAREER AT GANNON: Instructor, Chemistry, 1975-1978
Assistant Professor, 1978-1982
Associate Professor, 1982-1984

AFFILIATIONS: ACES

―――――――――

NAME: Camp, Terrence J.   BIRTHPLACE: Oil City, Pennsylvania

MARRIED: Yes   CHILDREN: 4

EDUCATION: B.S., Gannon University; M.S., University of Texas; M.A., Webster University

CAREER AT GANNON: Professor of Military Science, 1984-present

AWARDS AND HONORS: Bronze Star Medal - With Oak Leaf; Meritorious Service Medal - with 2 Oak Leaves; Army Commendation Medal - with Oak Leaf

―――――――――

NAME: Carney, William J.   BIRTHPLACE: Erie, Pennsylvania

MARRIED: Yes   CHILDREN: 2

EDUCATION: B.A., John Carroll University; M.A., Vanderbilt University

CAREER AT GANNON: Instructor in French, 1967-1972
Assistant Professor, June 1972-Present

AWARDS AND HONORS: Summer Grant from National Endowment for the Humanities

AFFILIATIONS: Pennsylvania Modern Language Association

NAME: Chapman, Thomas, Jr.   BIRTHPLACE: New York, New York
MARRIED: Yes   CHILDREN: 3
EDUCATION: B.S., University of Bridgeport; M.A., Iona College
CAREER AT GANNON: Head Basketball Coach, 1984-present

———————————

NAME: Chludzinski, Cary F.   BIRTHPLACE: Erie, Pennsylvania
MARRIED: Yes   CHILDREN: 2
EDUCATION: B.S., Edinboro University; M.S., Duquesne
CAREER AT GANNON: Faculty Member Accounting Department, 1982-present
AFFILIATIONS: American Institute of CPAs, Pennsylvania Institute of CPAs,
    Institute of Internal Auditors, Naval Reserve Association

———————————

NAME: Christy, James P.   BIRTHPLACE: Rockville Center, New York
MARRIED: Yes   CHILDREN: 1
EDUCATION: B.A., Wheeling College; M.Ed., Kutztown State University
CAREER AT GANNON: Director of Admissions, 1983-present
AWARDS AND HONORS: Outstanding Young Men of America (1981)
AFFILIATIONS: National Association of College Admissions Counselors,
    Northwest Pennsylvania Counselors Association

———————————

NAME: Cicero, Raymond F.   BIRTHPLACE: Erie, Pennsylvania
MARRIED: Yes   CHILDREN: 4
EDUCATION: B.S., University of Pittsburgh; M.S., Purdue University
CAREER AT GANNON: Instructor, Mathematics, 1968
    Director Evening & Summer Sessions, Continuing
    Education, 1968-1981
    Director, Earth Science Program, 1981-present
AFFILIATIONS: American Society of Photogrammetry, American Association
    for the Advancement of Science, Geological Society of America, Pennsyl-
    vania Academy of Science

———————————

NAME: Cultu, Mehmet   BIRTHPLACE: Tokat, Turkey
MARRIED: Yes   CHILDREN: 3
EDUCATION: B.S., M.S., Middle East Technical University, Ankara, Turkey;
    Ph.D., Northwestern University
CAREER AT GANNON: Assistant Professor, Engineering, 1978-1981
    Associate Professor, Engineering, 1981-present
AWARDS AND HONORS: Fulbright Scholarship
AFFILIATIONS: Institute of Electrical and Electronics Engineers, Power
    Engineering, American Society of Engineering Educators

PUBLICATIONS: (J. E. VanNess and H. Zimmer). 1973, "Reduction of Dynamic Models of Power Systems." *Proceeding of PICA Conference, Introduction to Electrical Engineering.* Erie, PA: Gannon University, 1983.

———————————

NAME: Dahlkemper, David E.   BIRTHPLACE: Erie, Pennsylvania

                                CHILDREN: 7

EDUCATION: University of Detroit

CAREER AT GANNON: Instructor, Industrial Management, 1981-present

AWARDS AND HONORS: ASME Man of Year (1971)

AFFILIATIONS: ASME

———————————

NAME: Danilovics, Richard A.   BIRTHPLACE: Sharon, Pennsylvania

MARRIED: Yes   CHILDREN: 1

EDUCATION: Sharon High School

CAREER AT GANNON: Administrtive NCO, Dept. of Military Science, 1983-present

———————————

NAME: Davies, Grace (Alstadt)   BIRTHPLACE: Albion, Pennsylvania

MARRIED: Yes   CHILDREN: 3

EDUCATION: B.S., Edinboro State College; M.S.L.S., Case Western Reserve University

CAREER AT GANNON: Technical Services Librarian (PT), 1969-1971
                  Acquisitions Librarian (PT), 1971-1980
                  Archivist/Gift Books Librarian, 1980-present

AWARDS AND HONORS: Faculty Senate Grant, Gannon University

AFFILIATIONS: Society of American Archivists, Erie County Historical Society

PUBLICATIONS: *For Christ and the Church* (Christian Endeavor); *Belle Valley Heritage Day,* 1976.

———————————

NAME: DeLaura, Nick R.   BIRTHPLACE: Erie, Pennsylvania

MARRIED: Yes   CHILDREN: 3

EDUCATION: B.S., University of Pittsburgh

CAREER AT GANNON: Instructor, Mechanical Engineering, 1970-1975
                  Assistant Professor, Mechanical Engr., 1975-present
                  Director/Chairman Engr. Tech., 1970-present
                  Director/Chairman Industrial Mgmt., 1980-present

PUBLICATIONS: Papers on "Industry in Cooperation with Industry" and "Engineering Technology Education and Relations with Industry" at ASEE Conferences.

NAME: DeLeon-Soto, Eron   BIRTHPLACE: Mexico
MARRIED: Yes   CHILDREN: 2
EDUCATION: B.S., Gannon College; M.S., Polytechnic National Institute;
    Ph.D., University of Buffalo and National University of Mexico
CAREER AT GANNON: Spanish Professor, 1950-present
                  Foreign Student Advisor, 1980-present
                  Ombudsman, Department of Humanities, 1979-present
AWARDS AND HONORS: Various service and Merit Awards, GECAC Director
    of the Year
AFFILIATIONS: Pennsylvania Bilingual Assoc., National Assoc. for Bilingual
    Education, Modern Language Assoc., Greater Erie Community Action
    Committee, Opportunities Industrial Center, City Planning and Devel-
    opment Commission, Human Relations Commission, Erie Economic
    Development Commission

————————————

NAME: DeSante, Paul J.   BIRTHPLACE: Erie, Pennsylvania
ORDINATION: Erie, Pennsylvania, May 7, 1959
EDUCATION: Gannon University; A.B., St. Mary's Seminary; M.A., Catholic
    University; Ph.D., St. John's University
CAREER AT GANNON: Director, Advanced Standing Program, 1974-present
                  Chairman, English Department, 1976-present
PUBLICATIONS: Book/Film Reviews for *Ave Marie, Screen Education Quar-
    terly*, et al.

————————————

NAME: DeWalt, Homer C.   BIRTHPLACE: Titusville, Pennsylvania
ORDINATION: Erie, Pennsylvania, 1950
EDUCATION: A.B., Canisius College; S.T.B., St. Mary Seminary and University;
    M.A., John Carroll University; Ph.D., University of Minnesota
CAREER AT GANNON: Instructor, 1956-1962
                  Assistant to the President for Diocesan Relations,
                  1983-present
AWARDS AND HONORS: Reverend Monsignor, Erie 1964
AFFILIATIONS: National Catholic Educational Association

————————————

NAME: Dipre, Gilio L.   BIRTHPLACE: Benezette, Pennsylvania
ORDINATION: Erie, Pennsylvania, May 19, 1955
EDUCATION: M.S., St. Bonaventure; Ph.D., St. Bonaventure
CAREER AT GANNON: Assistant Professor of Philosophy - present
AWARDS AND HONORS: Carnegie Summer Institute in Philosophy of Reli-
    gion, Notre Dame, 1969
AFFILIATIONS: AAUP Chapter, President 1970-1973
PUBLICATIONS: Crispo, Rev. Alphonse and Dipre, Rev. Gilio. "Metaphysics
    and The Philosophy of God." *Selected Readings*, 1968.

161

NAME: Dobiesz, Robert J.   BIRTHPLACE: Buffalo, New York
MARRIED: No
EDUCATION: B.A., Gannon College; M.L.S., University of Pittsburgh
CAREER AT GANNON: Director of Circulation, 1977-present
Student Supervisor, 1978-present
AFFILIATIONS: Member of the American Library Association, Past member of the Medical Library Association

————————

NAME: Drexler, Charles H.   BIRTHPLACE: Erie, Pennsylvania
ORDINATION: Erie, Pennsylvania, May 24, 1969
EDUCATION: B.A., Gannon College; S.T.B., M.A., Catholic University of America; S.T.L., S.T.D., Pontifical University of St. Thomas Aquinas, Rome
CAREER AT GANNON: Dept. of Theology, 1969-present
Director, Liberal Studies Program, 1977-1982
Director, Student Development, 1982-present
AFFILIATIONS: Catholic Theological Society of America, College Theology Society, Pennsylvania College Personnel Association
PUBLICATIONS: *The Authority to Teach: A Study in the Ecclesiology of Henry Edward Manning.* University Press of America, 1978.

————————

NAME: Duda, John J.   BIRTHPLACE: Milford, Massachusetts
MARRIED: Yes   CHILDREN: 4
EDUCATION: B.S., Massachusetts State College at North Adams; M.A., Hollins College; Ph.D., University of Rochester
CAREER AT GANNON: Faculty Member, Psychology Department, 1974-present

AFFILIATIONS: Society of Broadcast Engineers (SBE)
PUBLICATIONS: Duda, J.J. and Bolles, R.C. "Effects of prior deprivation, current deprivation, and weight loss on the activity of the hungry rat." *Journal of Comparative and Physiological Psychology* 56 (1963); "Threshold-gate limiter for CW reception." *Ham Radio.* 5 (1972).

————————

NAME: Dunford, Richard J.   BIRTHPLACE: Erie, Pennsylvania
MARRIED: Yes   CHILDREN: 5
EDUCATION: B.A., Gannon College; M.S., Syracuse University
CAREER AT GANNON: Instructor of Business Administration, 1964-1966
Assistant Director of Guidance and Placement, 1966-1969
Coordinator of Student Personnel Services, 1969-1972
Vice President Student Personnel Services, 1972-present

NAME: Ellis, Ernest S.   BIRTHPLACE: Duquesne, Pennsylvania
MARRIED: Yes   CHILDREN: 2
EDUCATION: B.S., Gannon College; M.S., University of Pittsburgh
CAREER AT GANNON: Physical Plant Director, 1971-present
AWARDS & HONORS: First Gannon graduate to achieve rank of General
AFFILIATIONS: Brigadier General, Ret.

_____

NAME: Elwell, Howard J.   BIRTHPLACE: Newark, Ohio
MARRIED: Yes   CHILDREN: 6
EDUCATION: B.A., Gannon University; M.A., Ohio State University
CAREER AT GANNON: Golf Coach, 1962-present
                  Asst. Basketball Coach, 1962-1966
                  Cross Country Coach, 1962-1968
                  Intramural Director, 1962-1968
                  Athletic Director, 1966-present
AWARDS AND HONORS: NAIA Cross Country Coach of the Year, 1967;
  Support our Sports Club Coach of the Year, 1967.
AFFILIATIONS: NCAA Golf Coaches Assoc., National Assoc. of Collegiate
  Directors of Athletics, NCAA Men's Committee on Committees, NCAA
  Council, Div. II Basketball Committee, NCAA Men's Div. II Basketball
  Committee, District 2 Chairman, NCAA Postgraduate Scholarship
  Committee, District 2 Chairman, NCAA Division 2 Golf Committee,
  EVAC Golf Committee, Tournament Director NCAA Div. II Nat. Golf
                  Championship, 1984.

_____

NAME: Falkewitz, Robert J.   BIRTHPLACE: Erie, Pennsylvania
MARRIED: Yes   CHILDREN: 2
EDUCATION: B.A., Gannon College; M.Ed., Edinboro State College; M.A.,
  Western Reserve
CAREER AT GANNON: Faculty Member, English Department, 1964
                  Speech Professor, Theatre & Communication Arts
                  Dept., 1973-present
AFFILIATIONS: NCTE, SCA, AAUP, AFM

_____

Fin, Robert C.   BIRTHPLACE: Budapest, Hungary
ORDINATION: Czechoslovakia, March 21, 1943
EDUCATION: B.Ph., Gregorian University, Rome; S.T.B., Studium Generale
  O.P., Budapest; S.T.L., Studium Generale O.P., M.Ed., State Teachers'
  College, Budapest; Ph.D., Pazmany Peter State University, Budapest;
  M.A., Middlebury College, Vermont
CAREER AT GANNON: Department of Theology, 1953-1964
                  Department of Education, 1953-1960

Department of Foreign Languages and Cultures,
1953-present

AFFILIATIONS: Pro-Synodal Judge, Diocesan Tribunal (1978-1984)

————————————

NAME: Fleming, John J.   BIRTHPLACE: Erie, Pennsylvania
MARRIED: Yes   CHILDREN: 3
EDUCATION: B.A., Gannon College; M.A., Fordham University; Ph.D., University of Ottawa
CAREER AT GANNON: Chairman, Psychology Department, 1952-1983
                  Professor, Psychology Department, 1984-present

————————————

NAME: Forsman, David R.   BIRTHPLACE: Erie, Pennsylvania
MARRIED: Yes   CHILDREN: 2
EDUCATION: A.T., B.T., Penn State University
CAREER AT GANNON: Instructor, Mechanical Engineering, 1983-Present

————————————

NAME: Franz, Edward Q.   BIRTHPLACE: Erie, Pennsylvania
ORDINATION: St. Peter's Cathedral, Erie, Pennsylvania, May 10, 1945
EDUCATION: A.B., M.A., Ph.D., Catholic University (Basselin)
CAREER AT GANNON: Professor, Philosophy, 1946-1962
                  Chairman, Philosophy and Religion, 1946-1951
                  Chairman, Philosophy, 1951-1953
                  Adjunct Lecturer, Philosophy, 1975-1982
                  Assistant Professor, Theology, 1982-present
AFFILIATIONS: American Catholic Philosophical Association, Metaphysical Society in America
PUBLICATIONS: *The Thomistic Doctrine on the Possible Intellect.* Catholic University of America Press, 1950; "The Unity of Knowledge," *Proceedings of American Cath. Phil. Assoc. Convention. Notre Dame, 1952.*

————————————

NAME: Frew, David R.   BIRTHPLACE: Erie, Pennsylvania
MARRIED: Yes   CHILDREN: 3
EDUCATION: B.S.I.M., M.A., Gannon College, Ph.D., Kent State University
CAREER AT GANNON: Director of Master of Business Adm. Program, 1971-1981
                  Assoc. Professor of Organization Theory and Behavior, 1973-1978
                  Professor of Organizational Theory and Behavior, 1978-present
AWARDS AND HONORS: Gannon University Outstanding Teacher Award; elected to American Men and Women of Science (1973); Gannon College Faculty Senate Research Grants

164 THE STORY OF GANNON UNIVERSITY

AFFILIATIONS: Academy of Management, American Institute of Industrial Engineers, American Sociological Association

PUBLICATIONS: *Experimental Approaches to Teaching Administrative Clinical Competencies: A Teacher's Handbook.* F. A. Davis, 1982; with Mary Ann Frew. *Administrative Operations in the Health Care Setting,* F. A. Davis, 1982.

NAME: Frew, Mary Ann · BIRTHPLACE: Erie, Pennsylvania
MARRIED: Yes · CHILDREN: 3
EDUCATION: M.A., Gannon College

CAREER AT GANNON: Director, Medical Assistants Program 1977-present

AFFILIATIONS: American League of Nurses, Pennsylvania Academy of Science

PUBLICATIONS: *Comprehensive Medical Assisting; Workbook for Medical Associates; Office Administrative Practice*

NAME: Gamble, Kenneth R. · BIRTHPLACE: Erie, Pennsylvania
MARRIED: Yes · CHILDREN: 3
EDUCATION: B.A., Gannon College; M.A., Boston College; Ph.D., Loyola University of Chicago

CAREER AT GANNON: Psychology Instructor, 1965-1968
Assistant Professor, Psychology, 1968-1972
Associate Professor, Psychology, 1972-present
Chairman, Dept. of Psychology, 1983-present

AWARDS AND HONORS: Diplomate in Clinical Psychology from American Board of Professional Psychology; Dean's List; U.S. Public Health Service Pre-Doctoral Fellow

AFFILIATIONS: Pennsylvania State Licensure, National Register of Health Service Providers in Psychology, Psi Chi National Honor Society in Psychology, Pennsylvania Psychological Assoc., American Society of Clinical Hypnosis, American Psychological Assoc.

PUBLICATIONS: "Paranoid Integration and Thought Disorder." *Journal of Clinical Psychology.* 31 (1975); "Comment on radical notion from Australia." *Schizophrenia Bulletin.* (Winter 1974).

NAME: George, Annmarie (Bernadowicz) BIRTHPLACE: Erie, Pennsylvania
MARRIED: Yes · CHILDREN: 3
EDUCATION: B.S., Damen (Rosary Hill) College; M.S., SUNY at Fredonia

CAREER AT GANNON: Lecturer, Fine Arts, Summer 1970
Instructor, Fine Arts, Fall 1973
Director/Alumni Recruitment Program, 1973-1976
Coordinator/Creative Arts Program, 1974-1977
Director/Schuster Gallery, 1974-Present
Assistant Professor, Fine Arts, 1977-Present

AFFILIATIONS: MENC, PMEA, PMTA, AAUP, NMTA.

PUBLICATIONS: Numerous articles in *Erie Times-News*, program notes for Erie Chamber Orchestra, et al.

NAME: Ghering, Harold A., III   BIRTHPLACE: Meadville, Pennsylvania
ORDINATION: St. Peter's Cathedral, Erie, Pennsylvania, May 16, 1980
EDUCATION: B.S., Penn State University; M.A., Christ the King Seminary
CAREER AT GANNON: Department of Computer Science, 1984-present

----

NAME: Glazer, Frank C.   BIRTHPLACE: McKeesport, Pennsylvania
MARRIED: Yes   CHILDREN: 1
EDUCATION: B.S., Gannon College
CAREER AT GANNON: Director, Annual Fund, 1980-1984
Campaign Director, 1982-Present
Director of Development, 1984-Present
AFFILIATIONS: Member of CASE.

NAME: Graves, Carl L.   BIRTHPLACE: Columbus, Ohio
MARRIED: Yes   CHILDREN: 2
EDUCATION: B.S., Bliss College
CAREER AT GANNON: Assistant Professor of Military Science (ROTC), 1982-present

----

NAME: Griesacker, Paul B.   BIRTHPLACE: Baltimore, Maryland
MARRIED: Yes   CHILDREN: 8
CAREER AT GANNON: Assistant Professor of Physics, 1967-1976
Chairman, Dept. of Physics, 1974-1978
Associate Professor of Physics, 1976-present

AWARDS AND HONORS: NSF Post Doctoral Appointment in Biophysics at Roswell Park Memorial Institute 1967, Gannon Faculty Research Grant 1969, Bendix Student Physics Project Award 1972, USAF-SCEE Summer Faculty Research Fellow 1981, Gannon University Research Grant 1983

AFFILIATIONS: American Assoc. of Physics Teachers; American Optical Society; Sigma Pi Sigma; American Assoc. of University Professors; Pennsylvania Academy of Science; Assistant Treasurer, PA Academy of Science, 1976-1980; Treasurer, PA Academy of Science, 1980-1982

PUBLICATIONS: "Construction of a Moderate Power CO2 Laser." Proceedings of the Chautauqua *Short Course on Lasers and Their Applications*. Penn State University, 1979; (W. Christian, C.F. Niederriter, J.B. Jacquel, D.C. Jordan, D.S. Shenk, and P.B. Griesacker), "Infrared Absorption Measurements with an Optoacoustic Cell." *Proc. of Pa. Aca. Sci., 1978, 99-102.*

NAME: Groszkiewicz, Frank W.   BIRTHPLACE: Erie, Pennsylvania
MARRIED: Yes   CHILDREN: 6
EDUCATION: B.S., Gannon College; M.S., Pennsylvania State College
CAREER AT GANNON: Instructor, Electrical Engineering, 1962-1969
                                  Assistant Professor of Engineering Technology,
                                  1969-1982
                                  Associate Professor of Engineering Technology,
                                  1982-present
AWARDS AND HONORS: IEEE Outstanding Member Award, 1975 Engineer
     of the Year, IEEE Centennial Medal and Certificate for Outstanding
     Service
AFFILIATIONS: IEE, AAUP, ASEE, PAS, Northwestern Inventors Council
———————————
NAME: Haas, Francis W.   BIRTHPLACE: Sharon, Pennsylvania
ORDINATION: Erie, Pennsylvania, 1964
EDUCATION: B.A., St. Bonaventure University, M.A., Catholic University of
     America; Ph.D., S.U.N.Y. at Buffalo
CAREER AT GANNON: Psychology Department, 1964
                                  Planning Department, 1979-1983
                                  Guidance and Placement, 1983-present
———————————
NAME: Haeger, Cherie Ann   BIRTHPLACE: Detroit, Michigan
MARRIED: No
EDUCATION: B.A., Marygrove College; M.A., Ph.D., Duquesne University
CAREER AT GANNON: Instructor, English, 1967-1970
                                  Assistant Professor, English, 1970-1975
                                  Associate Professor, English, 1975-present
AWARDS AND HONORS: National Defense Education Act Fellowship, NEH
     Summer Seminars for College Profs.; Junior Fellow, Southeastern Institute
     of Medieval and Renaissance Studies
AFFILIATIONS: Modern Language Association, Spenser Society, Milton Society,
     Renaissance Society of America, NWPCTE, NCTE, Western Pennsylvania
     Symposium on World Literature
PUBLICATIONS: "Dreamscape and Dream Vision," in *Spenser and the Middle
     Ages*, ed. David Richardson. Cleveland: Cleveland State, 1976. "The Defi-
     nitional Problem' in 'The Typological Problem.' in *Spenser at Kalamazoo*,
     ed. David Richardson. Cleveland: Cleveland State, 1978.
———————————
NAME: Hazen, Samuel L.   BIRTHPLACE: Greenville, Pennsylvania
MARRIED: Yes   CHILDREN: 3
EDUCATION: B.S., Penn State; M.S., University of Buffalo; Ph.D., University
     of Michigan
CAREER AT GANNON: Professor, Electrical Engineering, 1979-present

AWARDS AND HONORS: IEEE Oustanding Member 1984
AFFILIATIONS: IEEE, ASEE

————————————

NAME: Henry, Donald N.   BIRTHPLACE: Erie, Pennsylvania
MARRIED: No
EDUCATION: B.S., Slippery Rock State College
CAREER AT GANNON: Head Wrestling Coach, Recreation Supervisor,
          1984-present
AFFILIATIONS: MAT Tournament Calendar, "Top Technique," Body Lock
and Throws, Feb. 1983

————————————

NAME: Herbstritt, Richard L.   BIRTHPLACE: St. Marys, Pennsylvania
MARRIED: Yes   CHILDREN: 5
EDUCATION: B.A., Gannon College; M.A., Fordham University; D.Ed., Western
Reserve
CAREER AT GANNON: Assistant Registrar; Registrar
          Director of Admissions and Part-time
          Instructor
          Chairman of Department of Education
          Assistant to President
          Director of Admissions
          Director of Special Programs
          Dean of College of Education

————————————

NAME: Hultman, Carl A.   BIRTHPLACE: Milwaukee, Wisconsin
MARRIED: Yes   CHILDREN: 5
EDUCATION: B.S., University of Wisconsin; Ph.D., Penn State University
CAREER AT GANNON: Director Family Medicine Program, 1976
          Director Podiatry Program, 1978
          Coordinator, Science Center of Excellence, 1982
          Science Representative for Planning & Budget
          Committee, 1983
          Director Metalliding Institute, 1983
AWARDS AND HONORS: American Chemical Society Oustanding Member of
the Year, 1983
AFFILIATIONS: American Chemical Society, Pennsylvania Academy of Science,
Northwest Inventors Council
PUBLICATIONS: Hultman, Carl A. and G.M. Rosenblatt, "Vaporization of
Solids: Evidence for a Zipper Mechanism on the Retarded Vaporization of
Arsenic," *Science* 188, 145 (1975).

————————————

NAME: Jackson, George L.   BIRTHPLACE: Erie, Pennsylvania
MARRIED: Yes   CHILDREN: 3

EDUCATION: B.A., Gannon College; M.A., Penn State University

CAREER AT GANNON: E.O.P. Counselor, 1979-1980
                  E.O.P. Associate Director, 1980-present

AWARDS AND HONORS: Kiwanis Academic Award, DAR Good Citzenship Award, Gannon Alumni Scholarship

---

NAME: Jordan, Robert K.   BIRTHPLACE: Clearfield, Pennsylvania
                                       CHILDREN: 3

EDUCATION: B.S., Tufts College; Graduate Study, Brandeis University

CAREER AT GANNON: Director, Engineering Research Institute, 1980-1981
                  Co-Director, Metalliding Institute, 1983-present

AFFILIATIONS: Co-founder, Northwestern Inventors Council

NAME: Karlson, Eskil L.   BIRTHPLACE: Johnkoping, Sweden
MARRIED: Yes   CHILDREN: 3

EDUCATION: B.S., M.S., University of Pittsburgh; D.Sc., St. Louis University

CAREER AT GANNON: Fellow-Research and Development, 1978-present

AWARDS AND HONORS: Adm. Rickover Award for Development of Experimental Reactor for the Navy, NW Inventors Council Inventor of the Year, EESC Outstanding Member 1984, State of Pennsylvania Inventor of the Year, 1984.

AFFILIATIONS: Optical Society of America, Sigma XI, Health Physics Society, American Nuclear Society, American Gem Society, International Ozone Assoc., Who's Who of Science, Northwest Inventors Council, Erie Engineering Society, NW Pennsylvania Shrine Assoc., Inc.

PUBLICATIONS: Raman R. and E.L. Karlson. "The Treatment of Metal Wastes using Continuous Ion Exchange System." Presented at the 22nd Annual Meeting of Institute of Environmental Sciences. Philadelphia, April 1976.

NAME: Kelly, Philip H.   BIRTHPLACE: Marion, Ohio
MARRIED: Yes   CHILDREN: 2

EDUCATION: B.S., Mount St. Mary's College; M.A., University of Dayton; Ph.D., Carnegie-Mellon University

CAREER AT GANNON: Instructor, English Department, 1968
                  Open University Director, 1972-1979
                  Associate Professor, English Dept., 1979-present

---

NAME: Kiehlmeier, Shirley I.   BIRTHPLACE: Erie, Pennsylvania
MARRIED: Yes   CHILDREN: 3

EDUCATION: St. Vincent School of Nursing

CAREER AT GANNON: Part-Time Nurse, Health Center, 1971-1978

Full-Time Nurse/Director, Health Center,
1978-present

AFFILIATIONS: St. Vincent's Alumni Assoc., Mid-Atlantic College Health Assoc., Organization of College Health Services, American College Health Assoc., Occupational Health Nurse's Association of NW Pennsylvania

———————————

NAME: Kirkpatrick, M. Jude   BIRTHPLACE: Johnstown, Pennsylvania
MARRIED: Yes   CHILDREN: 3
EDUCATION: B.A., M.A., St. Francis; M.A., University of Colorado
CAREER AT GANNON: Teacher, Sociology Department, 1966-1968
                                    Chairman/Teacher, Sociology, Social Work,
                                    Criminal Justice, 1968-1976
                                    Director of Anthropology/Anthropology and
                                    Sociology Professor, 1976-present
AWARDS AND HONORS: Who's Who in the East by Who's Who in American, 1975-77-84
AFFILIATIONS: American Anthropological Association, American Archaeological Society, Ohio Valley Archaeological Conference, Eastern States Archaeological Federation, Society for Pennsylvania Archaeological
PUBLICATIONS: Environmental impact studies for Pennsylvania Electric Company, Monsanto Chemical Company, Pennsylvania Highway Department

———————————

NAME: Klempay, Janet   BIRTHPLACE: Pittsburgh, Pennsylvania
EDUCATION: B.A., Mercyhurst College; M.A., John Carroll University; Ph.D., University of Ottawa
CAREER AT GANNON: Assistant Director, Graduate School, 1970-1972
                                    Director, Mental Health Counseling
                                    Program/Professor of Psychology, 1972-present
AFFILIATIONS: American Psychological Assoc., Pennsylvania Psychological Assoc., American Assoc. for Counseling and Development, American Mental Health Counselor Assoc.

———————————

NAME: Klobchar, Thomas Richard BIRTHPLACE: Pittsburgh, Pennsylvania
MARRIED: Yes   CHILDREN: 2
EDUCATION: Physician Assistant, Hahnemann Medical College; B.S., Gannon College
CAREER AT GANNON: Clinical Coordinator, Physician Assistant Program, 1977-present
AFFILIATIONS: Warrant Officer Î29th Field Artillery Unit, New Castle, Pennsylvania

NAME: Kosar, Halit M.   BIRTHPLACE: Istanbul, Turkey

MARRIED: Yes   CHILDREN: 3

EDUCATION: M.S., Ph.D., Istanbul Technical University

CAREER AT GANNON: Dean, College of Science & Engineering

AWARDS AND HONORS: NATO Grant at Case Inst. of Tech., Outstanding
    Society Member Award from ASME 1976, Dedicated Service Award PSPE
    State 1982, Outstanding Society Member Awards from IEEE (1983) and
    PSPE (1980), Invitation from United Nations UNIDO to conduct seminar
    at Marmara Research Institute in Turkey on CAD/CAM Summer 1983.

AFFILIATIONS: Sigma Pi Sigma, Am. Soc. of Mechanical Engrs., Institute of
    Electrical and Electronics Engrs., Vice President PA Engr. Fndn., German
    Engineering Society, Turkish Mechanical Engr. Soc., Am. Soc. for Engr.
    Education, Soc. of Automotive Engr., Nat'l Soc. for Prof. Engrs., Soc. of
    Mfgrs, Engrs., Northwestern Inventors Council

PUBLICATIONS: Kosar, H.M. and J.B. Köeneman. "Kinematical Study of
    Man-Machine Systems." *Alliance for Engineering in Medicine and Biology*,
    1980.

——————————————

NAME: Kovacs, Katherine D.   BIRTHPLACE: Connecticut

EDUCATION: B.S., Gannon University; National Certification, National
    Commission on Certification of Physician Assistants

CAREER AT GANNON: Associate Clinical Coordinator, Physician Assistant
                         Program, 1981-present

AWARDS AND HONORS: PA Recertification by NCCPA, 1983

AFFILIATIONS: American Academy of Physician Assistants, Pennsylvania
    Society of Physician Assistants; Gannon/Hamot Respiratory Therapy
    Board Member

——————————————

NAME: Krahe, Michael J.   BIRTHPLACE: Erie, Pennsylvania

MARRIED: Yes   CHILDREN: 1

EDUCATION: B.A., M.S., Gannon College

CAREER AT GANNON: Director, Alumni Affairs, 1981-present

AFFILIATIONS: Erie Chamber of Commerce

——————————————

NAME: Kraus, Gerald A.   BIRTHPLACE: Erie, Pennsylvania

MARRIED: Yes   CHILDREN: 3

EDUCATION: B.A., Gannon College; M.A., The Pennsylvania State University;
    Ph.D., Southern Illinois University at Carbondale

CAREER AT GANNON: Assistant Professor of Mathematics, 1976
                         Associate Professor of Mathematics, 1981
                         Mathematics Department Chairman, 1983

AWARDS AND HONORS: Special Doctoral Assistantship from Southern Illinois

University, Graduate School Fellowship from Southern Illinois University, Faculty Merit Award from Gannon College

AFFILIATIONS: Mathematical Association of America

NAME: Krause, Edward C.   BIRTHPLACE: Worcester, Massachusetts

ORDINATION: Rome, Italy, December 19, 1966

EDUCATION: B.A., University of Notre Dame; S.T.B., S.T.L., Gregorian University (Rome); Ph.D., Boston University and the Boston Theological Institute

CAREER AT GANNON: Professor of Theology, 1980-present

AWARDS AND HONORS: Observer & Assistant, II Vatican Council (Rome), 1963-66; Language Study Award from University of Caen; addressed to American Academy of Religion, 1978; invited participant in Ethics Conference at Princeton, 1979; presentation at American Society of Christian Ethics, 1984.

AFFILIATIONS: Catholic Theological Society of America, American Society of Christian Ethics, American Academy of Religion

PUBLICATIONS: *Democratic Process in the Thought of John Courtney Murray and Reinhold Niebuhr.* Ann Arbor: Xerox International Inc., 1976; "Catholic Reflection on the American Proposition" in *The Constitutional Polity: Interpretations of the Founding Principles of the American Constitutional System.* Washington: University Press of America, 1983.

NAME: Krebs, Marjorie J.   BIRTHPLACE: Erie, Pennsylvania

EDUCATION: B.S., Penn State; M.A., Ph.D., University of Virginia

CAREER AT GANNON: Associate Professor, Psychology, 1982-present

AWARDS AND HONORS: NATO Fellowship to attend NATO Conference on Engonomics, Bellagio, Italy; Sigma Xi, Honorary in Science

AFFILIATIONS: Human Factors Society and subgroup on Organizational Design and Management

PUBLICATIONS: Krebs, M.J. and J. Wolf. "Principles for the Design of Color Displays," *Proceedings of the Society for Information Displays,* 1979.

NAME: Lafaro, Joseph R.   BIRTHPLACE: Brooklyn, New York

MARRIED: Yes   CHILDREN: 5

EDUCATION: B.A., St. Vincent College; M.A., Ph.D., St. Johns University

CAREER AT GANNON: Professor of Philosophy, 1976-present

NAME: Larrey, Martin F.   BIRTHPLACE: Fowler, California

MARRIED: Yes   CHILDREN: 5

EDUCATION: B.S., M.A., University of Santa Clara; Ph.D., University of California

CAREER AT GANNON: Director, Liberal Studies Program, 1974-1976
Dean, College of Humanities, 1976-present
——————————

NAME: Laurito, Gerard P.   BIRTHPLACE: Dunkirk, New York
MARRIED: Yes
EDUCATION: B.S., Penn State; M.S. Clarion University
CAREER AT GANNON: Microforms/Curriculum Librarian, 1983-Present
AFFILIATIONS: American Library Association, Pennsylvania Library Association
——————————

NAME: Lechner, Carl B.   BIRTHPLACE: Erie, Pennsylvania
MARRIED: Yes   CHILDREN: 4
EDUCATION: B.A., Villanova University; M.A., Gannon College; Ph.D., Case Western Reserve University
CAREER AT GANNON: Director, Physician Assistant Program 1977-Present
Director, Erie Postgraduate Medical Institute, 1982-Present
——————————

NAME: Leonardi, Thomas J.   BIRTHPLACE: Erie, Pennsylvania
MARRIED: Yes   CHILDREN: 2
EDUCATION: B.A., M.A., Gannon University
CAREER AT GANNON: Assistant Professor, Criminal Justice Program, 1982-Present
AFFILIATIONS: Abraxas II Group Home Advisory Board, Consultant with Erie County Adult Probation Department
——————————

NAME: Leu, Joseph A.   BIRTHPLACE: Charlevoix County, Michigan
MARRIED: Yes   CHILDREN: 3
EDUCATION: B.S.; Michigan Technological University; Ph.D., University of Alberta
CAREER AT GANNON: Assistant Professor of Physics, 1976
Associate Professor and Chairman of Physics, 1979
President, Faculty Senate, 1984-1985
AFFILIATIONS: American Association of Physics Teachers, American Association of University Professors
PUBLICATIONS: Lee, S.M., R.A., Mann, and J.A. Leu. "Raman Scattering in a Linear Crystal Lattice with Periodic Impurities." *Bull Am. Phys. Soc.* 15 (1970).
——————————

NAME: Levan, Sally L.   BIRTHPLACE: Williamsport, Pennsylvania
MARRIED: Yes   CHILDREN: 4
EDUCATION: B.S., Indiana University of Pennsylvania; M.A., Gannon University

CAREER AT GANNON: Teacher, English, 1976-1978
                  Adjunct Faculty, English, 1978-1981
                  Instructor, English and Director of Writing Center,
                  1981-present

AFFILIATIONS: Director, Northwestern Penna. Writing Project; National Council of Teachers of English; Writing Centers Association; Board Member, East Central Writing Centers Association; NWPCTE, Board Member

PUBLICATIONS: *Gannon University Writing Manual*

———————————

NAME: Levis, Robert J.   BIRTHPLACE: Erie, Pennsylvania

ORDINATION: St. Peter's Cathedral, Erie, Pennsylvania, May 5, 1948

EDUCATION: B.A., M.A., Ph.D., Catholic University of America, Washington

CAREER AT GANNON: Registrar, Admissions Chairman, 1949-1958
                  Student Personnel Director, 1958-1959
                  Chairman, Theology Department, 1964-1975
                  Director, Pontifical Center, 1972-present
                  Director, Liberal Studies Program, 1983-present

AFFILIATIONS: Association of Pontifical Centers, Society of Teachers of Religion, Catholic Biblical Society, Fellowship of Catholic Scholars

PUBLICATIONS: Two articles on Marriage, *New Catholic Encyclopedia;* Ph.D. dissertation, *The Ends of Marriage in the Catholic College Course on Marriage;* Co-editor of *John Paul II, Catechist;* columnist, *Lake Shore Visitor* 1980-present; columnist, *Toronto Register;* editor, co-author, *The History of Gannon University*

———————————

NAME: Lewis, Monica L.

CAREER AT GANNON: Public Relations Officer, External Affairs,
                  1979-present

———————————

NAME: Longo, Susan P.   BIRTHPLACE: Philadelphia, Pennsylvania

MARRIED: Yes   CHILDREN: 2

EDUCATION: B.B.A., University of Michigan; M.B.A., Gannon University

CAREER AT GANNON: Assistant Professor of Accounting, 1980-present

———————————

NAME: McCracken, Ward   BIRTHPLACE: Philipsburg, Pennsylvania

MARRIED: Yes   CHILDREN: 1

EDUCATION: B.S., M.Ed., Gannon College

CAREER AT GANNON: Resident Advisor (Wehrle), 1970-1971
                  Head Resident Advisor (Wehrle), 1971-1972
                  Resident Director (Wehrle), 1972-1975
                  Registrar, 1975-present

AFFILIATIONS: AACRAO, MSCRAO

NAME: McCullough, James   BIRTHPLACE: Punxsutawney, Pennsylvania
ORDINATION: St. Peter's Cathedral, Erie, Pennsylvania, May 30, 1957
EDUCATION: A.B., Gannon College; M.S., University of Michigan
CAREER AT GANNON: Associate Professor, Dept. of Mathematics,
                  1957-present
AWARDS AND HONORS: Bishop Gannon Award Outstanding ROTC Cadet,
    1952; Outstanding Student in Philosophy Award, 1953

———————————

NAME: McDonald, Thomas M. BIRTHPLACE: Rockville Center, New York
MARRIED: Yes
EDUCATION: B.S., SUNY at Stony Brook; M.S., Ph.D., Syracuse University
CAREER AT GANNON: Assistant Professor of Mathematics, 1981-present
AFFILIATIONS: American Mathematical Society, Mathematical Association
    of America

———————————

NAME: McGivern, James J.   BIRTHPLACE: Carbondale, Pennsylvania
MARRIED: Yes   CHILDREN: 3
EDUCATION: B.S., Iona College; Ph.D., University of Notre Dame
CAREER AT GANNON: Associate Professor of Biology & Director of
                  the Pre-Medical Program, 1976-present
AFFILIATIONS: American Genetics Assoc., Entomological Society of America,
    Genetics Society of America, Sigma Xi, and North East Association of
    Advisors for the Health Professions
PUBLICATIONS: Daly, Dogen and Ehrlich. *Insect Biology and Diversity*. Ed.
    James J. McGivern, et al. McGraw-Hill, 1978.

———————————

NAME: McGraw, Michael E.   BIRTHPLACE: Erie, Pennsylvania
ORDINATION: Erie, Pennsylvania, May 16, 1975
EDUCATION: B.A., M.D., St. Mary's Seminary and University; M.A., The
    Johns Hopkins University and Fordham University
CAREER AT GANNON: Instructor of Theology, 1980-present
AFFILIATIONS: Board of Trustees, Ecclesia Center

———————————

NAME: McSweeney, Thomas J.   BIRTHPLACE: Erie, Pennsylvania
ORDINATION: Blessed Sacrament, Erie, Pennsylvania, July 3, 1971
EDUCATION: B.A., St. Bonaventure University; S.T.B., M.A., Catholic Uni-
    versity of America
CAREER AT GANNON: Professor, 1971-present
                  Founder WERG-FM, 1973
                  Chairman, Dept. of Theatre & Communication Arts.
                  1973-1979
                  Director, Diocesan Communications Centre,
                  1980-present

AWARDS AND HONORS: Hall of Fame from Erie Theatre Arts Institute, 1980; Several "Best" in Directing, Acting Awards from Erie Theatre Arts Institue (BRAVO Awards)

PUBLICATIONS: Theatre critic for Erie Times publishing (1978-1980)

_____

NAME: Mailahn, Bruce Michael   BIRTHPLACE: Peoria, Illinois
MARRIED: Yes   CHILDREN: 1

CAREER AT GANNON: Payroll Dept., 1965-present
         Asst. Coach, Women's Basketball, 1977-1979

_____

NAME: Messina, Michael J.   BIRTHPLACE: Sharon, Pennsylvania

EDUCATION: B.A., John Carroll University; M.B.A., Youngstown State University

CAREER AT GANNON: Assistant Professor of Marketing, 1982-present

AFFILIATIONS: Academy of Marketing Science, American Marketing Association

_____

NAME: Miceli, Anthony J.   BIRTHPLACE: Chicago, Illinois
MARRIED: Yes   CHILDREN: 4

EDUCATION: B.A., University of Detroit

CAREER AT GANNON: Assistant Professor & Chairman of Theatre & Communication Arts, 1975-present

AFFILIATIONS: NABET, AFTRA, Alpha Psi Omega, Alpha Epsilon Rho, Arts Council of Erie

_____

NAME: Michalegko, Paula M.   BIRTHPLACE: Wellsville, New York
     CHILDREN: 1

EDUCATION: B.S., Mansfield University; M.Ed., Edinboro University

CAREER AT GANNON: Program Counselor, Family Medicine, 1983-present

AFFILIATIONS: American Association for Counseling and Development, American Cancer Society Board of Directors, Erie Association for Retarded Citizens, Barber Center Parent Group

_____

NAME: Miller, Larry J.   BIRTHPLACE: Rochester, New York
MARRIED: Yes   CHILDREN: 2

EDUCATION: B.S., SUNY at Stony Brook; M.S., University of Wisconsin; Ph.D., Louisiana State University

CAREER AT GANNON: Assistant Professor of Biology, 1982-present

AWARDS AND HONORS: Research Grant from Ben Franklin Partnership Fund, 1983; Faculty Research Grants from Gannon Unniversity, 1983 and 1984

AFFILIATIONS: Sigma Xi, American Association Advancement of Science, American Society of Zoologists, American Ornithologists Union

PUBLICATIONS: Articles in various science publications

―――――――――――

NAME: Minkiel, Stephen J.   BIRTHPLACE: Cambridge, Massachusetts

ORDINATION: Mary Immaculate Seminary, Northampton, Pa, May 30, 1957

EDUCATION: B.A., Mary Immaculate Seminary; Ph.L., Ph.D., Pontificium Athanaeum Angelicum, Rome

CAREER AT GANNON: Professor and Chairman, Philosophy Department

AFFILIATIONS: ACPA - National and Regional, Fellowship of Catholic Scholars, Maritain Association

PUBLICATIONS: *General Ethics in Light of St. Thomas.* 1959. *Man in Search of Man.* 1983.

―――――――――――

NAME: Minot, Walter S.   BIRTHPLACE: Woonsocket, Rhode Island

MARRIED: Yes   CHILDREN: 1

EDUCATION: A.B., Providence College; Ph.D., University of Nebraska

CAREER AT GANNON: Instructor, English Department, 1966-1968
Assistant Professor, English, 1968-1973
Associate Professor, 1973-1979
Professor, English, 1979-present

AFFILIATIONS: National Council of Teachers of English, Rhetoric Society of America, Wordsworth-Coleridge Association

PUBLICATIONS: *Rhetoric: Theory and Practice for Composition.* Winthrop, 1981.

―――――――――――

NAME: Mitchell, Barry J.   BIRTHPLACE: Braddock, Pennsylvania

MARRIED: Yes   CHILDREN: 1

EDUCATION: B.A., Duquesne University; M.A., University of Notre Dame; M.Ed., Gannon University

CAREER AT GANNON: Instructor of Theology, 1967-1970
Assistant Professor of Theology, 1970-1982
Assistant Professor Theology/Liberal Studies, 1983-present

AWARDS AND HONORS: American Society of Religion Who's Who in Religion, 1974

AFFILIATIONS: College Theology Society; American Assoc. of University Professors; PA State Education Assoc.; National Education Assoc.; National Council for Advancement of Humanities, Board Member and Treasurer; Erie County Library Board, Secretary; National Right-to Life; American Life Lobby

PUBLICATIONS: "Bring Back the Church Fathers." *Homiletic and Pastoral Review* (February 1975). "Is there a Business Ethic?" *Gannon Journal of Economics and Business* (Spring 1978).

NAME: Moffatt, Ann B.   BIRTHPLACE: Detroit, Michigan
MARRIED: Yes   CHILDREN: 3
EDUCATION: B.A., Villa Maria College; M.Ed., Gannon College; M.A., Du-
    quesne University

CAREER AT GANNON: Instructor of Sociology, 1975-present
                  Gerontology Program Director/Instructor,
                  1978-present
                  New Careers Center Assistant Director, 1981-1982
                  New Careers Center Director, 1982-present
                  Elderhostel Program Director, 1979-present
                  Instructor, Counselor Education, 1980-present

AWARDS AND HONORS: Outstanding Higher Education Guidance Program
    by PA Personnel and Guidance Assoc. 1981, National Exemplary Program
    for "Older People Project" by American Personnel and Guidance Assoc.,
    1981

AFFILIATIONS: American Assoc. for Counseling & Development, National
    Vocational Guidance Assoc., PA Personnel and Guidance Assoc., PA
    Vocational Guidance Assoc., Professional Assoc. of Specialists on Aging,
    National Employment Counselors Assoc.

PUBLICATIONS: *Counseling Older Adults, Guidelines for a Team Approach
    to Training,* Moffatt, Ann B. and Myers, Jane, ed. American Personnel
    and Guidance Assoc. on Aging.

——————————————

NAME: Moosa, Matti   BIRTHPLACE: Mosul, Iraq
MARRIED: Yes   CHILDREN: 3
EDUCATION: M.A., Ph.D., Columbia University

CAREER AT GANNON: Associate Professor of History, 1966-1969
                  Professor of History, 1969-present

AWARDS AND HONORS: United Nations Industrial Relations Award 1954,
    The Egyptian and Middle East History Award 1967

AFFILIATIONS: Middle East Studies Association

PUBLICATIONS: *The Origins of Modern Arabic Fiction, 1983.*

——————————————

NAME: Murphy, Charles M.   BIRTHPLACE: Erie, Pennsylvania
EDUCATION: B.A., Gannon College; M.S.W., State University of New York at
    Albany

CAREER AT GANNON: Social Work Program Director, 1974-present

AFFILIATIONS: Family Counseling Center Board of Directors (President 1978-
    79); United Way of Erie County; Erie NASW; Suicide Prevention Task
    Force Committee of Erie County; Pennsylvania Assoc. of Undergraduate
    Social Work Educators, treasurer; Deans and Director of Pennsylvania,
    treasurer; Family Crisis Intervention Services of Erie County, consultant;
    National Assoc. of Social Workers; Academy of Certified Social Workers;
    Council of Social Work Education.

NAME: Nelsen, Robert J.   BIRTHPLACE: Scranton, Pennsylvania
MARRIED: Yes   CHILDREN: 3
EDUCATION: B.S., University of Scranton; M.S., University of Scranton; Ed.D.,
     West Virginia University
CAREER AT GANNON: Assistant Professor, Counselor Education, 1971-1974
                              Associate Professor and Director of Graduate
                              Programs in Counseling, 1974-present
AFFILIATIONS: American Psychological Association, Pennsylvania Psycho-
     logical Association

———————————

NAME: Nies, Rita Ann   BIRTHPLACE: Erie, Pennsylvania
EDUCATION: B.A., Villa Maria College; B.S.L.S., Western Reserve University
CAREER AT GANNON: Librarian (cataloguing, circulation, reference &
                              periodicals), 1946-1949
                              Librarian (circulation, periodicals & reference),
                              1949-1954
                              Reference Librarian and Interlibrary Loan Librarian,
                              1955-present
AWARDS AND HONORS: Gannon College 25 Years of Service Award, 1971;
     Gannon University of Service Award, 1980
AFFILIATIONS: Erie Civic Music Association, Erie Philharmonic

———————————

NAME: Nishimura, Holly H.   BIRTHPLACE: Des Moines, Iowa
MARRIED: Yes

EDUCATION: B.S., Human Development, University of Hawaii at Manoa;
     M.P.H. (Public Health), UCLA
CAREER AT GANNON: Director of Student Activities (Stu. Personnel
                              Svcs. Div.), 1981-present
AFFILIATIONS: American Public Health Association; League of Women Vo-
     ters-Erie County; AAUW; Pennsylvania College Personnel Association

———————————

NAME: Ondrey, Gerald Stephen   BIRTHPLACE: Erie, Pennsylvania
EDUCATION: B.S., Chemistry, Gannon College; M.A., Physical Chemistry,
     Columbia University; M.Phil., Physical Chemistry, Columbia University;
     Ph.D., Physical Chemistry, Columbia University
CAREER AT GANNON: Instructor, Chemistry and Physics Department,
                              1983-1984
                              Assistant Professor of Chemistry, 1984-present
AWARDS AND HONORS: Gannon College Freshman Chemistry Award, 1975
AFFILIATIONS: American Chemical Society; Sigma Pi Sigma
PUBLICATIONS: Ondrey, G.S. and R. Bersohn. "Photodissociation Dynamics
     of 1, 3, 5-Triazine." *J. Chem. Phys.* (1984); Andresen, P., G.S. Ondrey,
     E.W. Rothe and B. Titze. "Nuclear and Electron Dynamics in the Photo-

dissociation of Water." *J. Chem. Phys.* 80 (1984) 2548; "The Photodissociation of Nitromethane at 193 nm," L.J. Butler, D. Krajnovich, Y.T. Lee, G. Ondrey and R. Bersohn, *J. Chem Phys.* 79, 1708 (1983). Other publications in profesional journals.

NAME: Orton, Geraldine (Leitl)   BIRTHPLACE: Pittsburgh, Pennsylvania

MARRIED: Yes   CHILDREN: 2

EDUCATION: B.S., Indiana University of Pennsylvania; M.S., Edinboro University; Ph.D., University of Buffalo

CAREER AT GANNON: Associate Professor, Mental Health Counseling, 1977-present

AWARDS AND HONORS: Member of Pi Gamma Mu, Social Science Honor Society

PUBLICATIONS: "A Comparative Study of Children's Worries." *The Journal of Psychology* (March 1982).

NAME: O'Toole, Austin J.   BIRTHPLACE: Bradford, Pennsylvania

ORDINATION: St. Peter's Cathedral, Erie, Pennsylvania, May 23, 1963

EDUCATION: B.A., Philosophy, St. Bonaventure University; Ph.D., Biology, Catholic University of America

CAREER AT GANNON: Dept. of Biology, 1963-present
                                Chairman, Dept. of Biology, 1973-1980

AWARDS AND HONORS: U.S. Dept. of Agriculture-Forest Grant in conjunction with the NW Institute of Research, Erie, PA; National Science Fndn. Instructional Scientific Equipment for Physiology and Biochemestry Grant; Gannon University Faculty Merit Awards; Science Program Grant for Gifted Jr. H.S. Students; N.W. Tri-County Intermediate Unit; other grants & awards.

AFFILIATIONS: Pennsylvania Academy of Science

PUBLICATIONS: "A Critique of the Ecological Land Type Concept in the Determination of Ecological Patterns within the Allegheny National Forest," *J. of the Penna. Academy of Science*, Vol. 56 No. 2, 1982; "A Vegetational Survey of the Allegheny National Forest," *J. of the Penna Academy of Science*, Vol. 55, No. 2, 1981; other publications in *J. of Penna Academy of Science*. Booklet: *Trees, Shrubs, and Woody Vines of Presque Isle*, 1970.

NAME: Ovnic, Louis J.   BIRTHPLACE: Bremen, Germany (FRG)

MARRIED: Yes   CHILDREN: 2

EDUCATION: B.A., Gannon University; M.Ed., Georgia State University

CAREER AT GANNON: Assistant Professor of Military Science, 1983-present

NAME: Penrod, Burger Bechtel   BIRTHPLACE: Johnstown, Pennsylvania
MARRIED: Yes   CHILDREN: 3
EDUCATION: B.S., University of Pittsburgh
CAREER AT GANNON: Director, Computer Center, 1981-present
AFFILIATIONS: Captain, U.S. Army Reserve

NAME: Peterson, Paul Ward   BIRTHPLACE: Erie, Pennsylvania
MARRIED: Yes   CHILDREN: 3
EDUCATION: B.A., University of Pittsburgh; M.A., New York University;
    Ph.D., New York University
CAREER AT GANNON: Instructor in Foreign Languages, 1946-1947
                              Instructor in Classics, 1950
                              Chairman, Dept. of Foreign Languages, 1951-1977
                              Vice President for Academic Affairs, 1977-present
AWARDS AND HONORS: Outstanding Language Teacher in Pennsylvania,
    1967; Coached Gannon's only Woodrow Wilson Fellow-Charles Em-
    mons-Linguistics
AFFILIATIONS: Secretary-Treasurer, National Federation of Modern Language
    Teachers; Delegate to Joint Council for Languages; Modern Language
    Assoc.; American Translators Assoc.; Linguistic Society of America.
PUBLICATIONS: Dialect Distribution in the Vercelli Homilies (Anglo-Saxon);
    Studies in Philology, (October 1947).

NAME: Pilewski, Timothy William   BIRTHPLACE: Erie, Pennsylvania
EDUCATION: B.A., Edinboro University; Continuing Education Certificate in
    Youth Ministry, Canisius College
CAREER AT GANNON: Associate Campus Minister, 1984-present
AWARDS AND HONORS: Boy Scouts of America Eagle Scout Award, 1976
AFFILIATIONS: Catholic Campus Ministry Association

NAME: Pizzat, Frank J.   BIRTHPLACE: Creekside, Pennsylvania
MARRIED: Yes   CHILDREN: 3
EDUCATION: B.S., University of Pittsburgh; M.S., University of Pittsburgh;
    Ph.D., University of Pittsburgh
CAREER AT GANNON: Director, Psychological Services, 1955-1974
                              Associate Professor, Counseling, 1974-present
AWARDS AND HONORS: Diplomate, Clinical Psychology, American Board
    of Professional Psychology, 1961
AFFILIATIONS: American Psychology Assoc.; Pennsylvania Psychology Assoc.;
    Society for Clinical and Experimental Hypnosis; International Society of
    Hypnosis
PUBLICATIONS: *Behavior Modification in Residential Treatment for Children:
    Model of a Program.*

NAME: Poulson, David Lee   BIRTHPLACE: Oil City, Pennsylvania

ORDINATION: Our Lady Help of Christians, Oil City, PA, June 22, 1979

EDUCATION: B.A., Gannon College; S.T.B., Pontifical University of St. Thomas in Rome

CAREER AT GANNON: Instructor of Philosophy, 1982-on leave for advanced study in philosophy at University of Toronto

AFFILIATIONS: Western New York Regional American Catholic Philosophical Association; National Right to Life Committee; Catholic League for Religious and Civil Rights.

———————————

NAME: Prokop, Duane R.   BIRTHPLACE: Youngstown, Ohio

EDUCATION: B.S.B.A., Youngstown State University; M.B.A., Youngstown State University

CAREER AT GANNON: Assistant Professor of Marketing

AWARDS AND HONORS: Phi Kappa Pi Scholastic Award, 1975; Youngstown State University Scholastic Award, 1974, 1975, 1976; American Marketing Association Oustanding Advisor Award, 1983

AFFILIATIONS: American Marketing Association, Academy of Marketing Science, Kiwanis, Honor Society of Phi Kappa Phi, Young Mens Christian Association, Sales and Marketing Executive Association of Erie

———————————

NAME: Quinn, J. Kevin   BIRTHPLACE: Dubois, Pennsylvania

MARRIED: Yes   CHILDREN: 4

EDUCATION: B.S., Gannon College

CAREER AT GANNON: Accountant, 1961-1964
                 Controller, 1964-1974
                 Vice President, Business Affairs, 1974-present

———————————

NAME: Radomski, Rose Marie   BIRTHPLACE: Erie, Pennsylvania

MEMBERSHIP IN RELIGIOUS COMMUNITY: Sisters of the Holy Family of Nazareth, Pittsburgh, Pennsylvania, September 1, 1957

EDUCATION: B.A., Carlow College, Pittsburgh; M.P.S., St. Paul University, Ottawa

CAREER AT GANNON: Associate Director, Campus Ministry, September 1982-present

AFFILIATIONS: Catholic Campus Ministers' Association; Pennsylvania Catholic Campus Ministers' Association

PUBLICATIONS: *Welcoming the Seasons: Advent, Christmas* and *Welcoming the Seasons: Lent, Easter,* co-author. "Leaflet for Advent Wreath Ceremony." Friedrich's, Erie. "Leaflet for Wedding Candle Kit." Friedrich's, Erie.

NAME: Reinhard, Gregor M.   BIRTHPLACE: Scranton, Pennsylvania
MARRIED: Yes   CHILDREN: 2
EDUCATION: B.A., M.A., Ph.D., Catholic University of America
CAREER AT GANNON: Professor, Dept. of Political Science
                                 Chairman, Dept. of Political Science, 1970-1981
                                 Director, Lawyer's Assistant Program
                                 Director, Graduate Master of Public
                                 Administration Program
                                 Pre-Law Advisor
                                 General Moderator Gannon University Model United
                                 Nations, 1969-present
AWARDS AND HONORS: Phi Beta Kappa; Pi Gamma Mu; Graduate Assist-
    antship, Catholic University; Woodrow Wilson Fund Grant
PUBLICATIONS: *City of Erie Budget Study, 1978-79;* co-author; *County of Erie
    Budget Study,* 1979; *County of Erie and City of Erie Budget Study Addenda,*
    1980; *City of Erie Government Study,* 1981; "The Origins of the Presidency"
    in *The Presidency Today: Policy Perspectives from Readings and Docu-
    ments,* David C. Kozak & Kenneth Ciboski, ed., Nelson-Hall Publishers,
    1984. ——————————

NAME: Roberts, Samuel Jacob   BIRTHPLACE: Brooklyn, New York
MARRIED: Yes   CHILDREN: 1
EDUCATION: B.S., Wharton School of Finance & Commerce, U. of Pa.; LL.D.,
    U. of Pa. Law School
CAREER AT GANNON: Distinguished Professor of Constitutional
                                 Democracy, 1984-present
AWARDS AND HONORS: Temple Men's Club 16th Annual Max C. Currick
    Brotherhood Award; Erie County Social Agencies Award of Merit; Erie
    Teachers' Association 11th Annual "Man of the Year" Award; Pennsylvania
    Trial Lawyers First Annual Award; University of PA Law School Order of
    the Coif; Editor, U. of PA Law Review, 1931.
AFFILIATIONS: Appellate Judge Seminar (Faculty Member), N.Y. University;
    Member of Bd. of Overseers, U. of PA Law School; Bd. of Trustees,
    Gannon U.; Bd. of Trustees, Phila, College of Osteopathic Medicine;
    Commissioner, National Conference on Commissions on Uniform State
    Laws; other memberships in professional organizations.
PUBLICATIONS: "The Adequate and Independent State Ground: Some Prac-
    tical Considerations," 19 *Land & Water Law Review* (1984); Foreword,
    "The Supreme Court of PA: Constitutional Government in Action," 54
    Temple Law Quarterly 403 (1981); "A State Court Judge Looks at the
    Federal Courts," 116 *U. of PA Law Review* 468 (1968); other law review
    articles and other materials in professional journals. ——————————

NAME: Rogan, Robert W.   BIRTHPLACE: New York State
EDUCATION: B.A., SUNY Buffalo; M.B.A., SUNY Buffalo; D.O., West Virginia
    School of Osteopathic Medicine

CAREER AT GANNON: Assistant Professor, Computer Science, 1984-present

AWARDS AND HONORS: Bausch & Lomb Honorary Science Award; N.S.F. Grant, Cornell University; Certified Data Educator

AFFILIATIONS: American Osteopathic Association; American College General Practitioners Ostepathic Medicine and Surgery

———————————

NAME: Rogers, Edward E.   BIRTHPLACE: Erie, Pennsylvania
MARRIED: Yes   CHILDREN: 3

EDUCATION: B.A., Gannon College; M.A., University of Detroit

CAREER AT GANNON: Mathematics, 1964-present

AWARDS AND HONORS: Gannon College Mathematics Award; University of Detroit Graduate Assistantship; National Science Foundation Grant

AFFILIATIONS: Sigma Pi Sigma

———————————

NAME: Ropski, Steven J.   BIRTHPLACE: Erie, Pennsylvania
MARRIED: No

EDUCATION: B.S., Gannon College; Ph.D., Indiana State University

CAREER AT GANNON: Instructor, Biology Department, 1984-present

AWARDS AND HONORS: Vice President and President of Life Sciences Graduate Student Union; Life Science Health and Safety Committee; Faculty Council of the College of Arts and Sciences

AFFILIATIONS: American Society of Mammalogists; Indiana Academy of Science; The Nature Conservancy; North American Wildlife Park Foundation; Tri-Beta Biological Honor Society

PUBLICATIONS: *Student Guide to Cat Dissection for Life Science 241L* (S. Ropski and W. Santee) Indiana State U. Printing Div., 1982; S. Ropski and K. Andersen. "Mammals of the Wattsburg Fen Natural Area," Pennsylvania Academy of Sciences, 1983.

———————————

NAME: Rouch, John S.   BIRTHPLACE: Cleveland, Ohio
MARRIED: Yes   CHILDREN: 6

EDUCATION: B.A., St. Bonaventure University; M.A., University of Michigan; Ph.D., University of Cincinnati

CAREER AT GANNON: Assistant Professor/Associate Professor/Professor —
                  English Department 1959-1975
                  Chairman, Education Department, 1965-1966
                  Chairman, English Department, 1967-1975
                  Dean, Graduate School, 1975-present

AWARDS AND HONORS: ADE-MLA Certificate of Excellence in the Teaching of English

AFFILIATIONS: Council on Graduate Schools in the U.S., Northeast Association of Graduate Schools, Pennsylvania Association of Graduate Schools

NAME: Rubino, David E.   BIRTHPLACE: Sewickley, Pennsylvania

ORDINATION: Erie, Pennsylvania, May 1973

EDUCATION: B.A., St. Francis College; M.Div., St. Francis Seminary/Catholic University; M.A., Edinboro State College; Ph.D., U. of Pittsburgh

CAREER AT GANNON: Assistant Director of Nash Library, 1976-1977
Director of Public Relations, 1977-1983
Lecturer, M.B.A. Program & Comm. Arts Department, 1977-1983
Director of Planning, Budgeting & Institutional Research, 1983-present

AFFILIATIONS: Assoc. of Communication Administrators; Assoc. of Institutional Research; CASE College and University Public Relations Assoc. of PA; Council for Advancement and Support of Education; Eastern Speech Communication Assoc.; Fellowship of Catholic Scholars; International Assoc. of Business Communicators; PA Assoc. of Colleges and Universities Information Committee; Speech Communication Assoc.; Membership in diocesan and community organizations

————————

NAME: Russo, Robert S.   BIRTHPLACE: Rochester, New York

MARRIED: Yes

EDUCATION: B.S., Wilmington College; M.A., Miami University

CAREER AT GANNON: Intramural Director/Soccer Coach, 1982-present

————————

NAME: Sarafinski, Dolores J.   BIRTHPLACE: Erie, Pennsylvania

EDUCATION: B.A., Villa Maria College; M.A., University of Notre Dame; Ph.D., Duquesne University

CAREER AT GANNON: Professor of English

AWARDS AND HONORS: Elected to American Benedictine Academy, 1961; Gannon Faculty Research Grants, 1977 and 1983.

AFFILIATIONS: National Council of Teachers of English; Modern Language Association

PUBLICATIONS: "Showing Staffers How To Do It," *Catholic School Editor*, 1953; Editor, *Notre Dame English Assoc. Newsletter*, 1959-61; "Book Length Studies of Ben Jonson Since 1919: a Review," *Research Opportunities in Renaissance Drama*, 17 (1974); *The Plays of Ben Jonson: A Reference Guide*. G. K. Hall, 1980.

————————

NAME: Schanz, John Philip   BIRTHPLACE: Erie, Pennsylvania

ORDINATION: St. Peter's Cathedral, Erie, Pennsylvania, May 18, 1950

EDUCATION: B.A., St. Mary's University; M.A., Catholic University of America; Ph.D., Western Reserve University

CAREER AT GANNON: Theology Department, 1950-present
Director of Adult Education Program until 1970

PUBLICATIONS: *Sacraments of Life and Worship*, Bruce, 1966; *A Theology of Community*, University Press of America, 1977; *Introduction to the Sacraments*, Pueblo Pub. Co., 1983; "The Crucifixion of Christ" and "The Wounds of Christ" (Articles in *New Catholic Encylopedia*); "The Eucharist as Covenant (article in *Emmanuel*)

————————————

NAME: Schauer, Richard C.   BIRTHPLACE: Pittsburgh, Pennsylvania

MARRIED: Yes   CHILDREN: 2

EDUCATION: B.S., University of Pittsburgh; M.S., North Carolina State; Ph.D., North Carolina State

CAREER AT GANNON: Associate Professor of Biology, 1978-present

AWARDS AND HONORS: Fellowship-Academic Year Institute at N. Carolina State U., 1967-68; NSF Instructional Equipment Grant for Physiology and Biochemistry (Co-author with Dr. A.J. O'Toole) Gannon University Faculty Research Grant; Research Council Grant; UNC at Greensboro; Human Cancer Research Grant, UNC-G; Sigmund Sternberger Fndn. Grant; other research grants.

AFFILIATIONS: Sigma Xi, American Society of Zoologists, American Association for the Advancement of Science, Pennsylvania Academy of Science, New York Academy of Science.

PUBLICATIONS: Rountree, R.C. and R.C. Schauer, "Effect of pyrodoxine and oestradiol on rat uterine ribonucleic acid, protein, and deoxyribonuclei acid synthesis." *J. Endocrinology*71, 1976; Schauer, R.C. and Donald E. Smith, "Effect of estradiol on *in vitro* nucleoside incorporation and methylation of rat uterine ribonucleic acid." *Hormone and Metabolic Research* 9, 1977; other research papers and abstracts, and *Gannon University Biology Lab Manual Vertebrate Physiology Supplements*, 3rd Ed., 1980.

————————————

NAME: Sharp, Patience (Hull)   BIRTHPLACE: Sharon, Pennsylvania

MARRIED: Yes

EDUCATION: A.S.R.T., Gannon University; B.S., Gannon University

CAREER AT GANNON: Director of Radiologic Technology, 1978-present

AWARDS AND HONORS: State Meeting First Award Scientific Exhibits: Zygomatic Arches, The Elusive Gall Bladder, Mandibular Studies

AFFILIATIONS: American Society of Radiologic Technologists; Pennsylvania Society of Radiologic Technologists; District Professional Society

————————————

NAME: Sitter, Richard E.   BIRTHPLACE: Erie, Pennsylvania

MARRIED: Yes

EDUCATION: B.A., Gannon College; Ph.D., SUNY/Buffalo

CAREER AT GANNON: Physics Department, 1968-present

AFFILIATIONS: American Institute of Physics, American Physical Society; Society of Physics Students

PUBLICATIONS: Sitter, Richard E. and R.P. Hurst. "Hyperpolarizationibilities in HARTREEE-Fock Atoms." *Physical Review A.* 5, 1 (January 1972).

———————————

NAME: Smith, Charles R., Jr.   BIRTHPLACE: Carmel, New York
MARRIED: Yes   CHILDREN: 5
EDUCATION: B.A. St. Peter's College; M.A., Marquette University; Ph.D., Syracuse University

CAREER AT GANNON: Instructor, English Department, 1962-1963
                                 Assistant Professor, English Department, 1963-1968
                                 Associate Professor, English Department, 1968-1974
                                 Professor, English Department, 1974-present
                                 Intersession Coordinator, 1969-1973

AFFILIATIONS: MLA, NCTE

PUBLICATIONS: Editor, *Greentree Press Study Guide: Introduction to Liberal Studies*

———————————

NAME: Smith, Howard C., Jr.   BIRTHPLACE: Richmond, Virginia
MARRIED: Yes   CHILDREN: 3
EDUCATION: A.S.S., Alfred State Tech. Inst.; B.B.A., University of Oklahoma; M.S., Alfred University; Ed.D., SUNY/Albany

CAREER AT GANNON: Dean, University College, 1984-present

AFFILIATIONS: Association of University Evening Colleges, National University Extension Colleges, Continuing Education Association of New York

PUBLICATIONS: Relating to interinstitutional collaboration, small business development, long-range planning

———————————

NAME: Snyderwine, L. Thomas .   BIRTHPLACE: Sharon, Pennsylvania
ORDINATION: Erie, Pennsylvania, May 18, 1968

EDUCATION: B.A., St. Mary's Seminary and University; M.A., Catholic University of Ameria; M.S.L.S., Case Western Reserve University; Ed.D., Nova University

CAREER AT GANNON: Assistant Director, Nash Library, 1979-1980
                                 Director, Nash Library, 1980-present

AWARDS AND HONORS: Beta Phi Mu, 9-28-83

AFFILIATIONS: ALA, ADS, NCCS, K of C

PUBLICATIONS: "Education: a Proper Apostolic Activity," *The Catholic Educator*, XL (April-June 1970); "Christian Suffering and Death," *Homiletic & Pastoral Review*, LXXIII (October, 19720; "Introduction of an Intra-Dep't. Supervisory Program at Cathedral Prep," *ERIC*, June 28, 1973; "Non-Threatening Supervision," *Scribe* (PASCD), June, 1975; "The Future of the Card Catalog," *Journal of Educational Media Science*, XVIII (Autumn, 1980); other publications.

NAME: Steele, Dennis C.   BIRTHPLACE: Erie, Pennsylvania
MARRIED: Yes   CHILDREN: 2
EDUCATION: B.S., M.B.A., Gannon College
CAREER AT GANNON: Staff Accountant, 1972-1975
                                    Controller, 1975-present
AFFILIATIONS: National Association of College and University Business
    Officers

————————————

NAME: Sullivan, Richard James BIRTHPLACE: Johnsonburg, Pennsylvania
ORDINATION: Erie, Pennsylvania, May 15, 1958
EDUCATION: B.A., M.A., St. Bonaventure University
CAREER AT GANNON: Theology Department, 1958-present
                                    Campus Ministry, 1965-present
AWARDS AND HONORS: Big Brothers/Sisters Award
AFFILIATIONS: Past Secretary, Priest Senate, Diocese of Erie; Past Secretary,
    Big Brothers/Sisters Board of Directors (Founding Member); Marriage
    Tribunal, Diocese of Erie; Director of Campus Ministry, Diocese of Erie;
    Higher Education Committee; Interchurch Ministries
PUBLICATIONS: Open University Manual: *Introduction to Sacred Scripture*

————————————

NAME: Sukitsch, Richard E.   BIRTHPLACE: Pittsburgh, Pennsylvania
MARRIED: Yes   CHILDREN: 1
EDUCATION: B.A., University of Pittsburgh; M.S., Duquesne University
CAREER AT GANNON: Director of Admissions, 1976-1983
                                    Director of Enrollment Services, 1983-present
AWARDS AND HONORS: Gannon University Faculty Achievement Award
AFFILIATIONS: National Association College Admissions Counselors, Penn-
    sylvania Association College Admissions Counselors

————————————

NAME: Susa, Robert P.   BIRTHPLACE: Sharon, Pennsylvania
ORDINATION: Erie, Pennsylvania, May 11, 1961
EDUCATION: B.A., St. Bonaventure University; M.A., Catholic University
CAREER AT GANNON: Instructor, Economics Department, 1961-1967
                                    Assistant Professor, Economics Department,
                                    1967-1974
                                    Chairman, Economics Department, 1973-1978
                                    Associate Professor, Economics Department,
                                    1974-present

NAME: Susko, John P.   BIRTHPLACE: Broughton, Pennsylvania

MARRIED: Yes   CHILDREN: 4

EDUCATION: B.S., University of Pittsburgh; M.A., University of Pittsburgh; Ph.D., University of Pittsburgh; Doctor of Laws (Honorary), Gannon University

CAREER AT GANNON: Teacher, Department of Business Administration, 1948-present

Chairman, Department of Business Administration, 1960-1970

Teacher, Economics Department, 1970-present

Dean, Business, 1974-1976

PUBLICATIONS: "The Price-Wage Spiral," *Labor Law Journal*, January 1960.

———————————

NAME: Szcypinski, Dorothy   BIRTHPLACE: Erie, Pennsylvania

MEMBERSHIP IN RELIGIOUS COMMUNITY: Sisters of St. Benedict, Erie, Pennsylvania, January 2, 1955

EDUCATION: B.A., Mercyhurst College and Gannon College; M.Ed., Edinboro, University

CAREER AT GANNON: Assistant Professor of Mathematics, September 1982-present

Adjunct Teacher of Mathematics (University College), January 1981-August 1982

AFFILIATIONS: MAA: NCTM; PCTM; MCWP; member of the Erie Diocesan Board of Christian Formation and Education

———————————

NAME: Szendrey, Thomas   BIRTHPLACE: Budapest, Hungary

MARRIED: Yes   CHILDREN: 2

EDUCATION: B.S., John Carroll University; M.A., Ph.D., St. John's University

CAREER AT GANNON: Assistant Professor of History, 1970-1976

Associate Professor of History, 1976-1982

Professor of History, 1983-present

AWARDS AND HONORS: International Research and Exchange Board Grant to spend six months in Hungary as an exchange scholar; three Gannon University Faculty Senate Research Grants; Gannon University Merit Award for Excellence in Research

AFFILIATIONS: American Catholic Historical Association; American Historical Association; American Association for the Study of Hungarian History; Group for the Study of Nationalism; Association for Bibliography in History; International Association for Hungarian Studies

PUBLICATIONS: *The History of the General Councils of the Roman Catholic Church*, 2 vols., Gannon University Press, 1978; "The Thought of St. Augustine in Hungarian Philosophy," *Proceedings of the 19th Hungarian Congress*, Arpad, 1980; "The Collection and Preservation of Hungarian Historical Documents Outside Hungary," *Proceedings of the 18th Congress*, Arpad, 1979; contributions to many scholarly books; publications in professional and scholarly journals.

NAME: Tassotti, Teresa Marie BIRTHPLACE: New Kensington, Pennsylvania

EDUCATION: B.A., Gannon College; M.S., Gannon University

CAREER AT GANNON: Associate Director, Operation Pathway, 1979-1980
Counselor, Upward Bound Program, 1980-1982
Director, Upward Bound Program, 1982-present

AWARDS AND HONORS: Outstanding Young Women of America, Inc., 1983, Outstanding Young Woman Award; Gannon University Upward Bound Student Body Outstanding Service and Dedication Award

AFFILIATIONS: Shiloh Day Care Center, Executive Board Member; Planning and Allocations Panel Member and Information and Referral Division Member, United Way of Erie County; American Personnel and Guidance Association; National Assoc. for Female Executives; Gannon University Professional Women's Assoc.; Mid-Atlantic Association for Educational Opportunity; Pennsylvania Association for Educational Opportunity Personnel; Erie Co. Political Assembly for Women

———————————

NAME: Thompson, Frederick, D. BIRTHPLACE: Erie, Pennsylvania

MARRIED: Yes CHILDREN: 2

EDUCATION: B.A., Gannon College; M.Ed., Gannon College

CAREER AT GANNON: Assistant Director, Upward Bound, 1968-1969
Director, Upward Bound, 1969-1974
Director, E.O.P., 1974-present

AWARDS AND HONORS: Erie Lyons Club Certificate of Appreciation; Erie Exchange Club Appreciation Award; Upward Bound Appreciation Awards (3); SWERI Exemplary Service in Education Award; Black Student Association of Erie Community Service Award; Central City NATO Educational Service Award; Congress of Black Basic Education Community Service Award for Education

———————————

NAME: Tillson, Scott E. BIRTHPLACE: San Diego, California

MARRIED: Yes CHILDREN: 1

EDUCATION: B.A., University of Pennsylvania

CAREER AT GANNON: Assistant Professor of Military Science, 1983-present

AWARDS AND HONORS: Army Commendation Medal; U.S. Army Parachutist Badge

AFFILIATIONS: U.S. Army Field Artillery Association; Erie Rugby Football Club

———————————

NAME: Torab, Hamid BIRTHPLACE: Tehran, Iran

MARRIED: Yes

EDUCATION: B.S.M.E., University of Tehran; M.S.M.E., Ph.D., University of Michigan

CAREER AT GANNON: Assistant Professor, Mechanical Engineering, 1984-present

AWARDS AND HONORS: Office of Energy Research, University of Michigan Fellowship; Department of Mechanical Engineering, University of Michigan Fellowships; Foreign Student Grant, University of Michigan; Pahlvai Foundation (Tehran) Fellowships

AFFILIATIONS: Associate Member of American Society of Mechanical Engineers; Associate Member of American Society of Heating, Refrigerating and Air-Conditioning Engineering

PUBLICATIONS: "Dynamic Behavior of a Heat Pump Water Heater," (With R.E. Sonntag), presented at 5th Annual Energy Symposium at Gannon University, March 1983; "Performance of an Integrated Heat Pump and Gas-Fired Water Heater System," (with R.E. Sonntag) presented at 19th IECEC Conference, August 19-24, San Francisco, CA, other papers presented at professional meetings

———————————

NAME: Treiber, James A.   BIRTHPLACE: Erie, Pennsylvania

MARRIED: Yes   CHILDREN: 1

EDUCATION: B.A., M.Ed., Gannon College

CAREER AT GANNON: Financial Aid, 1967-present

AFFILIATIONS: Current President, Downtown Board of Directors of the Y.M.C.A.

———————————

NAME: Twohill, Sister M. Dominic, O.P.

BIRTHPLACE: New York, New York

MEMBERSHIP IN RELIGIOUS COMMUNITY: Sisters of St. Dominic of Blauvelt, New York, New York

EDUCATION: B.A., Manhattan College; M.A., St. Bonaventure University; Ph.D., Fordham University

CAREER AT GANNON: Associate Professor of Philosophy

AFFILIATIONS: College Theology Society; American Catholic Philosophical Association; Fellowship of Catholic Scholars

———————————

NAME: Upton, Thomas Vernon   BIRTHPLACE: Antigo, Wisconsin

MARRIED: Yes   CHILDREN: 1

EDUCATION: B.A., M.A., Ph.D., Catholic University of America

CAREER AT GANNON: Assistant Professor of Philosophy, 1977-1980
                  Associate Professor of Philosophy, 1981-present

AWARDS AND HONORS: National Endowment for the Humanities Summer Seminar Fellowships, 1980 and 1983; Gannon University Faculty Merit Award; John K. Ryan Fellowship (CUA); Basselin Scholarship (CUA)

PUBLICATIONS: "The Role of Dialectic and Objections in Aristotelian Science," *The Southern Journal of Philosophy* 22 (1984); "Aristotle on Hypothesizing the *Genos* and Scientific Explanation," *Nature and System* 5 (1983); "Psychological and Metaphysical Dimensions of Non-Contradiction in Aristotle," *The Review of Metaphysics* 36 (1983); other publications in professional journals and papers presented at National Conferences.

NAME: Vartanian, Donald N.   BIRTHPLACE: Ypsilanti, Michigan
MARRIED: No
EDUCATION: B.B.A., Eastern Michigan University; M.B.A., Eastern University
CAREER AT GANNON: Assistant Professor of Military Science, 1982-present
AFFILIATIONS: American Volkssport Association, National Historian; organized the first Volksmarching Club in Erie (first Volksmarching Medal commemorated the 50th anniversary of Gannon University).

NAME: Volpe, Ronald J.   BIRTHPLACE: Martins Ferry, Ohio
MARRIED: Yes
EDUCATION: B.S.B.A., Gannon College; M.B.A., Xavier University; Ph.D., University of Pittsburgh
CAREER AT GANNON: Professor of Management and Marketing, 1969-present
Director of Admissions, 1974-1976
Co-Director of the Center for Management Development, 1976-1978
Dean, The Dahlkemper School of Business Administration, 1976-present
AFFILIATIONS: Academy of International Business; Academy of Management; Administrative Management Society; Alpha Kappa Psi Professional Business Fraternity; American Marketing Association; American Association for Higher Education; Eastern Association of College Deans; Small Business Institute Director's Association

NAME: Wallace, Robert A.   BIRTHPLACE: Erie, Pennsylvania
MARRIED: Yes   CHILDREN: 2
EDUCATION: B.S., M.B.A., Gannon College
CAREER AT GANNON: Adjunct Faculty Member, Management/Marketing 1972-1977
Assistant Professor of Finance, M.B.A., Program, 1978-present
Director, M.B.A. Program, 1981-present
AWARDS AND HONORS: Kent State University Teaching Fellowship
AFFILIATIONS: Financial Management Association; Southern Finance Association; Southwestern Finance Association; Eastern Finance Association

NAME: Walsh, Gerard Patrick   BIRTHPLACE: Rochester, New York
EDUCATION: A.B., University of Notre Dame; M.A., University of Texas at Austin
CAREER AT GANNON: Assistant Professor of History, 1965-present
AFFILIATIONS: American Historical Association; American Association of University Professors; Erie County Historical Association

PUBLICATIONS: Member of the Committee for the publication of *The History of Gannon University.*

NAME: Weber, Berta (Bertl) M.   BIRTHPLACE: Hollabrunn, Austria
MARRIED: Yes   CHILDREN: 3

EDUCATION: Master in Teaching, Ph.D., University of Vienna, Austria
CAREER AT GANNON: Faculty, Language Department, 1947-1965
                                  Associate Professor, 1965-1972
                                  Professor, 1972-present
                                  Chairperson, Department of Languages & Cultures
                                  1978-present
AWARDS AND HONORS: University of Bonn, Federal Republic, Fulbright Grant
AFFILIATIONS: Western PA Chapter, AATG; American Council on the Teaching of Languages; Modern Language Association; German-American National Committee; United German American Committee of the USA; Austrian Federation
PUBLICATIONS: "Herders Idee vom Genie im Vergleich mit Hamanns and Goethes Geniebegriff" Vienna, 1945; articles in professional journals.

NAME: Weber, Frederic F.   BIRTHPLACE: Clairton, Pennsylvania
MARRIED: Yes   CHILDREN: 1

CAREER AT GANNON: Director, Administrative Services, 1981-1982
                                  Director, Purchasing and Communications, 1982-
                                  present
AWARDS AND HONORS: U.S. Jaycees Outstanding Young Men of America; Butler Jaycees Jaycee of the Year; U.S. Jaycees National Jaycee Leadership Award; PA Jaycees President's Roundtable (two years)
AFFILIATIONS: Telecommunications Management Association

NAME: Wehrer, Robert A.   BIRTHPLACE: Juneau, Alaska
MARRIED: Yes   CHILDREN: 4

EDUCATION: B.S., Seattle University; M.S., Ed.D., Columbia University Teachers College
CAREER AT GANNON: Department of Education, 1968-present

NAME: Weibel, Marguerite M.   BIRTHPLACE: Milton, Pennsylvania
MARRIED: Yes   CHILDREN: 7
EDUCATION: B.S., Mercyhurst College
CAREER AT GANNON: Director, Secretarial Science Program, 1977-present

NAME: Wilson, Thomas C.   BIRTHPLACE: Denver, Colorado
MARRIED: Yes
EDUCATION: B.A., M.A., Ph.D., University of Colorado
CAREER AT GANNON: Instructor, Department of Sociology, 1977-1980
                  Assistant Professor, Department of Sociology,
                  1980-present
AFFILIATIONS: American Sociological Association
PUBLICATIONS: "White Response to Neighborhood Racial Change," *Sociological Focus*, 16:4, 1983; "Urbanism and Racial Attitudes: A Test of Some Urban Theories," *Urban Affairs Quarterly*, 1984.

————————————

NAME: Wozniak, Casimir John   BIRTHPLACE: Erie, Pennsylvania
ORDINATION: St. Peter's Cathedral, Erie, Pennsylvania, May 18, 1968
EDUCATION: B.A., St. Bonaventure University; M.Div., Christ the King Seminary; M.A., Gannon College; S.T.L., St. Paul University
CAREER AT GANNON: Department of Theology, 1975-present
AFFILIATIONS: Polish-American Historical Society

————————————

NAME: Yaeger, Kathryn (Greenholt) BIRTHPLACE: Hanover, Pennsylvania
MARRIED: Yes
EDUCATION: B.S., Gannon University
CAREER AT GANNON: Admissions Counselor, 1980-1982
                  Assistant Director of Admissions, 1982-1983
                  Associate Director of Admissions, 1983-present
AFFILIATIONS: National Association of College Admissions Counselors; Pennsylvania Association of College Admissions Counselors

————————————

NAME: Yehl, Addison   BIRTHPLACE: Olean, New York
ORDINATION: Christ the King Seminary, 1951
EDUCATION: B.S., M.S., St. Bonaventure University
CAREER AT GANNON: Chairman, Chemistry Department, 1951-1976
                  Professor, Chemistry Department, 1976-present
AFFILIATIONS: American Chemical Society; Fellow, American Institute of Chemists

————————————

NAME: Zagorski, Stanley J.   BIRTHPLACE: Pittsburgh, Pennsylvania
MARRIED: Yes   CHILDREN: 4
EDUCATION: B.S., Slippery Rock University; M.S., Edinboro State University
CAREER AT GANNON: Professor, Biology Department, 1968-present
                  Associate Dean, College of Science & Engineering,
                  1975-present
                  Director of Environmental Studies, 1979-present

Director of Science Education, School of Graduate Studies, 1972-present
Associate Director, Radiologic Technology, 1973-1978

AWARDS AND HONORS: Northwest Tri-County Intermediate Unit Educational Grants, 1976, 1977, 1978, 1979; Gannon College Faculty Research Grant, 1977; National Science Foundation Grants, 1977-78, 1978-79, 1981-82; EPA Grants, 1978, 1979, 1980, 1982; other grants.

AFFILIATIONS: Pennsylvania Academy of Science; International Association of Great Lakes Research; Pennsylvania Science Teachers Association

PUBLICATIONS: "Health Effects Related to Sewage Affluent Discharge Into Fresh Water Environments *Solid and Liquid Wastes: Management and Methods*, Pennsylvania Academy of Science, 1984; "The Changing Configuration of Presque Isle Peninsula," *The Journal of Erie Studies*, , Spring 1982, Vol. 11, No. 1; other publications in professional journals.

————————————

NAME: Zarnick, Gene G., Jr.　　　　BIRTHPLACE: Butler, Pennsylvania
MARRIED: Yes　　　　　　　　　　　　CHILDREN: 2
EDUCATION: B.S., Clarion State College; M.L.S., University of Pittsburgh
CAREER AT GANNON: Reference/Microforms, Nash Library, 1981-1983
Periodicals Librarian, Nash Library, 1983-present

AFFILIATIONS: Pennsylvania Library Association; American Library Association; Erie Association for Retarded Citizens; Sacred Heart Parish; Engagement Encounter; Local Chapter of Ground Zero

————————————

NAME: Zgainer, Margaret Anna　　BIRTHPLACE: Pittsburgh, Pennsylvania
EDUCATION: B.A., Point Park College; M.L.S., University of Pittsburgh
CAREER AT GANNON: Periodicals Librarian, Nash Library, 1982-1983
Head of Technical Services, Nash Library, 1983-present

AWARDS AND HONORS: Outstanding Young Woman in America Award

AFFILIATIONS: American Library Association; Pennsylvania Library Association

PUBLICATIONS: "We Keep Tabs (Colors) On Our Books," *Unabashed Librarian*, No. 24:11 (1977).

————————————

NAME: Zotov, Natalia V.
EDUCATION: B.Sc., M.Sc., University of Canterbury, NZ; Ph.D., University of Otago, NZ
CAREER AT GANNON: Assistant Professor, Mathematics, 1980-present
AWARDS AND HONORS: Institute of Astronomy, University of Cambridge, UK, Senior Visiting Fellowship
AFFILIATIONS: American Astronomical Society, Mathematical Association of America, Cleveland Astronomical Association

PUBLICATIONS: Zotov, Natalia V. and W. Davidson. *Australian J. of Physics*, 23, 127 (1970); Zotov, Natalia V. and W. Davidson. *Mon. Notices Roy. Astron. Soc.*, 162, 127 (1973); Zotov, Natalia V. and W. Davidson. *Aust. J. of Physics*, 29, 97 (1976); Angel, J.P.R., et al.: Proc. Pittsburgh BL Lac Conference, 1978; Zotov, Natalia V. and S. Tapia. *Astrophys. J. Lett.*, 229, L5-L8 (1979); other publications in professional journals.

FORMER FACULTY
(Teaching and Administrative)
OF
CATHEDRAL COLLEGE — GANNON UNIVERSITY

Adams, George
Agadjanian, Georges
Agnese, Lou
Ahearn, John J.
Aksogan, Orhan D.
Albanese, Anthony L.
Alberstadt, John William
Alcorn, Charles L.
Alessio, John
Allamon, Donald W.
Allard, Alexander
Allessie, Charles T.
Allgeier, Albert R.
Arena, Victor L.
Axtell, Frederick B.
Bacon, Michael H.
Baggiano, Maurice
Barber, Joseph C.
Barcio, Rev. Robert G.
Barclay, Lance
Barger, Lawrence E.
Barr, Joseph J.
Barrett, Charles F.
Barrett, Mary
Bart, John
Bates, Thomas F.
Baxter, Edward M.
Bayer, John D.
Becker, Robert H.
Bednarski, Joseph J.
Bell, Jack T.
Bess, Gail
Beverly, A. Louise
Beyer, Richard L.
Bicsey, John B.
Blewett, John H.
Bloomstine, William C.
Blystone, Eugene E.
Boag, Alexander
Boisot, Daniel
Bolash, William P.
Bolla, Lawrence
Bower, Robert F.
Brace, Jerry
Brairton, Barbara

Brasfield, James M.
Brault, Anne-Marie
Brennan, Edward T.
Bright, Jay
Brill, Robert J.
Brown, Henry
Brown, William G.
Browning, James M.
Brugger, James R.
Brugger, John E.
Buckley, John
Bukowska, Michalina
Burger, Noreen
Burgnon, Leroy
Burke, John R.
Burke, Paul
Burns, Raymond S.
Burns, Warren T.
Burroughs, Lloyd
Butler, Victor M.
Cacchione, Nunzio
Cairo, Eugene
Calabrese, Arthur D.
Caldwell, E. James
Caldwell, Ora O.
Cancilla, Paul F.
Cantoni, Dennis A.
Capella, Louis M.
Carandang, Amado
Carey, Ruth M.
Carlson, J. David
Carnahan, Robert E.
Carney, Mary Pat
Carney, Melvin E.
Cesa, Anita
Cevasco, George A.
Chapdelaine, Albert
Chellis, LaVerne
Chermack, Mary Grace
Cherry, Harold
Cherry, John F.
Cherubim, Sister
Chinchenko, John M.
Christenson, David
Ciccozzi, Attilio

Cicen, Randolph
Ciufoli, Bonaventure M.
Clay, Robert
Clemons, Awilda
Clingan, Mortimer James
Close, L. B.
Clough, Raymond J.
Coho, Owen
Cole, John
Colvin, Charles R.
Comerford, Steven J.
Conboy, Timothy J.
Connorton, Joseph J.
Cooley, James S.
Corzilius, Jo Ann
Counihan, Jeremiah M.
Craig, Michael F.
Craig, Winston A.
Crosby, Michael A.
Crotty, Tess
Culp, William H.
Cummings, Eugune H.
Currier, George
Curtis, Elsie
Czyzewski, Tadeusz
Daisley, William
Dapprich, Aloysius E.
Dargan, William E.
Darling, Ralph E.
Davis, Jeffrey J.
Davis, John B.
DeCramer, Gary M.
DeFazio, David
DeLabbio, Mary C.
Denues, Katherine
DeSante, David
DeSante, Joseph
DeSanto, Richard J.
Descoteaux, Albert R.
DeSlatte, Paula S.
DeWaelsche, Cynthia
DeMaio, Michael
Dinibutun, Talha
DiNicola, Pamela
DePlacido, Donald
Doemeny, Laslow
Donohue, Francis J.
Dougan, Donald E.
Dowdy, Robert
Drezga, Tihomil

Dudas, George J.
Duering, Aloysius
DuFief, Thomas A.
Dunn, James R.
Dymski, Jan
Edelman, Lorri Jane
Edwards, Dennis M.
Edwards, H. Rand
El-Sherbiny, Mohammed K.
Ellis, Robert T.
Emeruwa, Hart
Emma Therese, Sister
Emmons, Charles F.
Epolito, Joseph M.
Evans, Joseph C.
Falzone, Robert L.
Farantzos, Themos
Featherston, Robert J.
Finegan, Anna
Finegan, Owen Thomas
Finnecy, James R.
Fischer, H. Robert
Fisher, Kenneth J.
Fitzgerald, John M.
Fitzgibbon, John P.
Fitzpatrick, Matthew S.
Fleugel, Edna Rose
Flynn, Isabel
Fogarty, Timothy
Forston, John W.
Fox, Richard A.
Francis, Raymond J.
Frazier, G. Neal
Free, Suzanne
Freeman, James J.
Freeman, Thomas
French, Robert L. (F.W. DeMara)
Frew, John
Froelich, Gary D.
Funk, Hans D.
Gainer, Ronald
Gale, Bede Eric
Gallo, Robert D.
Garcia-Yglesia, Alfonso
Gardner, Arthur J.
Gardner, George A.
Garrittsan, Eleanor
Garvey, Robert
Garvey, William P.
Garzina, Francis

Gates, James C.
Gatewood, Claude V.
Gavin, Joseph A.
Geier, Roger A.
Gelinas, Jean-Paul
Gibbons. Alfred B.
Gibbons, Maurice C.
Gibbons, Paul F.
Gibney, Sean M.
Gilbert, William G.
Gildea, Martin M.
Gilewicz, John P.
Girard, David L.
Glover, John F.
Gnanasekaran, R.
Goebel, Bernardine
Goodenow, Theodore C.
Gorla, Rama
Gornall, M. Fletcher
Gorski, Thaddeus M.
Grady, Arthur C.
Gragg, Junior M.
Gray, Paul J.
Green, Floyd K.
Green, John C.
Green, Raymond
Green, Roger W.
Green, William C.
Green, William R., Jr.
Greer, Geoffrey, D.
Gregorek, Joseph C.
Greiner, Francis D.
Griffin, Thomas F.
Grignol, George E.
Groos, Almuth E.
Gross, Dawn O.
Groth, Charles C.
Guerrin, Robert
Guido, Thomas J.
Guiffrida, Alfred
Guzowski, Richard C.
Hackenberg, George R.
Haferman, Donald H.
Hahn, Sharon
Halperin, B. Bernard
Hamilton, Joseph H.
Hammer, Robert C.
Hanes, James G.
Hanlon, William J.
Hannes, Lance E.

Hansen, Richard S.
Haratine, Richard R.
Harding, James F.
Hardy, Coleman L.
Hari, Yogeshwar
Harper, Charles W.
Harris, William A.
Hartmann, Maurice M.
Hatton, Daniel
Haughney, Louis C.
Havican, George T.
Hayden, Francis
Healey, Gerald
Heath, Guy H., Jr.
Heibel, Edward J.
Heinlein, Albert Clayton
Henderson, Howard
Henneman, Dennis
Herr, James N.
Herrmann, Francis J.
Hesch, Paul
Hetra, Joseph
Heya, Zoltan
Hilbert, John J.
Hilbert, Mary
Hilinski, Bernadette
Hipp, Joseph
Hite, Anthony
Hoelter, Herbert G.
Hoffer, Arnold H.
Holbach, James
Holly, Patricia M.
Holmstrom, Ronald J.
Holzen, Herbert
Holzen, Stephanie
Hook, Albert G.
Horner, Walter B.
Hornfeck, William A.
Horton, Denise
Hrascenec, Rudolph J.
Hresko, Claire
Huang, Yun K.
Huckabay, Warren T.
Hummell, John
Hynes, John B.
Impeduglia, Giovanni S.
Innocenti, Gerard G.
Ismaila, Isa
Jewell, Marilyn M.
Jiang, Thomas J.

Joachim, Robert L.
Joern, William A.
John, Richard A.
Johnson, Carl A.
Johnston, Charles A.
Jones, Dana Sherwood
Jucaitis, Francis
Kahl, Alfred L., Jr.
Kaminsky, Theresa C.
Karcic, Mary (Heya)
Karcic, Milivoj Hrvoje
Karsznia, Barbara Ann
Kashmiry, Monir A.
Kavanaugh, Michael J.
Kazmierowicz, Eileen
Kean, Robert E.
Keefe, Leonard J.
Keeler, Harry, Jr.
Kelvington, James R.
Kennedy, Charles L.
Kennedy, Michael J.
Kennedy, Roger J.
Kennedy, Warren C.
Kenny, Robert J.
Kenwood, Joan
Kiley, James E., Jr.
Kilkis, Birol
Killian, Michael E.
Kim, Hyun Soo
Kingsley, Leonard E.
Kinney, Ludie E.
Kirk, Henry C.
Klein, Gregory
Koenig, Daniel J.
Kohlmiller, Elmer F., Jr.
Kokoros, James J.
Konopka, Michael A.
Koontz, Christian
Kopycinski, Clark
Kosc, Wieslaw
Kothapa, Julu
Krahe, Francis X.
Kroncke, Charles O.
Kuchta, Leslie
Kupetz, John
Kwiat, S. Thaddeus
Lacey, William J.
Lachowski, Joseph
Lafaro, Margaret
Lagomarsino, Elizabeth

Lall, Parshotam S.
Lambert, Richard E.
Lander, Edward
Lander, Joseph C.
Lane, Joseph
Lang, Betty L.
Larsen, Paul G.
Lasher, William C.
Latimer, Edward H.
Latimer, William N.
Lee, John T.
Lee, Joseph S.
Levin, Shirley
Lewis, V. Marion
Lockwood, Nile S.
Loh, Hsaio Chi
Lorei, Louis J.
Loring, Richard W.
Losty, James A.
Lotringer, Lucienne
Lovelace, Douglas C.
Lubiak, Casimir J.
Lucas, Mary Suzy
Lucas, Terry
Lucille, Sister M.
Lundy, Charles L.
Lynch, Carol
Maccoy, Joseph
Macy, John
Maczulski, Jane
Mai, Phan Than
Malinowski, John P.
Malone, Walter R.
Maloney, William T.
Mammen, Thampy N.
Mangin, Charles
Manus, Luther R., Jr.
Marciani, Louis M.
Marcy, Donald E.
Marin, Dennis
Marino, Frederick F.
Markey, David
Marsh, James E.
Marszalek, John F., Jr.
Martin, Frank L.
Martin, Richard J.
Martinez, J. Mauricio
Maskulka, James M.
Mason, Robert D.
Matthewson, Wilfred J.

Mayes, Kenneth J.
McCallum, George E.
McCarthy, Robert J.
McCluskey, Edward J.
McCormack, Donald M.
McCully, Calvin R.
McElhinney, Thomas J.
McGuire, M. Cornelia
McKeen, Robert W.
McKelvey, Charles E.
McKenzie, Carl H.
McLaughlin, Joseph W.
McManaman, Edward
McNelis, Gerald A., Jr.
McNierney, Leon Joseph
McQuaid, Ronald J.
McSweeney, Dennis D.
Meehan, John L.
Meier, Robert F.
Melanese, Dolores
Menz, Leo Joseph
Mercorella, Philip
Meyer, Albert Joseph
Mielcarek, Eugene John
Mihm, Xavier R.
Miller, Ralph Blair
Miller, Roy R.
Miller, Thomas C., III
Milloy, Patrick
Mish, Thomas F.
Moe, Wayne J.
Moffatt, Charles K.
Mollenhauer, James J.
Monahan, Robert E.
Monahan, Thomas A.
Montanari, Giovanni A.
Moore, Clayton D.
Moore, Thomas E.
Mor, Antonio
Morabit, Joseph L.
Moredock, M. Jeffrey
Morris, Karen
Morris, Michael
Morris, Rudolph E.
Moskowitz, Lester R.
Mostafa, Badria
Moye, Gary
Mueller, Lydia
Mundy, John L.
Murphy, David J.

Murphy, Edward F.
Murphy, John M.
Murphy, William
Murray, Paul J.
Muzzi, Caesar
Myer, Norman G.
Nania, Anthony J.
Napoli, Brian
Nees, John F.
Neimanis, George J.
Nellis, Violet P.
Nelson, Lawrence R.
Neurath, Herbert G.
Newhard, Dana F.
Nieb, Joseph E.
Niebling, Howard V.
Nies, Frederick C.
Novario, Olivio
Nussbaum, Erich
Nye, Mika
O'Brien, John P.
O'Connor, Gerard P.
O'Connor, James A.
Obidinski, Eugene E.
Olsavsky, Gregor M.
Overdyun, Richard
Ozment, Fred N., Jr.
Pagano, Bernard T.
Pallikunnen, Emmanuel A.
Palmer, David D.
Palmer, James E.
Palmer, Jesse T.
Paskus, Anthony
Patch, Aquinas R.
Paulucci, Philip M.
Payette, Bruce A.
Pegis, Paul C.
Pelinsky, Alex
Pelkowski, Jerome M.
Pendry, James D.
Peng, Jack
Perkins, Gary O.
Perotti, John M.
Peters, Elmwood J.
Peterson, James
Petronio, Vivetta
Petulla, Joseph
Pfadt, William F.
Pfeffer, Arthur A.
Phalan, Reed T.

Phillips, Leo J.
Pietrzak, Richard F.
Pilatowski, Frederick
Pine, Frederick P.
Pisoni, Joseph M.
Pitts, Arthur W., Jr.
Pizzat, Valerie
Plivelic, Mark A.
Pontrelli, Lawrence J.
Post, Robert J.
Powders, Kathleen
Powers, Eugene P.
Powers, Francis J.
Prah, John A.
Priest, Loring B.
Pulinski, Judy
Pupo, Salvatore
Puscas, Louis
Putko, Thomas H.
Quinn, Daniel G.
Quisenberry, James D.
Randoux, Henriette
Ranpollo, Randy
Ray, John W.
Reddinger, Edward G.
Reed, Keith G.
Reilly, Joseph F.
Reisenweber, Francis A.
Reisenweber, James H.
Reuwer, Mary Pat
Reynen, Ruth Ann
Rhee, Wansoo Theresa
Rhodey, William A.
Rice, Lewis A.
Richards, Jack
Riddle, Ronald W.
Rishell, John
Robbins, Phillip R.
Robey, Daniel
Robie, Henry J.
Rodzen, Phillip Louis
Rosen, Philip T.
Rossi, John F.
Roth, Andrew P.
Rothbein, Julius
Rothschild, Nora
Rotolo, Joseph
Rowland, J. Carter
Rubin, Mordecai S.
Russell, Bernard M.

Russo, Peter O.
Ryan, John W.
Ryan, Rita M.
Rybar, Richard H.
Rytz, Bodil
Saad, Francis
Sague, Conseulo
Salchli, Robert P.
Salvia, Frank J.
Salvia, Joseph A., Jr.
Santangelo, Francis A.
Sayles, Rapheal H.
Schaaf, Peter G.
Schaffner, James A.
Schauinger, J. Herman
Schauinger, Margaret J.
Schiegg, Jay
Schilling, Clarence
Schlessinger, Gert
Schmitt, Anthony
Schmitt, James
Schreckengost, Stanley E.
Schroeck, Bernard
Schroeck, George W.
Schubert, William A.
Schulz, John G.
Schumacher, John W.
Schwab, J. Donald
Sciamanda, Robert
Scollon, Robert W.
Scutella, Frank
Sedgwick, Michael J.
Sefcik, James F.
Seigel, Lawrence G.
Seiverling, Thomas W.
Seligman, Arthur M.
Sen, Pankaj K.
Sennett, William L.
Shapira, Gary J.
Shaw, Walter L.
Shea, Norris M.
Sheldon, Thomas F.
Shiffer, James
Shipman, John M.
Shiva, S.G.S.
Shively, Sharon
Shoulson, Abraham B.
Shoup, Maurice R.
Shu, H. Hunter
Simon, Martin

Simon, Milton
Simpson, Mamie L.
Sims, Barbara
Sinicropi, Anthony V.
Skrypzak, Stanley
Slater, John J.
Slavin, Lynn R.
Smaltz, Peter R.
Smellie, Larry
Smith, Edna May
Smith, Homer L., Jr.
Smith, Richard F.
Smith, Ronald P.
Smith, Walter R.
Snyder, Leslie M.
Somers, Eldon K.
Sopp, Mildred E.
Spaeder, Robert N.
Spangler, Conrad C.
Spannaus, Owen L.
Sparling, Edward L.
Speice, Lawrence T.
Stalsky, Igor
Stark, Norman H.
Starrett, Warren L.
Starrs, William M.
Stasenko, Stephen
Steckler, Gerard
Steckler, William E.
Steinwach, Gottlieb
Stephenson, Frank
Stout, Donald F.
Stout, George G.
Stouter, Vincent, P.
Straw, William H.
Strohmeyer, George E.
Sullivan, Lucille
Sullivan, M. Helen Jean
Sullivan, Mary Ann
Sullivan, Timothy
Sullivan, William L.
Sundie, William D.
Swartz, Joseph F., Jr.
Sweadner, Marie
Sweeney, Kathleen M.
Sweeting, Joy
Swift, Joseph A.
Syeda, Atzalunnisa R.
Sylvano, John B.
Symmons, Konstantin

Taglieri, Vincenzo P.
Tarbell, Raymond N.
Tascone, Joseph F.
Tatsch, Paul A.
Terrill, Alan
Teubner, John
Thomas, Ronald
Thompson, John
Thomson, John H.
Thornton, Daniel L.
Timmons, Robert G.
Tkach, Michael S.
Tocik, John Francis
Toperzer, Betty Cline
Trainer, Richard D.
Trimakas, Anthony
Tritschler, James J.
Tullio, Louis J.
Tullio, Robert
Twargowski, Stanley
Ugolini, Alex
Uhrmacher, Thomas
Van Aken, Shirley
Vanderbeck, Walter A.
Varga, George
Varrato, George M.
Vetrone, Leonard
Visnosky, Michael J.
Vladimiroff, Christine
Wachter, Joseph
Wacker, James T.
Wade, James N.
Wade, Richard E.
Wainwright, Harry, Jr.
Waldron, John E.
Wallach, John S.
Walpole, James R.
Walsworth, William A.
Walterhouse, Harry F.
Wang, Hwa-Lung
Ward, Judy
Warner, Bertille
Warren, Richard M.
Wasielewski, Ronald J.
Watson, Alfred M.
Weber, Gerald J.
Webster, Edward G.
Wedzik, Alphonse E.
Wehrle, Joseph J.
Weibel, Elmer

Weidle, Paul
Weigel, Gwendolyn
Weiland, Richard J.
Weis, Charles W.
Weis, James H.
Weithman, Charles
Weithman, Francis J.
Welch, George G.
Wellington, David
Wellington, John F.
Welsh, Thomas J.
Wesley, Joseph L.
White, James, Jr.
Wilder, Charles
Wilkerson, Juanita
Williams, Joan
Williams, John E.
Williman, Daniel H.
Willis, William E.
Wilson, Edward M.
Wilson, Glenn H.
Wilson, Robert

Witkowski, Stanley J.
Wolf, Norbert G.
Wolf, Norbert G.
Wood, Seth A.
Woods, Thomas
Wright, Corey J.
Wright, Ernest C.
Wrobel, Richard
Wroblewski, John E.
Wrubel, William M.
Yarbenet, Michael Randolph
Yochim, George J.
Yost, Janice E.
Young, John Jacob
Young, Steven
Zalas, John
Zand, Helen Stankiewicz
Ziegler, Richard G.
Zielonis, Gary P.
Zinober, Richard N.
Zipper, Joseph H.
Zynda, Thomas H.

204 THE STORY OF GANNON UNIVERSITY

SELECTED BIBLIOGRAPHY

Carney, John G. *Saga of Erie Sports*, Erie, PA: Carney, 1957.

Davies, Grace. Erie and a Brief History of Diocesan Institutions. Monograph.

Defarrari, Dr. Roy J. "Report to Bishop Edward P. McManaman," 19 December 1950.

_____, "Visit to Gannon," 20 January 1951.

Erie, A Guide to City and County, Federal Writers Project, American Guide Series, Philadelphia: William Penn Associates, 1938.

Elwell, Howard. "Development of the Sports Program: The Nash Era," Monograph.

"Evaluation Report for Gannon College," Gannon University Archives, Erie, Pennsylvania, 1957.

"Evaluation of Gannon College for the Middle States Association," Gannon University Archives, Erie, Pennsylvania, 1967.

Gannon College Catalogues, Erie, Pennsylvania, 1956-1978.

"Gannon College Statutes: Proposed Revision," 1 August 1956.

Garvey, William P. *The Ethnic Factor in Erie Politics, 1900-1970*, Doctoral Dissertation, University of Pittsburgh, 1973.

Glose, Rev. Joseph G. "Report on Master's Program," 28 February 1963.

Holmes, Oliver Wendell. "The Chambered Nautilus."

"Interim Report: Middle States Association," Gannon University, Erie, Pennsylvania, 26 April 1954.

"Items to be Fulfilled per Middle States Requirements," Gannon University, Erie, Pennsylvania, 10 November 1950.

"The Junior Leagues," *Fortune*, November 1934: (110-113).

Kruszewski, Sandra. "Gannon University Buildings," Gannon University Archives, Erie, Pennsylvania. 8 July 1983.

Lechner, Carl. Gannon College/Gannon University in Recent Years. Monograph.

Meder, A. E., Jr., "To Monsignor Wilfrid J. Nash." 26 April 1967. Letter. Gannon University Archives, Erie, Pennsylvania.

Nash, Monsignor Wilfrid J. "To C. W. Huntley." 18 Feburary 1969. Letter. Gannon University Archives, Erie, Pennsylvania.

_____. "To Taylor Jones about Graduate Programs." 1 October 1963. Letter. Gannon University Archives, Erie, Pennsylvania.

_____. "To Taylor Jones to initiate Gannon Graduate Programs." 19 March 1964. Letter. Gannon University Archives, Erie, Pennsylvania.

_____. "To Taylor Jones Requesting Evaluation of Curricula for Mechanical and Electrical Engineering." 16 March 1965. Letter. Gannon University Archives, Erie, Pennsylvania.

Nolen, John. *Greater Erie*. Erie: Ashby Printing, 1914.

Nyquist, Edward P. "To Reverend Wilfrid J. Nash." 2 May 1957. Letter. Gannon University Archives, Erie, Pennsylvania.

_____. "To Reverend Wilfrid J. Nash." 5 December 1958. Letter. Gannon University Archives, Erie, Pennsylvania.

Pishoc, F. P. "Letter to Reverend Wilfrid J. Nash." 8 May 1969. Letter. Gannon University Archives, Erie, Pennsylvania.

"Progress Report Submitted for Consideration of the Commission on Institutions of Higher Education Middle States Association of Colleges and Secondary Schools." Gannon College, Erie, Pennsylvania. September 1958.

Reed, John Elmer. *History of Erie County, Pennsylvania.* Topeka: Historical Publishing Company, 1925.

"Report of Gannon College to Middle States." 1967.

"Report of Inspection of Gannon College for Middle States Association of Colleges and Secondary Schools." 7-8 March 1949.

_____. 4-6 March 1951.

"Self-Study Report on Gannon College Presented to Middle States Association." 1977.

Stanford, Rev. Edward V., O.S.A. "Report on Awarding Charter." Gannon University Archives, Erie, Pennsylvania. 23 March 1964.

Walsh, Gerard, M.A. Monsignor Wilfrid J. Nash: The Man, the Priest and President. Monograph.

Wachter, Charles Frederick. *Cathedral College: Genesis of An Institution.* Master's thesis, Gannon College, January 1967.

STUDENT ROSTER OF
CATHEDRAL COLLEGE, 1933-1941

Richard Alberstadt	entered 9/17/34	Edward Grant	1933-34
Wilbur G. Baldwin	1936-37	Paul W. Green	1936-38
Robert George Baptist	1936	John P. Gregor	1936-37
James Barber	1939-40	Francis Greiner	1933-34
Robert S. Barrett	1934-35	William R. Griffin	1934-36
Ed W. Bauer	1938	Richard J. Grumblatt	1935-36
Frank Bauer, Jr.	1936-39	Victor J. Grumblatt	1933-35
John L. Becker	1934-35	Kenneth J. Gutshaw	1935-37
Joseph J. Bednarski	1934-35	Charles E. Hagan	1935-37
John H. Behringer	1936-37	Raymond C. Haibach	1935-36
Walter Bilski	1934-35	Urban Hanhauser	1933-34
William I. Blackwood	1934-36	Charles W. Hastings	1935-37
Vincent A. Boehm	1933-34	Charles R. Haughney	1933-35
John A. Bosner	1934-36	Herbert F. Heidt	1933-35
James W. Bothwell	1936-37	William J. Hepfinger	1940-41
Thomas J. Boyd	1936-37	William P. Heinlein	1934-36
Anthony N. Brown	1934-36	George Hickey	1933-34
Albert F. Brugger	1933-34	Harold F. Hynes	1933-35
Daniel Carboni	1933-34	Charles L. Johnson	1936-37
Gerard M. Carroll	1936-38	Edgar Jones	1933-34
Richard E. Carroll	1938-40	Stephen S. Kajencki	1937-39
James Cash	1935-37	John J. Kernan	1940-41
Bruno Cavallini	1933-34	David Kilpatrick	1933-34
George R. Christoph	1939	Adam Kornacki	1940-41
Thomas Clapper	1933-34	Edward Kownacki	1933-34
Eugene Coleman	1933-34	Raymond J. Krasinski	1936-38
Edwin Collins	1933-34	John R. Kinith	1934-35
Gerald Crane	1933-34	Raymond E. Kuntz	1936-38
Robert Crotty	1933-34	Robert C. Lachney	1933-34
Robert T. Daily	1935-37	Donald O. Larson	1939-41
Harry F. DeArment	1937-38	John F. Leary	1937-38
Maurice R. DeWalt	1936-37	Oscar E. Lecker	1937-38
Paul L. Disterdick	1937-38	Robert James Levis	1940-41
Edmund Donovan	1933-34	Walter Lohse	1933-34
John H. Downey	1936-37	Robert E. Lombard	1933-34
James Dudenhoefer	1939-40	James R. McGrath	1933-34
Robert J. Dugan	1935-36	Charles McIntosh	1933-34
James Dunigan	1933-34	William L. McLain	1936-38
Harold V. Edwards	1936-37	Matthew Mannarelli	1933-34
Edward F. Egg	1935-36	Theophil Markiewicz	1938-40
Francis Fischer	1933-34	Edward J. Marklow	1940-41
Edward Q. Franz	1936-38	Daniel J. Martin	1936-38
James J. Gannon	1935-36	Howard P. Miskell	1940-41
Francis J. Gerzina	1937-39	Charles A. Moore	1933-34
Matthew Gleisner	1937-38	Charles A. Moresco	1940-41
Martin A. Gloekler	1936-37	Russell P. Moscoto	1933-34

John E. Mullen	*	John J. Schaller	*
Leonard A. Mroszkowski	*	William J. Schnelzer	*
Douglas Murphy	*	Robert Schwane	1940-41
Paul Murray	1933-34	Richard J. Seavy	*
Donald J. Nash	*	Edward M. Semple	*
Wilfrid J. Nash	1933-34	Joseph J. Serafin	*
Hugh A. Nelson	*	Truman A. Shannon	*
Leo Neubert	*	William C. Shattuck	*
Frederick C. Nies	*	James B. Shunk	*
Clyde J. Nonamaque	1936-40	Jack A. Siegel	*
William J. North	*	John R. Siegel	*
Anthony J. Nowakowski	1935-37	George Small	1940-41
George T. O'Donnel	*	Edward R. Smith	*
Patrick O'Neill	*	Victor E. Snapp	*
Quentin R. Orlando	1937-38	Joseph J. Sova	1934
Richard J. Orn	*	Edward L. Spadacene	*
Reed T. Phalan	*	Carl Spaeder	*
Robert H. Phelps	*	James Sperry	1933-34
Edward M. Phillips	1937-38	William G. Spiegelhalter	*
Hobart R. Picard	*	Phil T. Sprickman	*
Stanley Pierzynski	1933-34	John Stanka	*
George J. Pleszewski	*	Anthony P. Stanopiewicz	*
Henry J. Pluskota	1937-41	Robert R. Stoltz	*
Thomas J. Prendergast	*	David Stout	*
William J. Pietrasanta	*	Robert W. Stout	1940-41
Ernest J. Prylinski	*	John A. Straub	*
William J. Purcell	*	David S. Strough	*
John M. Quigley	*	Edward J. Stutz	*
Charles E. Rabbitt	*	James M. Sullivan	*
John H. Rainsford	1934	Thomas J. Sullivan	*
Rowan C. Rastatter	1933-34	John W. Sunda	*
Edward G. Reddinger	1933-34	Charles E. Swaney	*
Daniel T. Regan	*	Donald L. Swanson	*
Bernard Reiser	1933-34	Edmund Thomas	1934
Robert J. Riddle	*	J. Gwynne Thomas	*
Edward J. Riley	*	Paul V. Thompson	1933-34
John Mark Riley	1933-34	James D. Timmons	1933-34
Paul R. Riley	*	Leo E. Trambley	*
Jack Robison	*	Francis P. Tushim	*
Leo J. Roland	1934-36	Fred J. Veith	*
James R. Rudy	1938-39	Albert P. Vicks	*
Robert P. Ruef	*	Joseph P. Vigorito	*
Edward J. Runser	1933-34	William Vollmar	1933
Robert J. Runser	*	Earl B. Wagner	*
Kendrick D. Salsibury	*	Howard M. Wagner	*
Theodore A. Sauers	*	Michael E. Walach	1933
William T. Sauers	*	Heyd R. Wallower	1934-35
Nicholas W. Scanlon	*	John Leo Walters	*
Vincent P. Schliff	1940-41	Paul F. Watson	1938-40

James H. Weber	1936-38	Melvin J. Wheeler	*
William D. Weber	*	Stanislaus J. Wisinski	*
Gerald Weibel	1933	Joseph E. Wolf	*
Charles H. Weiser	*	Regis E. Zacherl	*
Charles Weithman	1934	Frank J. Zbierski	*
Richard Welch	1934	Joseph Zipper	1937-38
John W. Wheeler	*	Harry W. Zirkelbach	*
Lemuel G. Wheeler	*	Edward J. Zymslinski	*

*Doubtful as to time of attendance.